An Outdoor Family Guide to

WASHINGTON'S

NATIONAL PARKS AND MONUMENT

VICKY SPRING
AND
TOM KIRKENDALL

THE
MOUNTAINEERS

Published by The Mountaineers
1001 SW Klickitat Way, Suite 201
Seattle, WA 98134

First edition, 1998

Published simultaneously in Great Britain by Cordee, 3a DeMontfort Street,
Leicester, England, LE1 7HD

Manufactured in the United States of America

Edited by Christine Clifton-Thornton
Maps by Tom Kirkendall
All photographs by Kirkendall/Spring
Chapter opening illustrations by Lauren Inness
Cover design by Watson Graphics
Book design by Bridget Culligan
Typography and layout by Gray Mouse Graphics
Cover photograph: *Mount Shuksan viewed from Heather Meadows Recreation
Area in North Cascades* © Kirkendall/Spring
Inset: *Children playing on the beach in Olympic National Park* © Kirkendall/
Spring
Frontispiece: *Mount Rainier reflecting in the still waters of Reflection Lake
near Paradise*

Library of Congress Cataloging-in-Publication Data
Spring, Vicky, 1953–
    An outdoor family guide to Washington's national parks and
    monument / Vicky Spring and Tom Kirkendall. — 1st ed.
        p.   cm.
    ISBN 0-89886-552-2
    1. Outdoor recreation—Washington (State)—Guidebooks.
    2. National parks and reserves—Washington (State)—Guidebooks.
    3. Family recreation—Washington (State)—Guidebooks. 4. Washington
    (State)—Guidebooks. I. Kirkendall, Tom. II. Title.
    GV191.42.W2S67 1998
    917.9704'43—DC21   98-11790
                                                                 CIP

Contents

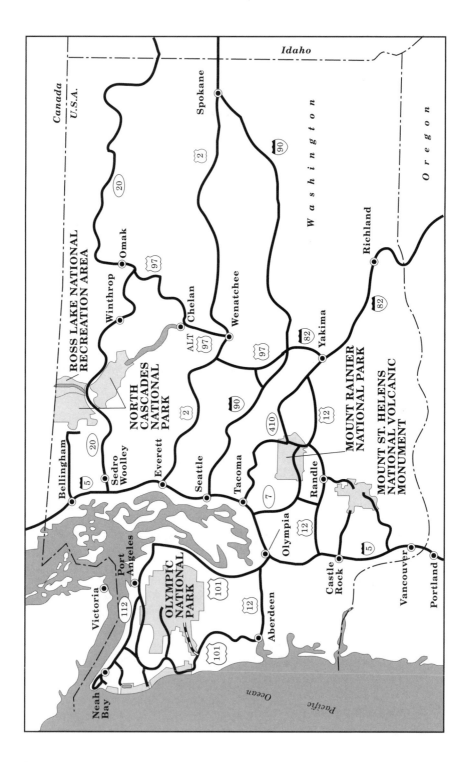

MAPS NOT INTENDED FOR NAVIGATION

KEY TO SYMBOLS

▲	Large hill or mountain top	▰	Backcountry shelter
◆	Object of interest	🛆	Picnic area
◪	Lookout	♿	Wheelchair accessible
Λ	Campground or campsite	◉	City or town
⬍	Ranger station	200	Forest Service road
🚶	Day hike	101	US highway
🚶🚶	Overnight hike	5	Interstate
⛴	Boat launch	20	State highway
⛴	Ferry boat	━━━━━━	Paved road
🚲	Bike ride	▀▬▬▬▬▬	Dirt road
---------------------· Main trail		━━━━━╋━━━ Gate	
---------------:::· Pass		—·——·——·— Park boundary	
----------------- Other trail		∿∿∿∿ River or creek	
▭▭▭▭▭▭ Trail or ski tour following road			

Introduction

Having a Good Time

The first and foremost rule of all family outings is to have a good time, together. At times, the diverse interests and ages of the family unit make this a seemingly gargantuan task. It takes some planning, but with a great deal of flexibility (and not a little ingenuity), the entire family can have a wonderful and memorable experience, to be laughed at or reminisced over for years.

This book is designed to help you plan the best trip possible in some of the most ideal areas in the state of Washington for family outings—our national parks. For toddlers and preschoolers, everything is new and interesting. A memorable day for a four-year-old child in a national park will be entirely unrelated to the glorious scenery. Most likely the preschooler will best remember splashing in a puddle, roasting marshmallows, or a particularly hilarious game of tag. As children grow, they may not like hiking but will tolerate it if they have a chance to see a marmot or a deer. Older kids may find excitement in achieving a goal, like catching a fish or reaching a destination. And teenagers, whom everyone believes to be so hard to entertain, may totally surprise you by quietly cherishing a half an hour spent talking to, or just being with, Mom or Dad.

Admittedly, lots of issues are difficult to resolve. As parents you probably already have encountered some of them once, twice, or innumerable times. These are issues like the big, heavy three- or four-year-old who is not willing to walk but can no longer be carried. Then there is the active eight-year-old who is mysteriously struck with exhaustion ten minutes after leaving the car. And we all know a teenager who is just too cool for words . . . if it's not electronic, it's not worth doing.

Dealing with these issues could spoil your trip, if you let them. However, if you accept the challenges and moderate your expectations, you will soon find yourself enjoying these park outings immensely. Think about each member of the family when you plan the vacation. Try to plan some activity that will particularly please that individual. Offer choices to the younger children and let the older ones help plan the trip. As parents, do not forget to please yourself as well. An afternoon or morning doing something you would particularly like to do (although you may have to do it by yourself) can be part of the plans . . . like a hike that exceeds the children's tolerance level, or a ranger-led nature walk where you would like to pay more attention to the information

Hikers on the Cape Alava Trail in the Ozette area of Olympic National Park

Campfires are endlessly fascinating for the young and young at heart.

given than to the children. Then there is the problem of the disenfranchised teenager: If a happy trip means that the boom box cannot be left at home, then bring it. (But please, for those of us so misinformed as to find the sounds of nature a bit more pleasant than Megadeth, insist that they use headphones.)

Just because you enjoy exploring the parks does not automatically mean that your children will love it too. Loving the outdoors is a learned skill. Although interest in bugs, beetles, and everything that moves is almost universal in young children, it must be fostered or it will disappear when they leave adolescence. If camping and hiking is something that you started to do when the children were older, you may have to work harder to make these activities as natural as watching television at home. Break the family in easy, with weekend trips to campgrounds with flush toilets, paved roads for riding bikes or roller blading, and campfire talks to fill the evening hours. For children, the fear of being in a strange environment can be greatly reduced by including extra playmates in the plans. Try to arrange your trip with another family so there will be plenty of kids to think up activities and plenty of adults to share responsibilities. These trips can also be ideal times to include grandparents or other relatives.

ON THE TRAIL

One of the greatest challenges of family outings is getting everyone moving up the trail. Children up to the age of three or four are usually carried on their parents' backs. Once children are too big for the pack, they spend the next year trying to get a ride. At this point you are not yet sure what the child is capable of, and do not want to push them beyond their limits. However, most parents find that boredom is the biggest factor in exhaustion.

All parents develop their own methods to deal with boredom. If you are still honing your techniques you may want to try some of the following: Bring a friend; read the trail description ahead of time and keep the kids interested in looking for the next intersection, creek, or bridge; carry treats (bribes) that can be handed out each time they attain an agreed-upon goal. Gifted parents spin stories as they go, often incorporating the terrain and history of the area into tales of the adventures of animals, favorite pets, or early peoples. For older children, promise a chance to wade, swim, or fish at your destination. As a child, I always rushed up the trail so that I could get to the viewpoint as fast as possible and bury my nose in a book for half an hour while my parents rhapsodized about the scenery. Now I plan extra time at the turnaround point so my son can play with the twenty or more little cars and trucks

"Hey Mom, does it bite?"

he carries wherever he goes. Teenagers are also a challenge when not motivated. I have seen some parents bribe their teens with money. Although I think the technique stinks, it's better than not going on the hike or dragging a moody, grumpy pre-adult along. Most teenagers can easily out-hike their parents, if you can find a goal that interests them. For example, if they prove themselves on the trail this year, offer them an extended backpack next year or plan to join the guides for a climb to the summit of Mount Rainier.

ON THE WATER

A canoe is a great way to travel into the backcountry. It is especially appealing to families with toddlers. A properly packed canoe will not only have room for diapers, but also for the quintessential teddy bear and favorite toy. Parents will even find room for a few luxuries of their own.

Traveling in a canoe with young children takes practice. The children have to learn what they can and cannot do and parents have to find a safe place for everyone to sit. Toddlers must be seated close to their parents so that their needs can be taken care of immediately. Parents have to be competent paddlers, ready to take up the slack while one or the other tends to a child.

The one essential piece of equipment to take on the water is a life vest for everyone. Then, it is a good idea to include plenty of distractions, such as books to read or boats to tow along, to entertain the children. Snacks are a great attention-getter and the longer they take to consume, the better. Bring a snack that can be pulled out at a certain time or used for distraction if the going gets rough.

Try to limit the time spent in the boat. Three to four hours is enough for most kids. Preschoolers can be encouraged to nap. Once the children are ready to paddle, they should be allowed to do so. By age five they may be ready to paddle for 5 to 10 minutes at a stretch. Of course, if they are racing another boat they may even try harder. After five years old it seems that paddling time increases exponentially every year.

The recommended kayak and canoe trips are on lakes where paddling is easy except when the winds come up. If new to paddling, do not attempt an overnight trip until you have practiced on several easy day trips.

BICYCLING

None of the parks are set up to accommodate young children on bicycles. Park roads are narrow and busy. Only Highway 20 over Washington Pass has a shoulder wide enough to be considered safe. However, the steepness of the road makes it a very hard ride, best left to durable teenagers or experienced adults. Campgrounds are always a popular place for bike riding. Helmets should be worn at all times and children must be cautioned about traffic. The bicycle trips within the parks are suited for mountain bikes only. All of these trips are challenging.

ON SNOW

Trips to the snow usually have only two outcomes. They will either be the absolute worst or positively the best outings of the entire year.

Ensuring that your winter trip is one of the great ones involves a lot of planning, research, and thought. First, there is no middle ground on the clothes. Everyone in the family needs long underwear, warm pants, jackets, mittens or gloves, a hat, and adequate footwear for snow. Second, check conditions beforehand; some years the snow fails to come, some years it arrives in such huge quantities that roads are unsafe and avalanches are daily occurrences.

Finally, be sure to have all the proper permits before leaving home. If a SnoPark permit is required, purchase it before your trip at your local sporting goods store or a nearby forest service office. In the Winthrop area, trail passes are available at the sporting goods store and at all of the lodges and resorts. All other trail passes can be paid for at the trailhead.

Try to plan more than one activity on a winter outing. For example, on a snowshoe trip you may want to bring a pair of skis or a sled for the kids to play with when you get back to the car.

When you pack lunch, think big and add a large thermos of warm soup or cocoa in addition to other liquids. A warm drink in the middle of a wet, sloppy day on the snow can keep the fun going.

FISHING

Many happy hours can be spent at lakes or streams if the kids have a fishing pole. Although the fascination eludes me, it does not elude my kids. They will walk great distances if they know they can fish when they get there. Younger children and nonswimmers need to be watched at all times and lines need constant untangling. Older kids will spend hours concentrating on those small, red bobbers. Teenage boys have been known to get up early, if there is a chance to fish. Non-fishermen can join in the family passion (personally, I just forget to put a hook on my line).

Rules vary for each of the national parks, monuments, and recreation areas covered in this book.

North Cascades National Park, Ross Lake National Recreation Area, and Lake Chelan National Recreation Area: A valid Washington State game fishing license is required. For information concerning regulations, check listings in the Department of Fish & Wildlife booklet or in the "Fishing in the North Cascades" brochure published by the park.

Mount Rainier National Park: No license is required and no official stocking has occurred in the lakes and streams of the park for over fifteen years. The result is less than exciting fishing. However, some lakes and rivers have managed to retain respectable populations, so carrying fishing poles is not a lost cause; just don't plan any meals around the catch.

Mount St. Helens National Volcanic Monument: A valid Washington State fishing license is required for all fishing in the monument and the surrounding reservoirs and rivers. Check regulations listed in the Department of Fish & Wildlife booklet for fishing in the forest lands, and check monument information for the most up-to-date regulations concerning fishing in the study and recovery areas.

Olympic National Park: A Washington State fishing license is *not* required *except* when fishing in the Pacific Ocean. Each valley and lake has its own set of regulations. Opening and closing of seasons vary from year to year. Call the park just before your visit and ask about the current regulations.

Safety

Safety in the out-of-doors requires the use of common sense and caution. Know the limits of each family member and never exceed them. Do not go out expecting accidents or problems, but be ready if one does happen. Knowledge is your best friend. Take a first-aid course and become familiar with the warning signs of heat exhaustion and hypothermia. Learn what to do in case of a sprained ankle or broken bone.

Never be afraid to turn back. Always watch the weather and head back before a storm hits. Never continue on if anyone in your party shows signs of exhaustion or dehydration.

Always carrry bug repellent and the Ten Essentials: extra clothing, extra food and water, sunglasses, pocket knife, candle or firestarter, flashlight with extra bulb and batteries, first-aid kit, waterproof matches, compass, and map.

AVOIDING TROUBLE

The best way to ensure a happy vacation is to avoid all possible trouble. The following are a few things to watch out for.

Water play

Most rivers, streams, and waterfalls in the national parks and national forests need to be approached with caution. The current in mountain creeks is often very swift and the rocks along the shore, often slippery. When approaching a river it is best to find a wide section with a large gravel bar with room for the family to move around safely. Do not attempt to wade or swim in the water unless it is clear and flowing slowly or not at all. Often mountain streams move surprisingly large rocks and submerged logs along their beds which could trap or injure anyone wading.

Wildlife

Do not feed or approach the wildlife. We have all heard this rule time and time again since we were young children. As parents we need to hear it again. No matter how much the children would like a better look, do not approach or feed any wild animal. Wild animals may strike out when they feel cornered. The hooves or antlers of the campground deer could cause serious injuries. Small

Your best chance to see a bear is at Northwest Trek wildlife park (see page 110).

animals such as squirrels and mice become pests when fed; they also die of malnutrition during the winter if they have eaten human food in the summer.

Cougars: These cats are expanding their population and returning to many of their old habitats. The cougar is dangerously strong, aggressive, and not afraid to attack a child. Parents should keep smaller children with them at all times. If older children (weighing 100 pounds or more) wish to forge ahead, they should only be allowed to do so in large, noisy groups.

If attacked by a cougar, always fight back. If you see a cougar, pick up young children and make noise. Try to make yourself look larger than life by standing on a fallen tree or a rock, holding your jacket or pack above your head, and putting your arms out. If a child is attacked, you must attack back. Find a large branch and beat the cougar with adrenaline-pumped arms, kick, and manually force it to release. Remember, it is the child's life you are fighting for.

Bears: Everyone is afraid of them, but everyone wants to see one. Bears live in all the national parks, recreation areas, and national monuments covered in this book. They are not social creatures and are rarely seen. Equally, they are not out hunting for families to devour. The most common is the black bear, which comes in a range of colors from tan to black. The grizzly bear, which the U.S. Government is attempting to transplant into the North Cascades, is extremely uncommon, almost never seen, and living quietly and contentedly almost everywhere throughout the Cascades except in the north.

The parks offer an excellent handout concerning bears. Read it and remember that humans are the greatest threat to the bear population. Try to keep your campsite neat and clean. Do not tempt these intelligent animals by leaving food and garbage lying around. When not in use, keep food and cooking gear in the car. If backpacking, hang it up. Bears who find food in a campground will come back, and so will their children. To keep bears from passing information from generation to generation, campground bears often are destroyed. Our thoughtlessness and their intelligence make a deadly combination.

If you see a bear on the trail, let the bear leave before you continue. Most bears will run and if it does not, it may be protecting a family. If the bear sees you but does not run, make lots of noise and head back the way you came. Wait a bit for the bear to move on before attempting the trail again.

Health and First Aid

Hypothermia: Hypothermia means a subnormal body temperature and is a constant hazard in the damp climate of the Pacific Northwest. This life-threatening condition is extremely difficult to reverse once started. The small body mass of children makes them more susceptible to hypothermia than adults. However, if one party member becomes hypothermic, the probability is high that the rest of the party is close to the same condition.

When the wind is blowing, hypothermia can occur at surprisingly warm temperatures. There have been cases of hypothermia that occurred when the air temperature was in the 50s.

The best way to avoid hypothermia is to always carry extra clothing for the entire family. Small items like hats and gloves take up very little room and can make a huge difference. Add windbreakers and, because this is the "Pacific Northwet," make sure they are waterproof. On the coast, in the rain forest, or on a wet day anywhere, put the kids' warm socks and rubber boots on to keep the feet dry. Finally, every member of the family should have something warm to wear, like a jacket or a sweater.

If this sounds like too much to carry, remember that the onset of hypothermia leads rapidly to death. . . . Maybe the load is not so big after all. (Be especially watchful of teens and pre-teens who refuse to wear a jacket or long pants. If you are the parent of such a child, you may want to introduce the word "hypothermia" and get the kids talking about it before heading out on your trip.)

Symptoms of hypothermia include loss of coordination, slurred speech, irrational behavior, or just general crankiness. All of these symptoms may also be found in a tired child.

Heat Exhaustion: The small body mass of children makes them extremely susceptible to heat exhaustion. On warm days, watch your children carefully for signs of overheating such as flushed cheeks and elevated body temperature. Lack of sufficient fluid intake is one of the prime causes of heat-related illness, so be sure that everyone gets plenty of liquids. Stop frequently, in the shade when possible, for drinks of water or sports drinks that contain carbohydrates and electrolytes.

Sunburn: Over-exposure to sun is one of the most common sources of vacation discomfort. Be especially careful on foggy or partially cloudy days when it is hard to keep track of how much sun exposure you have received. To avoid over-exposure and the resultant sunburns, always use a good sunscreen, ideally with an SPF rating of 30 or more. Babies and toddlers should wear hats to keep sun off the scalp. Sunglasses are equally essential to protect the eyes. A lifetime's worth of damage may be done by one day of play on snow without proper eye protection.

Ticks: Ticks are carriers of all sorts of unpleasant diseases including Lyme disease and Rocky Mountain spotted fever. Most ticks are found in the spring and early summer; however, be vigilant at all times. Ticks are common in the North Cascades and have recently been found in the Elwha and Lake Crescent areas of Olympic National Park.

Keeping the bugs away from your body is the best form of protection against ticks. During tick season, wear light-colored long pants and long-sleeved shirts. The lightness of color allows you to spot the ticks on your clothing. Tuck the pants into your socks to keep the ticks from getting in. Bug repellent with DEET is a proven deterrent (see Mosquitos and Other Bugs That Annoy).

Ticks often spend several hours on the body before attaching. Make regular tick checks of legs, clothing, hair, and neck at all rest stops. If a tick attaches, remove it immediately by pulling straight out with tweezers. Be sure all of the tick's legs, head, and body parts are removed then sterilize the area. If any of the tick is left in the skin, consult your doctor.

In the evenings, do a thorough tick check on each family member. Ticks like warm, tight places so check under the arms, waist bands, and private areas. Comb hair, then run hands over the scalp.

Mosquitoes and Other Bugs That Annoy: Nothing can spoil a trip faster than a couple of mosquitoes. Toddlers lack the coordination to slap them away, youngsters turn hysterical, and adults become easily annoyed. However, with a good dose of bug repellent the entire family can quickly relax and get back to the business of having fun.

The important ingredient in most effective bug repellents is DEET. Unfortunately, DEET, in concentrations high enough to repel bugs, can be harmful to young children. (It has, in a couple of rare cases, had negative side effects on adults, too). For children it is best to buy repellents that are made especially for them. Children's repellents contain DEET which stays on the surface of the skin rather than soaking in like the adult formulas do. Children's bug repellents wear off rapidly and must be reapplied every couple of hours.

Water: No matter how clear it looks, do not drink untreated water! This is especially important for children, whose small bodies rapidly become dehydrated by diarrhea.

On day hikes, always carry your entire water supply. That should be at least one quart per person, including the little people. On backpack trips, boil all water for three minutes then filter it for the best results. Do not use water purification tablets; the chemical's doses are often too strong for children.

First-aid Kit: Cuts and scrapes are commonplace, no matter where children are. Always carry a small bag of your family's favorite bandages and disinfectants for hurts real or imagined. Blisters are also frequent when kids are too busy exploring to stop and pull up a slipping sock or suddenly discover they have grown out of their favorite shoes.

Preserving Our Parks

Preservation of our parks is a herculean task, so who can blame the park rangers for getting upset when they see visitors trampling the meadows or picking the flowers? Children need to understand the fragile nature of the environment and how easily it is damaged. (As I personally hate lectures, I have avoided giving them to my children. What has worked well in my family is to explain the problem, then ask the kids what they would do to protect the resources if they were rangers. Thankfully, the rangers' solutions are much more restrained than those of the children!)

The following is a list of rules that must be followed if we are to preserve the parks for everyone:

1. Do not pick the wildflowers or any vegetation. Even if you and only a couple hundred other people pick just one flower each, a meadow would soon be denuded. It may also stop that plant from reseeding.

2. Stay on the trail. Walking off the trail tramples the vegetation and creates a maze of new trails which are confusing and ugly.

3. When stopping to rest or to picnic, look for a place off the trail where you can sit on a rock or a log. Never rest or picnic on a meadow.

4. Protect lakes and streams. Look for rocks, logs, or places where the soil has already been trampled when approaching the shore. Never enter a lake or creek if your skin is coated with sunscreen or bug repellent. Never use soaps or detergents, even ones that claim to be biodegradable, in lakes or streams.

5. In the national parks, campfires are allowed in established campfire rings only, with the exception of the ocean beaches where special rules apply. Firewood is sold at all the larger campgrounds; however, if you have space in your vehicle, economics indicate you should bring your own. If backpacking, carry a stove.

6. Pets—whether dogs or cats, pigs or chickens—are not allowed on trails in the national parks, except in designated pet walking areas. Pets are allowed in campgrounds but must be on a leash at all times. You may take your pet on trails in the national forests.

View of Mount Olympus from High Divide in Olympic National Park, (see page 277)

How to Use This Book

This book is divided into four chapters, one for each of Washington's three national parks and one for our national volcanic monument. Each chapter begins with an introduction, which focuses on special points of interest in the area, and on potential problems for families visiting that park. The parks are then divided into sections based on access. An introduction to each area describes nearby campgrounds, accommodations, and facilities. There are also suggestions on how to catch the area's highlights if you have only limited time to spend. The main focus of each section is one or more hikes, boat trips, or even bicycle rides. At the end of each section are more activities and hikes for families with time to thoroughly explore the area. The final section of each chapter describes two or more backpack trips, chosen with families and beginner backpackers in mind, as well as a couple of easy winter trips.

Each hike, boat trip, bicycle ride, or snow tour is rated for difficulty: easy, moderate, and challenging. Easy trips are on wide, well-graded trails, with little elevation gain. Some of these trails are designated barrier-free for wheelchair and stroller use. Easy hikes are usually no more than 2 miles round trip.

Moderate hikes are on well-maintained trails with more elevation gain and distance than the easy trips. Most moderate hikes are less than 5 miles long. Challenging hikes are as they sound. The trails with this rating may gain up to 2,000 feet of elevation and be as many as 8 miles round trip. The challenging designation is also given to rough trails, with big steps or narrow treads.

There is also a listing of activities you can do on each trip, so you'll know if you need to add swimming suits, extra film for your camera, or fishing poles to your pack.

Lower Curtis Glacier from Lake Ann Trail in the North Cascades National Park (see page 34)

Pay close attention to the "Best" category. This listing is designed to help you avoid planning hiking trips when the trails are still covered with snow, or heading out on a ski trip before the snow falls. Remember, the dates given are just estimates, and snowfall varies from year to year.

The "Map" listing is very important. Maps are not only a safety feature, they can also be a valuable tool to help inspire the group up the trail. Just pull out the map and have everyone try to locate their position. A compass is also helpful, if you know how to use one. If not, buy one and a good book to go along with it, and make learning how to use it a family project.

Noticeably absent from the trip descriptions is the amount of time it will take to complete each hike, ride, ski tour, or boat trip. The average adult walks about 2 miles per hour. Unfortunately, there is no such thing as an average child. For young people, walking time is based on how much fun they are having rather than distance. My recommendation is to start off with a couple of easy trips to get a feel for the amount of time it takes your family group to cover a certain distance, then make your best guess from there. Always allow lots of extra time, expecially if hiking with young children. If the trip goes faster than you planned, reward everyone with extra playtime when you get back.

An Additional Note About Safety

Safety is an important concern in all outdoor activities. No guidebook can alert you to every hazard or anticipate the limitations of every reader. Therefore, the descriptions of roads, trails, routes, and natural features in this book are not representations that a particular place or excursion will be safe for your party. When you follow any of the routes described in this book, you assume responsibility for your own safety. Under normal conditions, such excursions require the usual attention to traffic, road and trail conditions, weather, terrain, the capabilities of your party, and other factors. In addition, conditions may have changed since this book was written that make your use of some of these routes unwise. Always check for current conditions, obey posted private property signs, and avoid confrontations with property owners or managers. Keeping informed on current conditions and exercising common sense are the keys to a safe, enjoyable outing.

The Mountaineers

1

North Cascades National Park

North Cascades is a wilderness park with only minor incursions from roads or even trails. However, the national park is only part of a package that includes Ross Lake and Lake Chelan National Recreation Areas, Heather Meadows and Mount Baker Recreation Areas, and the North Cascades Scenic Highway. Wrapped together, the North Cascades offer an abundance of opportunities for explorations and outings.

North Cascades National Park is a celebration of biological diversity. Over 100 inches of rain fall in the western valleys of the park every year. From this lush rain forest environment the hills slope upward at dramatic angles, climbing with dizzying determination through the alpine zone to an arctic environment at the glacier-covered summits. Then, with equal swiftness, the land descends to parched slopes on the east side of the Cascade Range where ten inches of precipitation falls during the year and most of that in the form of snow. If you are impressed by numbers, there are 318 glaciers, 1,500 different species of plants, and thousands of different insects (bring your bug repellent) in the park.

This complex of park and recreation areas can be sampled by car, boat, or foot. The sprawling nature of the North Cascades has brought the administrating agencies (forest service and park service) together to jointly dispense information. Look for offices in Sedro Woolley, Marblemount, Newhalem, Early Winters, Winthrop, Chelan, and Stehekin.

Heather Meadows Recreation Area is a scenic paradise and a great place to spend an entire day of exploration. The meadows area is laced with trails

Canoeing past a waterfall along the shore of Ross Lake

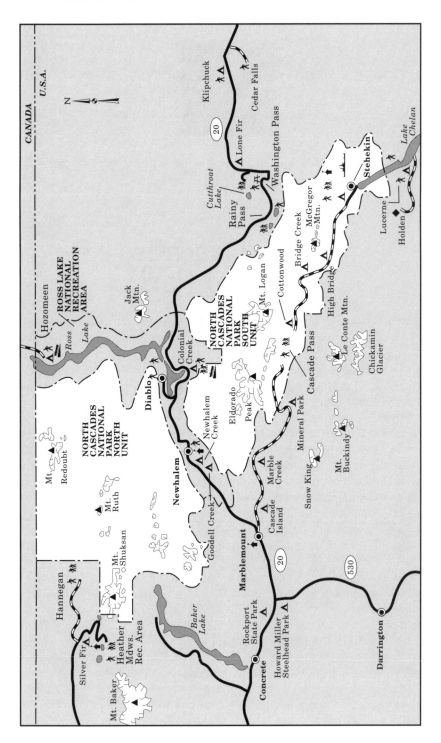

Mount Baker from Artist Point in Heather Meadows Recreation Area

ranging from toddler specials to airy walks up cliff faces. This area is favored by photographers who take advantage of the lakes, meadows, and rugged mountains to frame world-class pictures. Huckleberries grow well in this environment, and picking and eating berries is a favorite pastime of late-summer visitors.

Ross Lake National Recreation Area runs through the heart of North Cascades National Park and visitors can find views of glacier-coated mountains from the road and water. The National Recreation Area encompasses three man-made lakes that were created by Seattle City Light's hydroelectric power division long before the park was envisioned. The lakes lie deep in the Skagit River valley and look more like scenic fjords than reservoirs. Fishing and boating are popular activities. Seattle City Light offers tours of the hydroelectric projects which are not only informative but are extremely picturesque. Kids love them. For details, see the Newhalem area.

For families wishing to explore by car, the North Cascades Scenic Highway (Highway 20) offers excellent scenery for the adults and numerous activities for the kids. The highway cuts through Ross Lake National Recreation Area and brushes both the north and south units of the national park. Scenic viewpoints and short trails allow you to see and experience the forest and subalpine environments you pass through. The visitor center in Newhalem is a fascinating place, with thoughtfully designed displays. The highway exits the mountains at the western-style town of Winthrop, a popular cross-country ski area in the winter and a mountain biking and horse riding resort in the summer.

Lake Chelan National Recreation Area is administered by the national park. This 55-mile-long lake lies in a glacier-cut valley and was as beautiful as nature could make it—then man added 21 feet to the lake with a small dam at the town of Chelan. However, with or without the dam, the lake is one of the deepest in this country. The national park visitor center, at the upper end of the lake, is located in the small community of Stehekin and can be accessed only by foot, boat, or plane. From Stehekin, an upvalley road follows the Stehekin River to campgrounds and trailheads. A shuttle bus makes several trips a day to upvalley campgrounds and trails. Lodging is available.

Despite the sprawling nature of the North Cascades, satisfying visits can be tailored to fit almost any budget. For a single-day park blitz, pack a big picnic lunch and plenty of snacks for a long drive over the North Cascades Highway. Plan stops at the Newhalem Visitor Center and at all the viewpoints along the road. Take a short nature walk at Happy Flats. At Rainy Pass walk the mile-long trail to Rainy Lake. Stop again at Washington Pass Overlook to gaze at the impressive granitic masses of Liberty Bell and Early Winters Spires. If time allows, drive on an additional 30 miles to the western-style town of Winthrop to buy an ice-cream cone and get a feeling for the dry side of the mountains before heading back.

The boat trip up Lake Chelan to Stehekin can also be a single-day adventure.

Rainy Lake, an easy walk from North Cascades Scenic Highway

At Stehekin, check out the visitor center then ride the bus, rent a bike, or walk the 3 miles upvalley to Rainbow Falls before returning to the boat.

If you have several days, plan to do one or more boat trips and hikes.

As this is truly a wilderness area, accommodations and services are not numerous. On the west side of the park, the nearest accommodations are located in Marblemount. There are no gas stations for the 89-mile stretch of highway between Marblemount and Winthrop. Campgrounds are also limited and available only on a first-come basis. Arrive before noon to secure a site on a summer weekend.

Accommodations are easier to find on the east side of the park. Motels and bed and breakfasts are in plentiful supply along Highway 20 from Methow to Twisp, with the largest number being located at Winthrop. Restaurants and grocery stores are equally easy to find. Campgrounds are also relatively plentiful.

Winter visitors can sample only the extreme fringes of the park and the adjacent recreation areas. Highway 20 is closed between milepost 130 at Colonial Creek and milepost 175 at Early Winters. The Newhalem Visitor Center is open on weekends only. Stehekin remains open year round with the lake boats running on a limited schedule. Skiing is the chief winter activity.

Permits: National park entry fees are not charged in this wilderness park. Backcountry permits are required for all overnight stays away from your car. (No fees in 1997; expect to pay for the permits in the future.) On forest service lands, you will need a parking permit, obtainable at all information centers and forest offices.

Heather Meadows Recreation Area

Backpacking, berry picking, hikes, nature walks, photography, scenic drive, visitor center

Mount Shuksan, whose glaciated reflection in the clear waters of Picture Lake is the most photographed alpine scene in the world, and Mount Baker, a smoldering volcano cloaked in ice and snow, create an almost surreal backdrop to the Heather Meadows Recreation Area. During the fall, when conditions are the best, the meadows are dotted with an international group of photographers whose huge cameras are mounted on massive tripods.

You do not have to be a professional photographer nor do you have to visit in the fall to enjoy one of nature's finest works of art. Simply pack a large picnic lunch and get an early start for a long day of scenery viewing. Heather Meadows is an ideal area for families young and old. Baker-Snoqualmie National Forest, the area's administrators, has made an effort to create trails for all, from relatively short, barrier-free paths for wheelchairs and strollers, to steep routes blasted into rock walls for the nimble footed.

Fire and ice are the main themes of this meadowland. The effects of the volcanics and glaciers can be seen everywhere. Columnar basalt dots the meadows and excellent examples can be seen along the road to Artist Point. Mount Baker is a dormant volcano whose slumbers were interrupted by a snort and a snore as recently as the mid-1970s. Ice has sculptured the volcanic land, creating basins, valleys, and hills. Glaciers are still at work today, carving the flanks of Mount Shuksan and Mount Baker even as you read these words.

Heather Meadows lies at the edge of the very popular Mount Baker ski resort and the road to the base of the meadows is open year-round. The forest service shuts down operations in mid-September, closing the visitor center and removing trailhead and informational signs. The road from Heather Meadows to Artist Point is often closed by snow until mid-July. (It is best to call ahead before an early summer visit.)

Although extremely popular throughout the entire year, many people prefer to visit Heather Meadows in the late summer and early fall (August and September), taking advantage of the short season between the snowmelt and the new snowfall. August is a great time for hiking, with warm days and, hopefully, good weather. September brings a quick coolness at these high elevations, and Heather Meadows and the surrounding countryside yield a rich crop of mountain huckleberries. Blue-mouthed berry pickers can be seen roaming the trails with overflowing pails of succulent berries. If you come to photograph, spend a September afternoon in lower Heather Meadows with your camera pointed toward Mount Shuksan. At sunrise, you and your camera should be at Artist Point, taking advantage of the early morning light and its rich shadows on Mount Baker.

If you have only one day to spend in the Heather Meadows area, plan to explore the three nature trails, and if time allows add a walk to Table Mountain or Bagley Lakes. Stop at the visitor center for a short but interesting glimpse of the area's history. Families with more than a single day may consider a hike to Chain Lakes or Lake Ann.

The closest accommodations to Heather Meadows are located 18 miles west in Glacier. The wide variety of available lodgings there serve the ski trade and reservations are essential in the winter. During the summer, vacancies are common, especially mid-week. You will also find a couple of restaurants, a small store, and a gas station in this small town. The Visitor Information Center, at the east end of Glacier, is open from July to mid-September.

The area campgrounds have a limited number of sites. Douglas Fir Campground, 0.8 mile east of Glacier, offers thirty-six sites. Silver Fir Campground, 13.6 miles east of Glacier, provides another thirty-one sites. Groups have access to the facilities of the Excelsior Camp, by reservation only. NO camping is allowed in Heather Meadows Recreation Area. Due to the limited number of available campsites, side roads and turnouts are heavily exploited as overflow areas during the summer. If you are considering this kind of camping, bring your own water and a shovel to bury all human waste.

Upper Bagley Lake

Nature Trails

ROUND TRIP: up to 1 mile
TRAIL DIFFICULTY: easy to moderate
ELEVATION GAIN: up to 200 feet
ACTIVITIES: hiking, geological information, photography
BEST: August to September
MAP: Green Trails: Mount Shuksan
Map on page 30

Heather Meadows Recreation Area has three nature walks designed to introduce the natural history and showcase the scenic highlights.

Picture Lake: This 0.5-mile, barrier-free lake loop is a favorite of photographers and berry pickers. On clear, windless days you will see a crisp image of Mount Shuksan in the lake. The trail begins 21 miles east of Glacier. When State Route 542 reaches Heather Meadows, it divides. Go right and immediately begin to look for parking. The trail can be picked up from several locations around the lake. At one point, on the north side of the lake, the road must be walked for a few hundred feet. Although the trail is well marked, it is essential that you keep children close.

Fire and Ice: This is a 0.5-mile round trip on a barrier-free trail to an overlook of Upper Bagley Lake, Herman Saddle, and Table Mountain. The surrounding hillsides are covered with heather, in summer colors of pink and

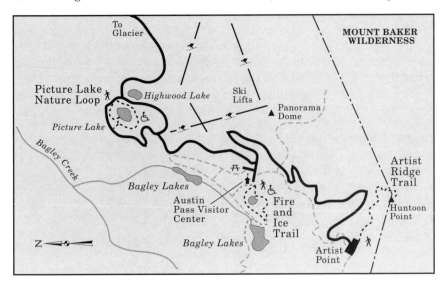

Mount Shuksan rising photogenically above Picture Lake in Heather Meadows

white, and a medium-sized tarn fills the small basin. Interpretive signs along the route explain the volcanic and glacier-created features.

If you enjoyed the barrier-free section of the trail, you may continue your walk on the gravel trails in this same area. One trail loops from the restrooms, making a popular stop at the edge of the small lake (tarn) in the middle of the meadow. This trail joins the barrier-free trail for the return to the visitor center. Another trail, starting at the visitor center walkway, heads down a rock face with the aid of a few steps. Once off the rock you may go left to an overlook of Bagley Lakes, or right to the Bagley Lakes access trail.

To reach the trailhead, drive 1.1 miles from Picture Lake then take the second right. Continue up until the road makes a sharp switchback. Go left and park near the Austin Pass visitor center.

Artist Ridge: Mount Baker and Mount Shuksan look equally impressive from this well-named ridge. The trail begins as a very short, barrier-free walk to a viewpoint, then continues on for another 0.5 mile along the ridge. The ridge trail is not easy, but for this classic walk it is worth helping the little ones over the steps and up the steeper grades. Most children simply follow the crowds of other children and do not question the difficulty. However, for the determined nonwalkers, there are information signs to look at, rocks to be climbed, and a small tarn to throw rocks in at the end of the loop.

To reach the trailhead drive State Route 542 east from Glacier 21 miles to

Hikers ascending the Table Mountain Trail, Mount Baker in the distance

Heather Meadows, where the road divides. The ascent continues another 1.1 miles then take the second paved road on the right. The road is steep, narrow, and designed for two-way traffic. Continue up 2.8 miles to road's end at Artist Point. The Artist Ridge Trail starts at the southeast corner of the parking lot.

Lake Ann

ROUND TRIP: 8 miles
TRAIL DIFFICULTY: moderate
ELEVATION GAIN: 900 feet in; 800 feet out
ACTIVITIES: hiking, backpacking, and fishing
BEST: August to September
MAP: Green Trails: Mount Shuksan
Map on page 33

This hike is a family pleaser with plenty of water for the kids to play in and exquisite scenery for the adults. The trail is wide with well-graded switchbacks and the downhill at the start tends to hook reluctant walkers into going a long way before they utter their first complaint. If the distance seems too long, shorter hikes can be made to a boulder-strewn meadow at 1 mile or a small open basin at 2 miles. You might also wish to consider an overnight stay at Lake Ann, giving everyone time to fish, splash in the lake, explore, and watch the sunset on Lower Curtis Glacier.

Drive State Route 542 east from Glacier 21 miles to Heather Meadows where the road becomes one way around Picture Lake. Continue up 1.1 miles then take the second paved road on the right. Switchback up 1.8 more miles to find the Lake Ann trailhead on the left (4,730 feet).

The trail starts off following the contours of the ridge and the road. At 0.1 mile, when a service road intercepts the trail, go right and head into the forest, starting a switchback descent. Huckleberry bushes blanket the hillsides and, in early September, it is easy to lose sight of the objective when faced with the choice of walking or taste-testing berries.

After descending for 1 mile, the trail levels off to cross an open basin. The creek in the middle of the basin requires some boulder-hopping skills. Beyond, the trail crosses a rocky hillside then hops and skips across the creek for a second time. This is followed by a nearly level traverse through a huckleberry-covered forest. A final, short descent leads to an intersection with the Swift Creek Trail at 2 miles. The wildflowers here are the best of the hike.

After descending a full 800 feet the trail now begins to climb. Cross the infant Swift Creek and begin a switchbacking ascent out of the huckleberries and forest to meadows and boulder fields. Young feet will have their greatest challenge on the uneven rocks that make up the trail. Mount Baker comes into view, its gleaming whiteness causing most hikers to scramble for their sunglasses before taking a good look.

Before long, the objective, a saddle on the ridge above, can be seen. At 3.9 miles the trail crosses the 4,880-foot high point and Mount Shuksan comes into

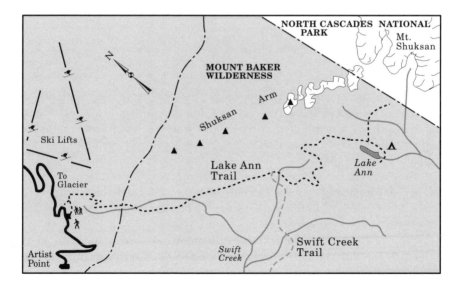

view, just a few feet in front of you. Just below is Lake Ann. If overnighting, rush on to find the best campsites at the far end of the lake. On a weekend they will probably already be taken.

With Mount Shuksan and the Lower Curtis Glacier presenting such a powerful view, many people find themselves compelled to follow the well-defined trail into Shuksan Creek Basin for a closer look. Stick with the well-maintained trail; do not follow the rough tracks of the climbers' route into the Fisher Chimney area, which is dangerous even for experts. Once you have had your fill of the mountain, head down to the lake for a look at some wonderful metamorphic boulders whose swirls and spirals make beautiful patterns.

Mother and son together on the trail to Lake Ann

Chain Lakes

ROUND TRIP FROM ARTIST POINT: 4 miles
TRAIL DIFFICULTY: easy
ELEVATION GAIN: 200 feet in; 500 feet out
ACTIVITIES: hiking, backpacking, fishing
BEST: late July to September
MAP: Green Trails: Mount Shuksan
Map on page 35

Lakes, loops, and nature's finest scenery provide the winning combination that makes Chain Lakes a very popular destination for families, scout troops, retirement home outings, and everyone else who does not fit into the above groups. Campsites are numerous; however, it is not uncommon for them to fill on summer weekends.

The Chain Lakes group is comprised of four lakes, each with a personality and scenery distinctly its own. The four lakes can be accessed from three different directions on trails ranging from easy to very challenging (and somewhat dangerous).

Drive State Route 542 east from Bellingham to Glacier then continue 21 miles to Picture Lake. After the road turns into a one-way loop through the meadows area, head up for 1.1 miles then take the second paved road on the right.

This narrow, steep road climbs for a final 2.8 miles to end at the Artist Point parking area (5,060 feet).

The trailhead is located at the southwest corner of the lot and begins in conjunction with the Table Mountain Trail. Confusion between the two trails is avoidable as long as you remember that the Chain Lakes Trail begins by decending 60 feet off the south side of the ridge. The initial descent is followed by a sweeping traverse across the rocky sides of Table Mountain. The high alpine atmosphere is magnificent with splashes of red paintbrush and dabs of blue lupine poking between the boulders.

After 1 mile the trail divides (5,200 feet). The Chain Lakes Trail heads right, over a grassy ridge then down through alternating bands of huckleberry and colorful wildflowers to Mazama Lake at 1.7 miles. The trail does not actually touch the shore of the lake, so visitors must find the official way trail to the water. Once at Mazama Lake (4,700 feet), find a boulder to sit on for your snack or picnic and avoid trampling the already much-abused lakeshore. Campsites are located in the trees to the west.

Continuing on, the trail arrives at Iceberg Lake, the largest in the chain, at 2 miles. This lake offers a classy reflected view of Mount Baker. Icebergs linger in the chilly waters, occasionally avoiding the sun for the entire summer. Numerous campsites are found here. About halfway around Iceberg Lake, a trail angles off to the left for a short jaunt over to Hayes Lake. A narrow path continues on to Arbuthnet Lake, the last member of the chain.

Most families will want to return the way they came, on the well-graded

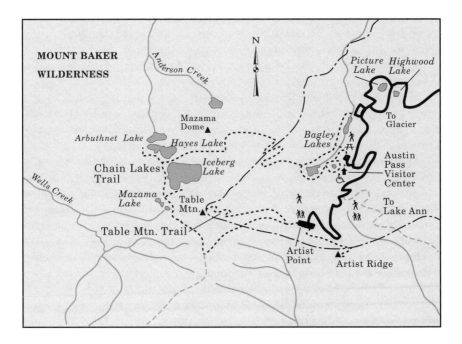

trail to Artist Point. However, for strong hikers, the trail continues beyond Iceberg Lake to reach Herman Saddle at 3 miles. The climbing does not stop here. The trail ascends to the 5,440-foot point on Mazama Dome before beginning the long descent through an open basin to Bagley Lakes at 5.5 miles. From Bagley Lakes walk up to the visitor center where one or more party members must climb the final mile on the Wild Goose Trail back to the start at Artist Point.

On the map there is an inviting route over Table Mountain to Chain Lakes. This is only a route, with a long unmarked section from the summit of Table Mountain to the boot path down to the Chain Lakes Trail. Hikers on this route must be prepared to cross a very steep and often rock-hard permanent snowfield. Slips could easily result in injury.

Table Mountain

ROUND TRIP: 2 miles
TRAIL DIFFICULTY: moderate
ELEVATION GAIN: up to 680 feet
ACTIVITIES: hiking, scenic views
BEST: mid-July to September
MAP: Green Trails: Mt. Shuksan
Map on page 35

More like a mesa than a member of the Cascade Range, flat-topped Table Mountain is composed of a deep, solid plateau of lava. The summit lies in the alpine zone and offers a great playground of rocks, tarns, and man-built cairns. The views will make you dizzy as you rotate around and around to look at Mount Baker, stare at Mount Shuksan, and gaze at Mount Sefrit, Goat Mountain, Yellow Aster Butte, Winchester Mountain, and on north to the Boundary Peaks.

The trail, blasted into the cliffy hillside, is an engineering feat. Although airy, it is very wide. However, if you or anyone in your group are not comfortable in exposed areas you should consider a different hike. (After all, you really cannot go wrong in this area).

Following the directions given for Chain Lakes, drive to the road's end at Artist Point (5,060 feet).

The trail starts on the southwest corner of the parking lot and immediately climbs over a rocky hump. The views are already outstanding and the trees on the south side of the ridge are masterpieces of environmental art. The trail descends, passing a small pond on the right, then climbs again. Most youngsters, and the young at heart, will be tempted to leave the trail at one point or another to scramble over the rocks. If you stray from the trail, please remember to keep your feet on the rocks and stay off the already overly trampled vegetation.

Before long, the trail heads up a narrowing ridge where the tread is blasted into the solid rock. After two switchbacks, the trail swings over the crest of the cliff and onto a deep green meadow where it splits. To the right, a spur trail climbs to the first rocky knoll at the east end of the Table Mountain plateau (5,553 feet). Numerous cairns have been built by visitors to celebrate the summit. The trail to the left traverses the rolling mountain crest, passing several small and photogenic tarns, pocket meadows, and sturdy alpine trees.

After about 1 mile, the trail disappears into the rocky terrain. Footpaths and rock markers delineate a route on across the plateau which connects to the Chain Lake Trail. Unfortunately the only way off the west side of Table Mountain requires descending a long, steep, permanent snowfield, suitable for hikers carrying ice axes only.

Adding a rock to a giant cairn at the top of Table Mountain

MORE ACTIVITIES
Map on page 39

Nooksack Falls: This is a dramatic falls which can be reached by car. Drive Highway 542 east from Glacier 7.1 miles then go left on Forest Road 33 (Wells Creek Road). Descend 1 mile to the falls parking area near the bridge. Walk to the fence for a view of the 175-foot drop.

Bagley Lakes: An easy, 1.5-mile walk takes you to two lakes located in a cirque at the base of Table Mountain and Mount Herman. Around the lakes, the hillsides are covered with heather and huckleberry bushes (bring a berry bucket for September visits). The upper end of Upper Bagley Lake has a shallow beach for wading but do not be surprised if the water remains cool the entire summer.

To reach the Bagley Lakes trailhead, drive Highway 542 east from Glacier 21 miles to Heather Meadows. Where the road divides at Picture Lake continue 1.1 miles then go right on the road to Austin Pass and Artist Point. Head uphill for a couple hundred feet then go right again into a large, paved parking area. The trail begins by heading downhill to Lower Bagley Lake. An alternate access to the lakes starts at the Austin Pass Visitor Center. The Bagley Lakes Trail connects with Wild Goose Trail and Chain Lakes Trail.

Wild Goose Trail: This trail was designed to alleviate the area's terrible parking difficulties. Although most people prefer to drive to their destinations, when parking is a problem, this trail may be the lifeline that saves the day.

Mount Shuksan viewed from the crest of Panorama Dome

The lower end of the Wild Goose Trail is located at the Bagley Lakes trailhead (see previous section). The trail climbs through the meadows and huckleberry fields to Austin Pass Visitor Center (an elevation gain of 150 feet).

The second section of the trail is a long 1.2-mile ascent to the trail's end at Artist Point parking area (a climb of 1,000 feet). Wild goose markers along the trail keep you on the right path. The trail connects all the major trails in the area.

Panorama Dome: This short, 2-mile trail begins by descending into Galena Basin then climbing through open meadows dotted with the towers and wires of the chairlifts for the Mount Baker Ski Area. Views from the 4,801-foot summit of the dome include Mount Shuksan, Shuksan Arm, and the ski area. Berry picking, in season, is excellent. And although the chairlift towers and cables steal something from the wilderness aspect of the area, their presence may actually inspire some of the junior members of the family to walk, talk, and ask questions. The trail ends at the summit where a couple of chairlifts come together.

The trailhead is located on the left, 0.4 mile up the Artist Point Road (4,380 feet). There is parking for one, squeeze two, cars on the right. Additional cars should park at the Austin Pass Picnic Area.

Austin Pass Visitor Center: A warming hut, used by an older version of the Mount Baker Ski Area, has been converted into a small visitor center. The

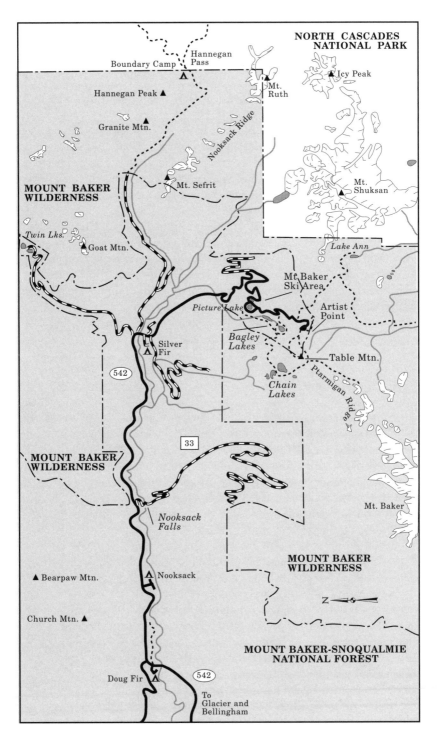

NORTH CASCADES
NATIONAL PARK

Hannegan
Boundary Camp   Pass

Hannegan Peak ▲

▲Icy Peak

Granite Mtn. ▲

Nooksack Ridge

Mt.
Ruth

MOUNT BAKER
WILDERNESS

▲ Mt. Sefrit

Mt.
Shuksan

Twin Lks.

▲Goat Mtn.

Lake Ann

Mt. Baker
Ski Area

Picture Lake

Artist
Point

Silver
Fir

Bagley
Lakes

542

Table Mtn.

Chain
Lakes

Ptarmigan Ridge

33

MOUNT BAKER
WILDERNESS

Nooksack
Falls

Mt. Baker

MOUNT BAKER
WILDERNESS

▲ Bearpaw Mtn.

Δ Nooksack

N

Church Mtn. ▲

MOUNT BAKER-SNOQUALMIE
NATIONAL FOREST

Doug Fir   542

To
Glacier and
Bellingham

building was built in the 1930s by the CCC and remains, today, a beautiful example of a structure from that period. Inside is a cultural museum of the Heather Meadows area covering the mining and ski area history. The visitor center, located next to the Austin Pass Picnic Area, is open daily from July 1 through mid-September. This is also a great place to inquire about current trail conditions.

Ptarmigan Ridge: Both finalists in the North Cascades Beauty Pageant (that is, Mount Baker and Mount Shuksan) are seen from this high alpine ridge. This is not an easy hike; the rocky ground and a couple of steep sections give it a minimum of a moderate rating. Steep snow slopes cover the trail until mid-August or later. Save this hike for good weather; it is easy to wander off the trail and become lost in fog or mist.

The Ptarmigan Ridge Trail starts in conjunction with Chain Lakes Trail at the Artist Point Parking Area. After 1 mile the trail divides; go straight and soon begin descending 160 feet before leveling off to traverse an open basin. At 1.7 miles the trail begins to climb. There is usually a snowfield to cross at this point. Take a look and determine if this crossing is appropriate for you and your family. (If not, head back and explore Chain Lakes.)

Newhalem

Hiking and camping

At an elevation of just 520 feet, Newhalem is one of the lowest areas of the North Cascades National Park complex. Water is the most important resource of this area. The Skagit River, having passed through Ross, Diablo, and Gorge Dams, runs free at last and its gravel bars are important breeding grounds for salmon. The young hatch in the sandy soil along the river's banks, mature, then head out to the salt water. They return to the Skagit to continue the life cycle by laying more eggs and dying. During the winter, bald eagles line the shores, waiting to feast on the salmon carcasses.

Trails in this region all have something to do with water. Water is everywhere, and don't be surprised if it should be falling from the sky. Newhalem receives 100 inches of rainfall a year, making it a temperate rain forest.

Newhalem is a quaint little company town with manicured lawns, clean streets, and neat houses, in a dramatic setting at the base of a narrow, rocky gorge. This little town is perfect for families, with short walks and swing sets. You can even crawl up on the old Seattle City Light No. 6 train engine, look into the engineer's cabin, then ring the bell. At the east end of town, you may look at giant turbines from the viewing room of the Gorge Powerhouse then walk outside to explore the surrounding gardens along Ladder Creek Falls Trail. If you have time, come when it's dark and check out the lights.

The nearby National Park Visitor Center features interactive displays for the younger, tactile members of the party, a sight and sound format for the older kids, and an intelligent progression through the life zones from the rain forest to a walk-through glacier (to check out the ice worms, of course) for the adults. The forest fire display, with its realistic thunder and lightning, is fascinating. Take time to watch the movie; it is also well presented.

The National Park Visitor Center at Newhalem is the best place to inquire about the North Cascades' Junior Ranger program designed for children ages 6–12. The program encourages them to think and learn, then goes a step further by asking them to teach.

One of the most popular activities of the Newhalem area are the Skagit Valley Tours offered by Seattle City Light. Newhalem is also a good jump-off point for a day drive to Winthrop and back, and a great base for day hikes to Diablo and Ross Lakes.

No hotel, motel, or food service is available at Newhalem. The nearest accommodations are in Marblemount, 14 miles west. Campers have Goodell Creek Campground, located at the west end of Newhalem (111 sites and vault toilets) and Newhalem Creek Campground, situated on the road to the visitor center (120 sites, including thirteen very private walk-in sites, and flush toilets). Other nearby campgrounds are Colonial Creek, Rockport State Park, Steelhead County Park, and the primitive forest camps of Cascade Island, Marble Creek, and Mineral Creek on the Cascade River Road.

Campground programs are offered on Friday and Saturday nights at Newhalem Campground. Ranger/naturalist walks are given at the visitor center.

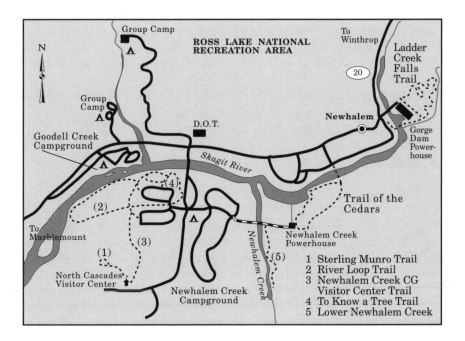

Trail of the Cedars Nature Walk

ROUND TRIP: 0.3 mile
TRAIL DIFFICULTY: easiest
ELEVATION GAIN: 20 feet
ACTIVITY: hiking
BEST: all year
MAP: park handout: Newhalem area
Map on page 41

A carefully tended garden, a long suspension bridge, information signs, and a peek into a working powerhouse ensure that the family will not get struck by a case of exhaustion (boredom) on this forest loop. Run, skip, hop, or just amble and enjoy. The trail surface is hard enough for strollers.

Drive Highway 20 to Newhalem and park near the old train engine (520 feet).

Walk past the grocery store then follow the street to its end at a carefully tended garden. Head through an arch then follow the paved pathway past a garden circle. Cross the Skagit River on a suspension bridge. Below, salmon can be seen in the clear waters during spawning season. Once across, the trail divides. Stay left and walk though the forest to Newhalem Creek and a small powerhouse. After peeking in the windows at the machines, head back along the Skagit River.

Ladder Creek Falls Trail

ROUND TRIP: 0.4 mile
TRAIL DIFFICULTY: moderate
ELEVATION GAIN: 150 feet
ACTIVITIES: walking, powerhouse information, gardens, lights
BEST: March to October
MAP: park handout: Newhalem area
Map on page 41

From end to end this trail is a sure kid pleaser. Test it out by walking the loop during the day then come back in the evening, just after the sun goes down, and do it again under the lights (bring a flashlight to negotiate the stairs in the dark).

Ladder Creek Falls Trail is maintained by Seattle City Light. It is full of steep steps and narrow pathways, which may be difficult for older family members. Strollers are not practical. If this were a normal trail, young kids would

Bridge spanning the Skagit River on the Trail of Cedars Nature Walk in Newhalem

hate the difficult walking, but here there is too much to see and do for youngsters to notice the problems.

At night the trail is lit by a wonderfully garish string of lights that appears to be powered by a small waterwheel. The lights have a strong appeal to all primary color lovers, and young children tend to rush from one light to the next to see what color their skin will change to.

Note: This trail can be hazardously slippery when icy or wet.

Drive Highway 20 to the east end of Newhalem and park in the gravel lot on the south side of the road across the Skagit River from the Gorge Dam Powerhouse (520 feet).

Walk to the far end of the parking lot then follow the trail down to a narrow suspension bridge over the Skagit River. Once across, cross the manicured lawns, passing flower gardens and a small pool to reach a point where the trail divides. Go straight, heading uphill along the edge of Ladder Creek. Before long, the trail divides again; go right for a short side trip to a dead-end bridge over the base of the falls then return to the main trail.

Waterwheel generator in a small pool at the edge of Ladder Creek Falls Trail

After a short, brisk climb along Ladder Creek Gorge, the trail divides a second time. Stay right and continue to climb; the trail on the left is a shortcut route for anyone having difficulty negotiating the steps. After a dramatic view of the falls, the trail descends to meander along the hillside, passing below the waterwheel and along the edge of several ponds. The finale is a descent through terraced gardens to the Gorge Dam Powerhouse visitor entrance and restrooms. The view of the big machines and the few historic pictures will not keep you long. Head down a final steep stairway and go left through a tunnel to end the loop.

MORE ACTIVITIES
Map on page 41

Seattle City Light Tours: These tours start from the town of Diablo, located 1 mile off Highway 20 at milepost 126. Following the signs, drive through town, then along the base of the Diablo Dam hydroelectric plant to a large parking area. The museum and information center are open Thursday through Monday during the summer and on weekends only during the fall.

The tours come in two varieties. The short, 90-minute tour is relatively inexpensive and includes a history video, a ride up an incline railroad, and a walk across Diablo Dam. No reservations are required. Call ahead for times. The regular tour is 4 hours long and includes the history of the Skagit project, a ride on the incline railroad, a cruise on Diablo Lake, a tour of the Ross Dam hydroelectric project, and a dinner. Children under five are free. Reservations are advised.

Thornton Lakes Trail: The trail climbs 2,100 feet in 5.3 miles to a lake. Views are moderate. Camping is poor. The access road is rough and may be difficult for some cars. Drive Highway 20 for 11 miles east of Marblemount then turn right at milepost 117.2. Head up the steep gravel road for 4.7 miles. This trail is rated as challenging.

Sterling Munro Trail: This 330-foot-long, barrier-free trail starts at the National Park Visitor Center in Newhalem. The trail winds through the forest and ends on a hillside with a view of the Picket Range in the heartland of the North Cascades National Park. The Picket Range is inaccessible except to experienced mountain climbers.

River Loop Trail: This 1-mile trail loops through the forest to a rocky river bar. The Skagit River is too swift and cold for wading or swimming; however, it is a great place for throwing stones. The trail starts between Loops A and B in Newhalem Creek Campground and connects with the "To Know a Tree" Trail and the Visitor Center Trail. The River Loop is rated easiest and is an ideal afternoon stroll for campers.

Newhalem Creek Campground—Visitor Center Trail: This trail offers safe pedestrian access between the visitor center and the campground. In the campground the trailhead is located between Loops A and B. This 0.4-mile trail is rated easiest.

"To Know a Tree" Trail: This easy, 0.5-mile loop introduces the native trees of the Newhalem area. The only criticism possible of this thoughtfully designed trail is the lack of signs at the many intersections. If you do not find an information sign soon after an intersection, go back and try the other way. This trail is accessed from the restroom in Loop A, the amphitheater, or the entrance station to Newhalem Creek Campground. Parking is located at the amphitheater.

Lower Newhalem Creek Trail: This old trail ambles through the forest and ends in a grove of stately trees. Along the way, the trail passes near the site of an ancient Native American rock shelter. The park has plans to develop this site in the future. The trail begins in Newhalem Creek Campground between Loops C and D. Walk a service road for 0.3 mile. After crossing Newhalem Creek on a steel grated bridge take an immediate right on an unmarked trail and head up through a forest of stick trees. After 0.2 mile, look for a well-trampled path on the right which heads to the creek and the site of the rock house. The trail ends in 0.2 more mile at an excellent creek access point with cascades above and below. This trail is rated moderate.

Stetattle Creek Trail: Just a short stroll up this trail will reward families with grand picnic sites. The creek paints a pretty picture as it cascades over white granitic boulders. Unfortunately, the trail has suffered from recent flooding and some sections are narrow and exposed. Young children should stay close to their parents. The best portions of this hike are found on the first 0.8 mile. Drive Highway 20 east from Newhalem and turn left at milepost 126 at the Diablo spur road. After 1 mile the road crosses Stetattle Creek and enters Diablo. Find a parking place along the street then begin your hike near the bridge. This hike is rated as moderate because of slide areas.

Sourdough Mountain Trail: If you are looking for some place to expend a great deal of energy, this is the perfect trail. After gaining 5,085 feet of elevation in just 5.7 miles, the trail arrives at one of the most amazing views in the entire area. Take plenty of food, water, and spare clothes for the hike and plan a full 10 hours to complete it. Drive Highway 20 east from Newhalem, then turn left at milepost 126. Follow the signs 1 mile to Diablo. Once in town, stay left where the road divides the first time and right the second time. The trailhead is located on the left. This trail is extremely challenging.

Diablo and Ross Lakes

Backpacking, boating, camping, hiking

Although both of these lakes are man-made, their locations deep in the mountains assure excellent scenery along with guaranteed family fun. Ross Lake is an amazing 22-mile-long reservoir where waterfalls tumble straight off cliffs to land in the dark lake waters. Diablo Lake is a sparkling blue gem in a setting of glacier-covered mountains. The two lakes are ideal for exploring with canoes, kayaks, motorboats, or even small rubber rafts. Or, if you do not want the hassle and stress of dealing with a boat, take a ferry ride. The Diablo Lake

Diablo Lake ferry

ferry runs twice a day from mid-June through mid-September. The return may be made by ferry or trail. The Ross Lake Resort runs an "on-demand" ferry service to all the major trailheads and lakeside camp areas; or you may rent one of their small motorboats or canoes.

If boating is not on your list of fun ways to spend a vacation, try some of the local trails to dams, viewpoints, lakes, or big trees.

Except for the Ross Lake Resort, which floats on the lake and is without road access, accommodations in the Diablo and Ross Lakes area are nonexistent. The easiest way to reach the resort is to take a ferry to the upper end of Diablo Lake then ride up to Ross Lake in a truck. The final leg of the journey is by boat. The resort may also be reached by a 1.5-mile hike from Highway 20. Reservations are a must. Call (360) 386-4437. Other motels and restaurants are located in Marblemount, 24 miles west of Diablo Lake.

The best bet for camping is Colonial Creek, located on a narrow offshoot of Diablo Lake known as Thunder Arm. Surrounded by glacier-clad mountains and deep blue lake water, it is a beautiful area. Colonial Creek is centrally located for most exploration along the Highway 20 corridor. Besides boating, there are ample opportunities for hiking or driving excursions. The campground has 162 sites, including several walk-in sites right along the lakeshore. The amphitheater offers nightly programs and ranger- or naturalist-led walks up Thunder Creek on summer weekends.

For the economy minded, Gorge Lake Campground is ideal. There is no

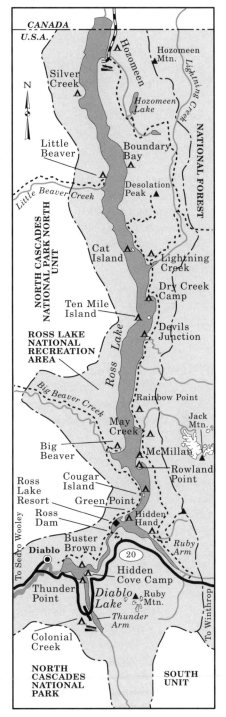

charge for staying at this small, six-site area which has a pit toilet but no running water. Parents with young children should note the steep drop-off from the bluff to the lake and plan to be extra vigilant. This small campground is located near the town of Diablo, 6 miles east of Newhalem on Highway 20. Because it is free, it is frequently full.

You will also find camping at the north end of Ross Lake at Hozomeen. Hozomeen is a sprawling campground that features 122 sites, vault toilets, and running water. This is the only place where boats can be launched on Ross Lake. Seattle City Light tries to time the filling of the Ross Lake reservoir so that water will reach Hozomeen by the start of fishing season (around the first of July). How long the launch facilities stay afloat depends on the snowpack and therefore varies from year to year. Hozomeen is very isolated. To reach it by car, you must drive north from Bellingham 27 miles to Sumas where you cross into Canada. Head east for 49 miles toward Hope. The final leg of the journey is a 40-mile drive south on a road that gets progressively rougher as you go.

Diablo Lake

ROUND TRIP: up to 10 miles
PADDLING DIFFICULTY: easy
ACTIVITIES: canoeing, kayaking, camping, and fishing
SEASON: April to October
MAP: Green Trails: Diablo Lake
Map on page 47

Surrounded by the glacier-covered peaks of the North Cascades, a water adventure on Diablo Lake is not only exciting for children but also a scenic feast for adults. The lake has four campgrounds. Colonial Creek Campground is a fee area with lakeside campsites, running water, restrooms, and a boat launch. The other three campgrounds are accessible by water only. Each of these camps has a dock, picnic tables, and an outhouse. A free, backcountry camping permit is required for all overnight stays.

Although Diablo Lake is ideal for beginning paddlers and first-time water campers, there are certain hazards that must be considered before embarking. The first consideration is motorboats, which pose potential problems on two fronts. The boats set up wakes that are especially troublesome in the narrow arm of the upper end of the lake. They also tend to bring in a rowdy element to the campsites. It is the second consideration, the wind, however, which poses the greatest hazard to paddlers. Canoeists and kayakers should be moderately comfortable with rough-water paddling before venturing out of Thunder Arm.

The winds usually blow stronger in the afternoon, so normally (but not always) the day can be planned with a morning or evening paddle and an afternoon of fishing or playing on shore.

The best boating campsite for younger children is Thunder Point, located 1 mile from the boat launch. This campground is fairly open, with room to roam and play. Hidden Cove and Buster Brown Camps are smaller and thickly forested. Hidden Cove is located on a steep hillside. A good bug repellent and a daily tick check is recommended at all campsites.

Paddle west from the boat launch at Colonial Creek to the narrow passage under Highway 20. Linger a few moments under the bridge to listen to cars rattle and your voice echo before continuing. A log boom is often strung across Thunder Arm to stop logs from drifting into the lake. When in place, you must pass through a narrow opening, marked by cones. At 1 mile, pass Thunder Point Camp on the left then glide into island-dotted Diablo Lake. When the water is calm, it is fun to explore the islands while paddling west across the lake toward the old Diablo Lake Resort. An exciting trip, which requires only a half mile of open water paddling, is Diablo Arm. At the end of Thunder Arm head right, up the narrow channel of the now-flooded Skagit River, to a point near the base

of Ross Dam. The lake becomes a narrow gorge where trees and wildflowers have only a toe-hold on the sheer rock walls. Waterfalls dominate the view.

Two small docks mark the upper end of Diablo Lake, 5 miles from Colonial Creek. You can continue on a couple hundred feet and peek around the bend of the river at the imposing face of Ross Dam before heading back. If you land, leave your boat out of the way of other users. For walks you may head up toward the power plant where the Diablo Lake Trail crosses the water on a high bridge. Or, with advance reservations, you can contact the Ross Lake Resort by phone from the power plant and they will transport you (and your small boat, if desired) for a fee up to Ross Lake where you can hike or rent a motorboat or canoe for more exploration. See Ross Lake for more canoeing and kayaking opportunities.

This toddler loves the canoe ride, but couldn't care less about the scenery.

Ross Lake

ROUND TRIP: up to 42 miles
PADDLING DIFFICULTY: moderate
ACTIVITIES: canoeing, kayaking, camping, fishing, and hiking
SEASON: Memorial Day to September 15
MAPS: Green Trails: Diablo Lake and Ross Lake
Map on page 50

Ross Lake is ideal for an extended canoe or kayak camping adventure. For the mature members of the party, who care for such ethereal pleasures, the scenery is stunning (better than the famous Bowron Lakes in Canada). Glaciated summits tower over the lake, waterfalls plunge down cliffs to end in cold waters, and the tributary streams and rivers offer exciting excursions up narrow canyons to the base of rapids. For everyone else, the fishing is excellent after July 1, campsites are numerous, and there are plenty of trails to relieve the tedium of paddling a boat.

This is not a trip for inexperienced paddlers. Winds frequently turn the lake into a frothing cauldron. Even if you are comfortable paddling in rough water, a short distance can become a marathon when heading into the winds. Best chance for calm water is early morning and late afternoon. Plan quick breakfasts or snacks that can be consumed in the boat and strive for early starts.

Just getting to Ross Lake is quite a challenge. The only car access is at the northern end of Ross Lake at Hozomeen, approximately 5 hours from Seattle. The final 40 miles from Hope, British Colombia, are on a narrow, rarely maintained gravel road and not recommend for low-clearance vehicles. The boat ramp at Hozomeen is generally useable July through mid-September but it is

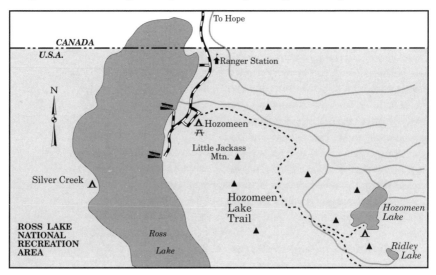

A fully loaded canoe approaching Lightening Creek Boat Camp on Ross Lake.

best to check with the Newhalem Visitor Center before making the long drive. The best water access is from Diablo Lake. This means starting the trip at Colonial Creek and paddling 5 miles to the end of Diablo Lake. Boats and gear are then portaged up a mile-long road which gains 600 feet while climbing over Ross Dam. You may do the portage yourself—wheels are recommended—or pay a fee and take advantage of the portage service offered by Ross Lake Resort. Arrangements should be made in advance by calling the resort at (360) 386-4437. The third option is to backpack your gear down the Ross Dam Trail 1.5 miles and rent a canoe from the resort.

Before you start you will need a backcountry permit, which can be picked up at ranger stations in Marblemount, Newhalem, or Hozomeen. The permit helps distribute people around the lake and ensures an available site when you arrive. Campsites vary in size from singles to room for seven tents. Three of the camps are located on islands. Write ahead to the park for a map of the lake showing the location and size of the camps to help plan your trip.

Paddling distances are relatively short and active families will have time for afternoon hikes. Big Beaver Boat Camp is located near the intersection of the West Bank and Big Beaver Trails. A moderate 6- to 8-mile round-trip hike up the nearly level Big Beaver Valley leads to 1,000-year-old cedars. However, short hikes along the river are also rewarding. A 0.2-mile trail from May Creek Camp leads to the East Side Trail and is a great place to stroll through the forest. The popular Lightning Creek Boat Camp lies at the junction of Lightning Creek Trail and Desolation Peak Trail. Desolation Peak is a classic: 9 miles round trip, with a 4,400-foot elevation gain and an unforgettable view of the lake, recommended for hyperactive teenagers and any parents that can keep up. For an easier afternoon stroll head north on the East Bank Trail as it climbs 1,000 feet in a long mile to views over Ross Lake. Families with very young children can spend an agreeable afternoon throwing rocks off the Lightning Creek Bridge or walking south to Lodgepole Camp. Little Beaver Camp at the Little Beaver trailhead is another place for an afternoon leg-stretching. Finally, the car camp at Hozomeen (accessible from the water) offers a chance to stretch your legs on an easy 6-mile round trip to forested Hozomeen Lake.

Scenery does nothing but improve as you go, no matter which end of the lake you start at. Colonial Peak, Davis Peak, and Ruby Mountain dominate the southern end of the lake. Jack Mountain towers over the center and Desolation and the awesome Hozomeen eclipse all competitors at the northern end.

Be sure to visit Big Beaver and paddle to the edge of the waterfall. Do not pass up a trip to Devils Creek. Lightning Creek and Little Beaver are a must. Finally, when the lake is calm, take time to cruise along the base of Skymo Creek Falls.

Plan at least 6 days to tour the entire lake. Throw in an extra day's worth of food just in case you get weathered in. June trips are recommended, as the lake is inaccessible to most motorboats at that time.

Diablo Lake Trail

ONE WAY: 4 miles
TRAIL DIFFICULTY: moderate
ELEVATION GAIN: 800 feet
ACTIVITIES: hiking and ferry ride
BEST: June to mid-September
MAP: Green Trails: Diablo Lake
Map on page 53

It is not the impressive vista of snow- and ice-wrapped mountains, rising straight up from Ross and Diablo Lakes, that will be remembered by the younger family members. And while the massive face of Ross Dam may cause some small show of interest by the over-eight crowd, and almost everyone will agree that spotting boats on the lake waters far below is fun, it is the ferry ride that will make this a memorable hike.

Diablo Lake Trail is in good condition and much of it can be walked two abreast. However, the trail climbs without respite for the first mile then continues on up at a moderate pace for the second mile, much to the distress of younger hikers. For parents to take note of, there is a short (it just seems long) section of exposed trail along the upper arm of Diablo Lake near the 2-mile point. If heights and exposure are a problem, then this section will not be enjoyed. Keep the family together, hold the young ones' hands, and make sure that everyone's attention is focused on the trail. When you wish to look at the scenery, stop. Do not walk and look at the same time.

Drive Highway 20 east 7.1 miles from Newhalem to milepost 127.1. Go left and descend the Diablo Dam access road. Cross the dam then turn right and head along the lakeshore 0.5 mile to the second dock and park (1,208 feet).

The ferry makes two runs a day, at 8:30 A.M. and at 3:00 P.M. It leaves the upper end of the lake at 9:00 A.M. and at 3:30 P.M. You may take the boat up and walk back at your own pace, or hike up and let the family anticipate the ride back. If you choose to start by hiking, walk the road past the City Light dock and work area, then around a cove to a large gravel turnaround just before the gated entrance to the old Diablo Lake Resort. The trail, which is unmarked, heads uphill through the woods.

If riding up the lake on the ferry, after disembarking, walk past the passengers boarding the truck that heads up to Ross Lake, and go right toward the Ross Dam Powerhouse. Once you reach the lawn, look for a trail sign and a suspension bridge on your left then head across the water. Ross Dam looms

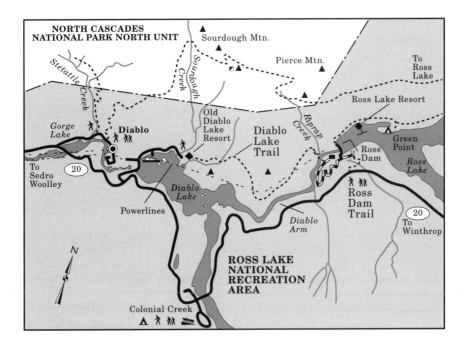

above. Once across, the trail begins climbing past a few remaining artifacts of the construction crews' abandoned living area.

After a couple switchbacks, a side trail heads right to a very exposed viewpoint of the dam. Viewing space is extremely limited and views are better above.

Near the 1-mile point, when the trail reaches the powerline swath for the second time, pause for the best view of Ross Lake and Jack Mountain. Beyond, the tempo of the climb relaxes and the trail begins to traverse south. After crossing a small creek near the 2-mile point, head across the exposed slopes above Diablo Arm. Keep together here. When you reach the powerlines for a third time, look left for a spur trail to a bench overlooking Diablo Lake. This is a great lunch spot and the last of the expansive views.

The trail then plunges down a boulder-strewn hillside before entering the forest to reach, at 3.4 miles, an old road. Stay to the right and follow the trail uphill to yet another old road which is walked for about 20 feet before veering left back on the trail. Continuing down, the lake comes into view and at 3.8 miles the trail ends at the road. Go right to return to the ferry dock.

Ross Dam

ROSS DAM
> ROUND TRIP: 2 miles
> TRAIL DIFFICULTY: moderate
> ELEVATION GAIN: 600 feet on return
> ACTIVITY: hiking
> BEST: May to mid-October
> MAP: Green Trails: Diablo Dam
> Map on pages 47 and 53

BIG BEAVER
> ROUND TRIP: 14.8 miles
> TRAIL DIFFICULTY: difficult
> ELEVATION GAIN: 500 feet in; 600 feet out
> ACTIVITY: backpacking
> BEST: May to September
> MAPS: Green Trails: Diablo Dam and Ross Lake

Ross Dam is an ideal destination for enquiring minds that want to know. The only hazard on this hike is for the parent, who must come up with answers for the blizzard of questions that pours forth as the dam gets closer and closer. Be forewarned, it will require a little advance reading about hydroelectric power generation to keep your super-parent status alive.

If you're looking for a backpack trip, the trail around the west side of Ross Lake is a great one. When you pick up your backcountry permits at Marblemount,

View from the top of Ross Dam

request a site at the boater's camp rather than the hiker's site. Although the boater's camp is 0.4 mile farther, the larger tent spaces, picnic tables, and easy lake access make it better for families than the primitive hiker's area.

Drive Highway 20 east 14 miles from Newhalem to milepost 134.2. Park on the left (west) side of the road in a wide gravel turnout (2,800 feet).

The trail heads immediately down. Almost before anyone has time to ask "Are we there yet?" the trail crosses Happy Creek. This shady, cool spot has two bubbling waterfalls and makes a good rest stop on the way back up.

Before long the trail crosses an open hillside overlooking the dam. Each view is better than the last. At 0.8 mile the trail arrives at a road and ends. Go left and descend 100 yards then go right on a road to the dam.

Upon reaching their destination, most adults tend to sit down and soak in the view. However, the gung-ho smaller hikers will focus on the massive dam. After walking the length of the dam and exploring the other side, the best way to stem the questions about why the electricity does not fall out of the wires is to head back up to the parking area. This is a good time to switch the discussion from electricity to gravity while you explain that all hikers who go down must go back up to return to their car.

If you're backpacking to Big Beaver, cross the dam and go right. The trail stays close to the lakeshore for the next mile until it passes the floating Ross Lake Resort. Ignoring the temptation to rent a canoe, stick with the trail as it begins to climb. At the 2.5-mile point a spur trail branches right to Green Point Camp—an excellent alternate to Big Beaver. The gradual but steady climb continues until the 3.8-mile point, at which time the trail begins a rolling traverse. Shortly after passing the hiker's camp at 7 miles, the trail crosses Big Beaver Creek. Go right for the final 0.4 mile to Big Beaver Camp.

MORE ACTIVITIES
Map on page 56

Pyramid Lake: This completely forested walk to a small puddle with limited views is best left for a long rainy weekend when there is a need to "just get out and do something." The trail is accessed from Highway 20 at milepost 126.9, located 5.8 miles east of Newhalem. Park on the north side of the road. The trail starts on the south side of the road and gains 1,500 feet in the 2 miles. The hike is rated as challenging.

Thunder Woods Nature Trail: This is a refreshing and thoroughly enjoyable walk, once you get over the shock of a nature trail that is not a leisurely amble. Rather than exploring the level valley bottom, this trail scales the steep hillside on its 1.5-mile loop. Of course, all the climbing leads to some unusually interesting ecology. A brochure, picked up at the start of the loop, discusses the plant and animal life of the hillside. The trail starts from Colonial Creek Campground at milepost 130.2. Drive into the south side camp area and follow the trail signs to the far end of the camp. Walk upvalley on Thunder Creek Trail for 0.1 mile to the well-signed nature loop trailhead. The rating for the loop is moderate.

Thunder Creek Trail: A venerable old forest is the object of this short hike. Although most people turn around when the trail crosses the Thunder Creek suspension bridge at the 0.8-mile point, the 1.5 miles beyond are true magic to lovers of beautiful forests. There are easily accessible backcountry

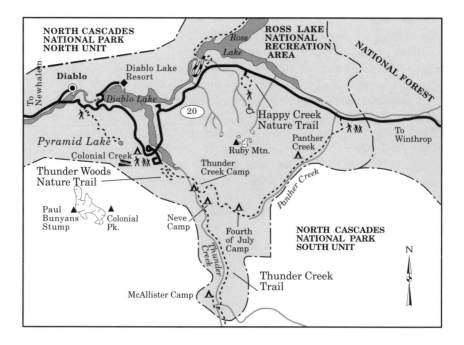

camps at 1.8 miles and 2.6 miles. The trail starts in conjunction with Thunder Woods Nature Trail; see above for directions.

Happy Creek Nature Trail: This 0.1-mile loop is a favorite with everyone who takes the time to walk or ride it (it is a barrier-free trail so wheelchairs, walkers, and strollers all work here). The entire trail is elevated on wood decking, adding to the fun for kids. Information signs discuss habitat and forest ecology. In late spring and early summer watch for slippery slugs sunbathing on the planks. The trail is located on the south side of Highway 20 near milepost 134.5, just 4.3 miles east of Colonial Creek. The trail is rated easiest.

North Cascades Scenic Highway

Backpacking, camping, hiking, scenic drives

North Cascades Scenic Highway cuts through the northern reaches of the Cascade Range between Ross Lake National Recreation Area to the resort areas of the Methow River valley. Although the highway is not actually part of the park, views of the interior of the North Cascades Range from the road make this drive a key element to any visit of the national park. The road climbs over two mountain passes; at 4,855 feet, the densely forested cut in the mountains called Rainy Pass is the lower of the two. The 5,477-foot Washington Pass lies in a subalpine wonderland between meadows dotted with islands of trees and towering rocky summits.

Horseback riders near Sun Mountain Resort in Methow Valley

The contrast between the rain-soaked west side of the Cascades and its dry eastern slopes is startling. Coming from the west, the trip begins in the rain forest and climbs thickly forested hillsides all the way to Washington Pass. As soon as you start down the east side of the mountains, the change is immediate and dramatic: pines replace the moisture-loving cedars and the greens of the understory give way to browns. The forest floor is open, blanketed with a mat of thick grass rather than the typical west-side tangle of ferns, alders, and Oregon grape. The Scenic Highway ends as the road abruptly exits the mountains to enter the dry, open, and nearly level plains of the Methow River valley.

Although viewpoints along the highway are numerous and spaced to allow travelers the best possible sampling of the scenery from their vehicles, to really experience this area you must get out and walk. The road passes within a couple miles of four subalpine lakes set in deep cirques. Groups with very young children, or older members with stiff knees, should try the level, paved walk to Rainy Lake. Families that have achieved an age of increased mobility can consider adventuring to Lake Ann, Blue Lake, or Cutthroat Lake.

Accommodations and food service along the North Cascades Highway between Ross Lake National Recreation Area and Early Winters are nonexistent. The nearest lodging is located at Marblemount on the west side of the mountains and at Mazama on the east side. When exploring the highway, visitors are advised to pack a substantial picnic lunch and bring plenty of liquids. (Make sure the car has enough gas to travel through this wilderness.) For campers, there are three forest service campgrounds to choose from on the east side of Washington Pass. Lone Fir at milepost 168.4 has twenty-seven sites, drinking water, and pit toilets. At milepost 175.1, Klipchuck Campground offers forty-six sites in a shady valley bottom setting, as well as water and flush toilets. Early Winters Campground at milepost 179 provides another twenty-six sites along the edge of Early Winters Creek with running water and pit toilets. More sites are available on the west side at Colonial Creek and Newhalem. There is also a state park at Winthrop (almost always full), and several private camping areas for tents and motor homes.

The North Cascades Scenic Highway officially ends when you exit the mountains at Early Winters. For many visitors, the entrance to the Methow River valley is where the fun begins. The Methow offers a fascinating opportunity to sample a high desert environment. There is a host of activities to choose from, including horseback riding, mountain biking, hiking, and rafting. Horseback rides are available at Sun Mountain Lodge for guests only; however, Mazama Country Inn offers daily signups for walk-ins. Children should be age ten or older for these rides. If you have questions, talk to the wranglers. For longer excursions into the wilderness, inquire at the Forest and Park Information Center located on Highway 20 at the north end of Winthrop for a list of local outfitters.

Liberty Bell Mountain and Early Winters Spires viewed from the Washington Pass Overlook

Methow Valley is famed for its excellent mountain bike rides. Most of the roads and trails have steep climbs and equally steep descents, making this area best for sturdy teenagers and their parents. However, there are some rides that can be completed by riders of any age. Mountain bikes may be rented in Winthrop and at Sun Mountain. No bikes are available for young riders. There is limited availability of 24-inch-wheel bikes which generally fit kids ages twelve and up.

Lake Ann and Maple Pass Loop

LAKE ANN
> ROUND TRIP: 3.5 miles
> TRAIL DIFFICULTY: moderate
> ELEVATION GAIN: 620 feet
> ACTIVITIES: hiking, backpacking, fishing
> BEST: mid-July to September
> MAP: Trails Illustrated: North Cascades National Park
> Map on page 61

MAPLE PASS LOOP
> LOOP HIKE: 7.2 miles
> TRAIL DIFFICULTY: challenging
> ELEVATION GAIN: 1,800 feet
> ACTIVITIES: hiking, backpacking, fishing
> BEST: mid-August to September
> MAP: Trails Illustrated: North Cascades National Park

Only 600 feet above the thickly forested draw that is Rainy Pass lies a world of flower-carpeted, subalpine meadows and gem-like lakes sheltered by towering cliffs. Lake Ann, the most accessible of these lakes, is an ideal day hike or an easy overnight backpack. Maple Pass Loop is a challenging walk which climbs to high alpine splendor while crossing three passes with views so stunning that every hiker of the scenery-appreciating age will have at least one "Ohhhh" pop out of them.

Although only 7.2 miles in length, Maple Pass Loop is very demanding. The climb is relentless and the descent to the Rainy Lake Trail very steep, requiring shoes with soles that really grip. Carry plenty of water, lots of snacks, and extra clothes.

Drive Highway 20 to milepost 157.5 at the summit of Rainy Pass. Exit to the south and find space in the large trailhead/picnic area parking lot which has running water and bathrooms (4,855 feet).

Walk to the well-signed Lakes Trail trailhead. The trail divides at the large information sign. Go right and head toward Lake Ann. (The paved trail on the left goes to Rainy Lake and will be used by Maple Pass Loop hikers on the return.)

Lake Ann Trail climbs steadily up the forested hillside. The trail is wide enough for younger hikers to walk side by side. Several wide points along the trail offer great places for rest stops. Keep watch over your food; the resident camp robbers are adept at stealing things right out of your hands.

Near the 0.7-mile point, leave the trees and begin a climbing traverse around a rocky basin brightened by masses of wildflowers. At 1.1 miles the trail divides. Lake Ann is now an easy stroll to the left. When the trail enters the meadows at 1.5 miles look for two campsites on the left. A third campsite can be found below the first. Camping at the lake is not allowed.

Lake Ann (5,475 feet), reached at

Young hiker helps his grandmother over a rough section of the trail to Lake Ann

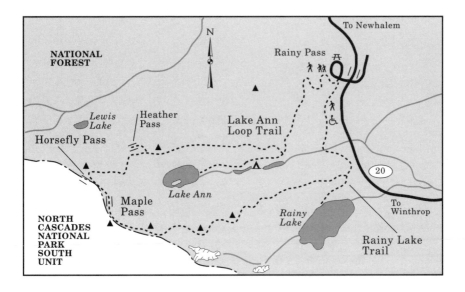

1.8 miles, is a feast for the eyes only. Enjoy the view, have a snack, and, if the kids want to try out the water, retreat downvalley 0.3 mile and head to the ponds. These are fascinating places brimming with aquatic life and easily accessible for young legs.

Hikers doing the entire Maple Pass Loop should stay right at the Lake Ann intersection and continue climbing. At 2.3 miles pass an open meadow on the right. This is 5,800-foot Heather Pass. A boot path branches to the right for a mile-long traverse to isolated Lewis Lake.

The trail continues to climb, switchbacking high above Lake Ann. Horsefly Pass, 6,400 feet, is reached at 3.1 miles. This pass earns its name and before you get a chance to sit down and enjoy the view, you will be under siege by those pesky bugs. Because you cannot sit here without being bitten, you will soon be studying the ant farm of trails that radiate out from the pass. The correct trail follows the ridge crest to the left and in 0.5 mile reaches the 6,600-foot high point of the loop at Maple Pass.

If you have not taken the time to study the view, stop here and do so. Glacier Peak, the North Cascades, and the Pasayten Wilderness spread out around your feet.

From Maple Pass, descend rapidly into the forest. At 6.7 miles the dirt trail ends. Go left and join the crowds strolling the paved Rainy Lake Trail back to the parking lot at 7.2 miles.

Rainy Lake

ROUND TRIP: 2 miles
TRAIL DIFFICULTY: easy
ELEVATION GAIN: none
ACTIVITY: hiking
BEST: mid-July to September
MAP: Green Trails: Washington Pass
Map on page 61

This 1-mile-long barrier-free trail ends at the shores of a deep glacier-carved lake. Far above, melt water from the Lyell Glacier and several small permanent snowfields begins a tumbling, 1,500-foot journey, dancing down long cascades and plunging over cliffs in lacy waterfalls to reach the lake. Above the glaciers, the towering ramparts of Frisco Mountain and Rainy Peak do their best to hide this beautiful lake in deep shadows.

The paved trail provides a solid base for strollers, wheelchairs, and canes. In other words, this is a walk for the entire family. Even the family pet is invited.

Drive Highway 20 to milepost 157.5 at the summit of Rainy Pass. Exit to the south and find a space in the busy trailhead/picnic area parking lot which has running water and bathrooms (4,855 feet).

Follow the LAKES TRAIL sign to the actual trailhead, then go left on the paved and level Rainy Lake Trail. For the adults there are several small marshy meadows with rich carpets of wildflowers to enjoy and informational signs to read. Younger members of the group will probably prefer the benches and the wooden bridges over the creeks. The second creek is energetic enough to float sticks down until late summer. At the 0.5-mile point, pass the Maple Pass Loop/Lake Ann Trail. Continue on pavement, heading through dense timber.

At 1 mile, the trail ends at a paved overlook. This is the best viewing area of the lake. Paths head down to the shore, but the steepness of the terrain and the accumulation of avalanche debris keeps water contact at a minimum. Look, enjoy, rest, and then head back.

Blue Lake

ROUND TRIP: 4.4 miles
TRAIL DIFFICULTY: moderate
ELEVATION GAIN: 1,100 feet
ACTIVITIES: hiking, fishing
BEST: mid-July to September
MAP: Green Trails: Washington Pass
Map on page 63

A short distance from the hustle of Highway 20 lies a true wilderness cirque at the edge of the barren world of high alpine tundra. This teardrop-shaped lake abuts a vertical wall that soars 2,000 feet into the sky. To the east, Liberty Bell and neighboring Early Winters Spires form what appears to be a turreted wall of a giant's castle, beautiful and just a bit foreboding.

The trail to the lake is wide and well maintained. However, the constant climb can be discouraging to younger walkers. Once at the lake, the whining

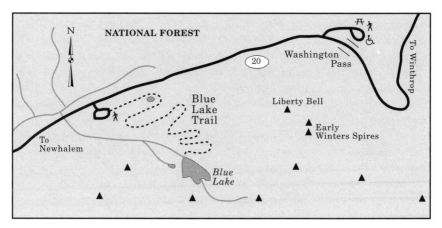

Blue Lake

will stop and exhaustion will disappear like magic. The old, broken-down miner's cabin at trail's end simply demands exploration, while the lake's outlet stream begs to be splashed in and the deep bluish waters cry out for a fishing pole.

No camping is allowed in the lake basin. There is room for one tent in the meadow 0.1 mile below.

Drive Highway 20 to milepost 161.5, located 0.9 mile west of Washington Pass and 4 miles east of Rainy Pass. Turn south off the highway into a gravel parking area (5,230 feet). If arriving in the early morning hours, carefully step over the sleeping forms of climbers sprawled on the ground. Later in the day you will share the trail with these climbers as they head up to Liberty Bell and Early Winters Spires.

This is a National Recreation Trail. In the lower sections, as you parallel the highway, you may wonder why. Do not worry; before long the trail switchbacks away from the road and heads up through thinning forest speckled with wildflower-brightened meadows. The trail emerges briefly from the trees at the 1-mile point to switchback over the lower section of a rocky slope. However, it is not until the trees are left behind at 1.6 miles and you head across an open meadow with a full palette of colorful wildflowers and views of Liberty Bell that the true visual impact of this area is appreciated.

At 2.2 miles the trail crosses the outlet stream and ends at Blue Lake (6,300 feet). Paths radiate out in every direction, but, unless you scramble all the way around the lake, it is hard to improve on the initial view. Meadows and wildflowers are everywhere. Snowfields dip into the lake for much of the summer and water lovers will find that they are quickly afflicted with a case of the cold shivers.

Cutthroat Lake

CUTTHROAT LAKE
>   ROUND TRIP: 4 miles
>   TRAIL DIFFICULTY: easy
>   ELEVATION GAIN: 440 feet
>   ACTIVITIES: hiking, swimming, backpacking, fishing
>   BEST: mid-July to September
>   MAP: Green Trails: Washington Pass

CUTTHROAT PASS
>   ROUND TRIP: 11.4 miles
>   TRAIL DIFFICULTY: difficult
>   ELEVATION GAIN: 2,300 feet
>   ACTIVITIES: hiking, backpacking
>   BEST: late July to September
>   MAP: Green Trails: Washington Pass
>   Map on page 66

In its wide cirque below the ramparts of Cutthroat Mountain, this shallow lake is an ideal day trip. (Pack some wading shoes; the lake bottom is messy.) Along the way there are creeks for throwing rocks and sticks and large granitic boulders for scrambling. Families who prefer a longer stay will find several passable campsites 0.3 mile below the lake. No camping is allowed at the lake.

For more ambitious crews, the long hike to Cutthroat Pass rewards hikers with a top-of-the-world destination and open meadows. The perception minded will find the pass has marvelous scenery.

Drive Highway 20 to milepost 167 located 4.8 miles west of Washington Pass and 11 miles east of Early Winters Campground. Go north on Cutthroat Road for 1 mile to the trailhead parking area and informal campground (4,500 feet).

From the often dusty parking lot, work your way around the horse loading ramp then walk along the old river terrace. Horses and mountain bikes also use this trail. Both can be dangerous if improperly controlled so keep younger children close.

After passing a couple of unofficial spur trails, the main route crosses Cutthroat Creek on a sturdy bridge then heads upvalley. The climb starts with a steep Z, after which the rate of ascent moderates to an almost imperceptible upward ramble. On hot days, groves of trees provide shade between sections of exposed hillside. Early season walkers will have several hazardous creeks to cross. By late summer, these are nothing but dry channels.

The trail divides in a shady fold of the hill at 1.7 miles. For Cutthroat Lake, go left and descend to cross the creek then climb a short hill. If camping, go left on a well-beaten boot trail to the unmarked tent sites. Continuing to the

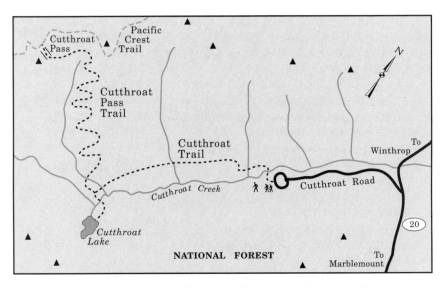

lake, the trail is rough and sandy. At 2 miles reach the grove of trees marking the edge of the lakeshore marsh (4,950 feet). Pick some solid ground for your picnic then explore the rough round-the-lake trail to find the best splashing site. Swimmers will find large rocks just off the east shore appealing on warm days.

If continuing on to the pass, get set to climb. The trail is well graded but the climb is constant. Trees get shorter and meadows larger. The 6,800-foot pass, reached at 5.7 miles, is an exotic rock garden decorated with lichens and miniature flowers. No matter how tired you feel, find some energy for a short stroll to a small knoll just south of the pass. Views encompass Cutthroat Peak, Liberty Bell, and even the glaciated mass of Dome Peak. (There is no reliable source of water near the pass; backpackers are advised to use the campsites near the Cutthroat Lake turnoff.)

Cedar Falls

ROUND TRIP: 4 miles
TRAIL DIFFICULTY: moderate
ELEVATION GAIN: 560 feet
ACTIVITIES: hiking and backpacking
BEST: June to mid-October
MAP: Green Trails: Mazama
Map on page 67

Thanks to its proximity to Klipchuck Campground, Early Winters Campground, Mazama, and Winthrop, this is a very popular trail. And, of course,

Cedar Falls itself is amazing. The upper part of the falls splits into two channels and tumbles down to a rocky pool. The lower falls gathers all the water from the two upper sections and makes a giant free-fall down an even larger cliff.

Unfortunately, the falls are hard to see. The best views are atop rocky overhangs where one missed step will plant you 50 or more feet down the hill. In short, Cedar Falls is not the sort of destination where the family can relax, enjoy the view, then allow the children to play unattended before heading back.

Drive Highway 20 to milepost 175.4, located 2.5 miles west of Early Winters Campground or 13.6 miles east of Washington Pass. Turn north on Spur Road 200 and head uphill on a rough dirt road 0.9 mile to its end at the Cedar Creek trailhead (3,040 feet).

The trail starts off by ascending the steepest hill of the entire hike. Before long, enter the forest where the climb abates and the trail begins a long upvalley traverse. With no views and no creeks to see or cross, it is only the anticipation of seeing the falls, or maybe of some special treat you are carrying, that keeps the smaller feet moving. Listen for bird calls and try to guess what they are saying. Listen for the squirrels and try to hear the differences between the squirrels and birds. If all else fails, stop and draw pictures in the dust.

At 2 miles the roar of the falls can be heard. Look for a small campsite/picnic place on the left and follow one of the footpaths that leads from it to the viewpoints perched high above the abyss. After viewing the upper falls, walk down the cliff line to a view of the lower falls. A steep, rocky trail descends from the top of the cliff to the pool at the base of the upper falls. If you choose to descend, do so with extreme caution.

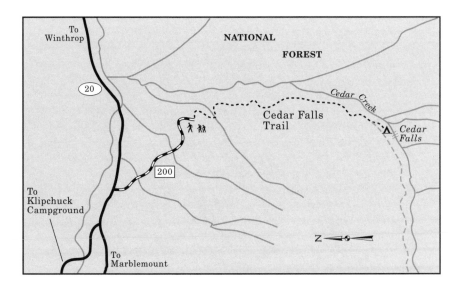

Patterson Mountain Loop

LOOP TRIP: 3 miles
TRAIL DIFFICULTY: moderate
ELEVATION GAIN: 700 feet
ACTIVITIES: hiking, views, wildlife
BEST: May to October
MAP: Sun Mountain Trails Map
Map on page 68

Views, high desert rangeland, and wild birds keynote this recently developed trail. Late spring and early summer see the hillsides covered with a carpet of wildflowers. Grouse seem to be everywhere and snowcapped mountains pierce the crisp blue sky.

This trail is part of the Sun Mountain Lodge Trail system and is open to all hikers without charge. For information, inquire at the Sports Shop and Activity Desk at the lodge. Carry plenty of water. During the summer months it is best to hike in the early morning or evening hours when the air is cooler.

Drive Highway 20 to the south end of the western-style town of Winthrop. Cross the bridge over the Methow River then immediately head west on the Twin Lakes Road. After 3.3 miles go left on Patterson Lake Road and head up 4.2 miles to Patterson Lake. The trailhead is located across the road from the Public Fishing parking area (2,440 feet).

The hike begins with a potentially discouraging climb. As a distraction, encourage everyone to look and listen. Grouse often hide in the thick brush along the trail. After an initial 200-foot elevation gain, the trail reaches a broad saddle, several fences, and an intersection which marks the start of the loop. The South Side Trail offers the easier ascent and is the recommended route

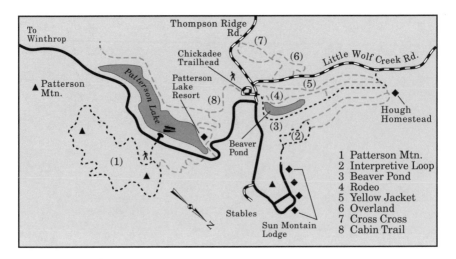

unless you arrived midday and wish to take advantage of the North Side Trail shade.

The South Side Trail crosses a fence then proceeds to switchback up the hillside. Views expand exponentially as you go. At first you see just Patterson Lake. Before long Sun Mountain Lodge comes into view. Soon after you are looking north to Pasayten Wilderness and a broad expanse of the North Cascade Range.

This is a range area and cows roam the slopes. Fences divide the hillsides and cattle are moved around during the summer, but the result is a lot of cow trails cutting and meandering over the hillsides. Put the kids out in front and give them the challenge of following the bits of orange tape, lines of rocks, and arrows etched in wood that help you stay on the route. Young children may have a hard time on the steeper slopes.

Steps provide a fun way to cross cattle fences on the Patterson Mountain Loop.

After climbing steadily for 1.7 miles the trail suddenly reaches the crest of the ridge (3,140 feet). From this point you can try to convince the group that a 0.5-mile cross-country stroll to the true summit would be fun, or just enjoy the view you have and head down on the North Side Trail. The descent is quick and the occasional shade is usually occupied by the occasional cow.

At 2.8 miles is an intersection with a trail to Sun Mountain Lodge. Go left and cross a fence to close the loop.

MORE ACTIVITIES

Map on pages 68, 70, and 72

Canyon Creek Trail: This is an interesting and fun stop to relieve the tedium of a long drive over the pass. In just 0.2 mile, you will cross two bridges and explore two old buildings. The trailhead is located 11.4 miles east of Colonial Creek Campground on the north side of the road. Follow the trail upvalley to cross Granite Creek then head downstream to an intersection. Go straight to find the old, beautifully constructed Beebe Cabin around the corner. To reach the old barn, cross Canyon Creek on a narrow log (short people should have their hands held by taller people who, in turn, can hold onto the railing wire). Go left and head downvalley 200 feet. The barn is rotten; explore with caution.

Washington Pass Overlook: This is a must stop for first-time visitors to the North Cascades. From a cliff top overlooking Highway 20, watch cars crawl up to the pass and, in the opposite direction, zoom down from the summit beneath a giant fortress of cliffs that puts the Great Wall of China to shame. The wall is topped by Liberty Bell and Early Winters Spires. Let your attention wander, crossing the snowfields to Kangaroo Ridge, Snagtooth Ridge, and even part of Silver Star Mountain. The short 0.1-mile Overlook Trail crosses the cliff tops then heads up a rocky staircase before descending back to the parking area. The Overlook has a picnic area with running water and a massive, $1.2 million designer bathroom featuring composting toilets. A small kiosk is open during the months of July and August. Forest service personnel are on duty to answer questions.

Lone Pine: The Lone Pine was a landmark used by travelers for over 100 years. A section of the tree is preserved in Lone Pine Campground.

Lone Pine Loop Trail: From Lone Pine Campground, this barrier-free interpretive trail heads upvalley for a nearly level 0.4 mile to Early Winters Creek. Wheelchair drivers may need a push on a short uphill section toward the end. For walkers who wish to explore further, a well-marked 2-mile loop trail continues upvalley on the route used by Indians and early European explorers.

Klipchuck Campground—River Loop: This 0.2-mile loop trail provides access to Early Winters Creek from Klipchuck Campground. The creek is a great place to splash, throw rocks, and cool off after a warm day.

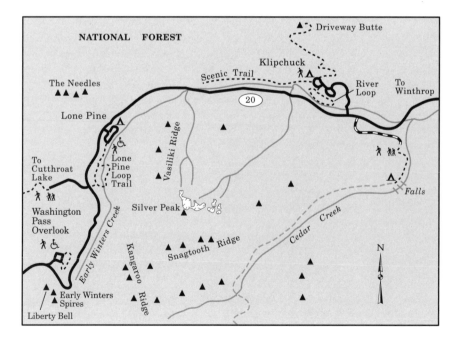

Klipchuck Campground—Scenic Trail: This valley explorer starts in Loop B and ends 4 miles upvalley. Few views and no spectacular scenery, just pleasant walking through a lodgepole forest highlights this trail. Look for deer and wildflowers in early summer.

Klipchuck Campground—Driveway Butte: A rewarding view of the east side of the North Cascades and the Pasayten Range can be had by anyone willing to make the long, steep, very hot, and very, very dry trek to the site of the old lookout at the crest of Driveway Butte. It is 4 miles from the trailhead at the entrance to Klipchuck Campground to the 5,982-foot summit. The trail gains 3,100 feet of elevation, making this hike extremely challenging.

Goat Peak Lookout: This is a challenging hike to the top of a 7,000-foot peak with magnificent views. The mountain and the fire lookout building at the summit can be seen throughout the Methow Valley, allowing clever parents to point out this exotic destination, days before you go there. Drive Highway 20 to the Lost River Road, located on the east side of the bridge over the Methow River. After 2 miles go right on Road 52. Follow it 3.7 miles then go left on Road 5225 for another 4.6 miles. Take a right on Spur Road 200 for a final 3 miles to the trailhead.

Sun Mountain Interpretive Loop: This 1-mile loop is one of the best introductions to the high desert environment found anywhere. The trailhead

Mountain biker on a trail near Sun Mountain resort

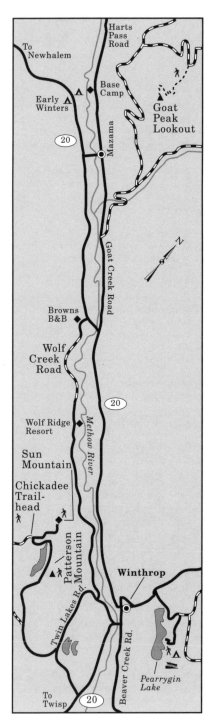

is located at Sun Mountain Lodge. From the parking area, follow the paved road past the lodge's Gardner and Robinson Units. Head up Kraule Trail and follow it past the Water Tanks. Return on the View Ridge Trail.

Wolf Creek Loop—Mountain Bike: This easy ride follows paved and dirt roads along the Mazama River. Expect traffic along the entire loop. The route begins at Highway 20 on the south side of Winthrop and returns to Highway 20 at Brown's Bed and Breakfast, just south of Mazama. The return leg of the loop is on Highway 20. From Winthrop, head west on Twin Lakes Road 1.4 miles. Go left on Wolf Creek Road and head up the nearly level valley for 3 miles to an intersection where you leave the pavement. Go right on Lower Wolf Creek Road. After 1.5 miles the route divides; stay left and begin a steady climb on loose gravel. Turn around if any of the group has reached the end of their comfort zone. The climb lasts for a long 0.9 mile and is followed by a gradual descent. At 10.7 miles from Winthrop the Wolf Creek Road intersects Highway 20 and ends.

Beaver Pond Loop—Mountain Bike: This easy 3-mile loop is ideal for novice trail riders. The first time around, ride Beaver Pond Trail to Hough Homestead then return on Little Wolf Creek Road. Once you have mastered the basic skills, go around the pond a second time and try the Yellow Jacket Trail on the way back. To reach the trailhead, drive Highway 20 to the south side of Winthrop then go right on Twin Lakes Road for 3.3 miles. Take a right on Patterson Lake Road. One mile beyond the lake go left and park at the Chickadee trailhead.

Stehekin

Backpacking, biking, bus tours, camping, fishing, food service, hiking, horse rides, lodging, rafting, ranger talks, visitor center

Accessed only by boat, plane, or trail, Stehekin is an isolated community located at the upper end of Lake Chelan. Without a road connecting it to the outside world, Stehekin may sound like a mellow place, with no appeal to the needs and desires of boisterous and energetic families. Admittedly, there are no video arcades, radio reception is lousy, and television is conspicuously absent. However, despite the lack of modern amenities, visitors, no matter what their ages, rarely have time to be bored.

If allowing only a single day for your Stehekin visit, arm yourself with a camera and binoculars for spotting wildlife along the open hillsides above Lake Chelan, and pad the pocket with a few extra dollars. Bring books and toys for younger family members. In order to maximize your time at Stehekin, you may want to ride up the lake on the faster, and more expensive, *Lady Express* and, after three and a half hours on shore, make your return on the slower *Lady of the Lake II*. If you ride the economical *Lady of the Lake II* both directions, you will have only a brief 90-minute layover at Stehekin.

Once at Stehekin, there are possibilities galore. The trip to Rainbow Falls is very popular. A bus waits at the dock to whisk you upvalley 3.5 miles and back in about 40 minutes. However, if you need to release some pent-up energy after the boat ride, you can rent bikes instead (riders must be tall enough to straddle a 24-inch-wheeled bike). For the preschoolers, parents may rent bike trailers. In-between-sized riders need to bring their own bikes (expensive for a one-day visit).

If the trip to the waterfalls sounds too hectic, try a very scenic hike on the Lakeshore Trail, 0.5 mile to Hazard Creek and back, followed by a stop at the visitor center to view a slide show. On warm days, end your visit with an invigorating wade or swim in the lake.

Longer visits are better, allowing

Mountain bikes are ideal for exploring Stehekin.

for a leisurely sampling of the valley. Accommodations are numerous, the two largest being the North Cascades Stehekin Lodge located at the boat landing and the Stehekin Valley Ranch located about 9 miles upvalley. There are also bed-and-breakfasts and a couple cabins to rent. If you bring your tent, campsites are located within 0.2 mile of the boat landing and eight more campgrounds are scattered along the Stehekin Valley Road. You must have a campsite reservation. Calling ahead is advised. You may call the Golden West Visitor Center Stehekin at (360) 856-5703, or try the main park office at Sedro Woolley: (360) 856-5700. Check at the visitor center for evening programs on the weekends.

Once at Stehekin, you can tailor the visit to fit your family's time, energy, and financial budget. Possible activities include a horse-drawn wagon tour from the bakery to the historic Buckner Orchard, raft trips, horse rides (minimum age is 10 years old), bike rides up or just downvalley, hikes, nature walks, and boat rentals. Bus rides up and down the valley are expensive. During the summer months, two buses are required to reach the road's end. In 1997 the driveable road ended at Bridge Creek and only hikers, horses, and bicycles could go all the way to Cottonwood Camp. It is uncertain when the road will be repaired. Information and sign-up for raft trips, horse rides, and wagon trips can be done at the Courtney Log Office, located just west of the post office and opposite the shower and laundry building. A radio telephone is located there also and calls out of the valley can be made for a hefty fee.

Rainbow Falls

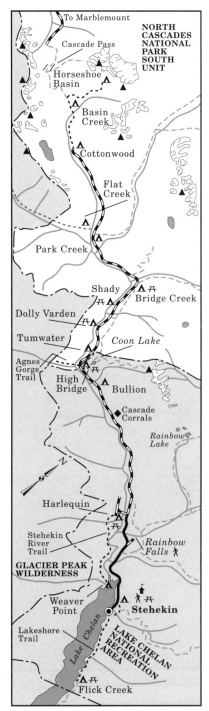

Lakeshore Trail

ROUND TRIP: up to 7.4 miles
TRAIL DIFFICULTY: moderate
ELEVATION GAIN: up to 300 feet
ACTIVITIES: hiking, backpacking, views, water play
BEST: April to October
MAP: Green Trails: Stehekin
Map on page 75

This fun and scenic hike is a great way to spend an hour or a day. The views are excellent and sure to please the adults, while watching the nearly constant passage of boats and floatplanes will keep the kids busy. Turnaround points

View over Lake Chelan from the Lakeshore Trail

are numerous; however, Flick Creek, at 3.6 miles, with its shelter, picnic table, boat dock, and beach access, makes an ideal destination. Energetic hikers may prefer to continue on over scenic Hunts Bluff to the old hotel site at Moore Point, a 14-mile round trip.

The trail has several narrow sections where, for the parents' peace of mind, younger hikers should be escorted. As always in the Lake Chelan area, keep a vigilant eye out for snakes and do daily tick checks.

From the boat landing, head uphill and to the left. Walk in front of the Golden West Visitor Center, passing the restrooms to reach an intersection. Continue straight, following signs to Lakeshore Trail. Pass a house, then walk through the overflow camp area. The trail takes you on a short scramble up some rocks to the first views over the lake to Domke Mountain.

After skirting the lakeshore for 0.5 mile the trail heads into a fold in the hills and crosses Hazard Creek just below a lacy waterfall. Continuing on, pass a summer home at Adams Point and shortly after return to the lakeshore to cross another rocky point. At 2.7 miles the trail traverses Fourmile Creek, then passes a couple of good-looking campsites. At 3.6 miles the trail passes above Flick Creek Campground. Follow one of the unsigned trails down to the shelter, campsite, restroom, and boat dock. (Boaters tend to treat the place as private property; however, the campsite is open to everyone.)

Stehekin Valley Road

ROUND TRIP: up to 17.1 miles
TRAIL DIFFICULTY: easy to challenging
ELEVATION GAIN: up to 1,600 feet
ACTIVITIES: mountain biking, hiking, backpacking
BEST: July to September
MAPS: Green Trails: Stehekin and McGregor Mtn.
Map on page 75

Although bikes are recommended, exploring the Stehekin Valley can also be fun on foot, if you are an adult, that is. Most normal kids will tend to ask that difficult "Why" question, leaving you to fumble for workable answers as cars, buses, and bicycles cruise by.

The valley road is scenic from start to finish. The first 1.3 miles are right along the lakeshore. The next 15.8 miles are spent following the Stehekin River as it winds between snow- and ice-covered mountains. The route initially is in the forest then gradually enters the subalpine world where the road ends. Trails continue on, ending only when they reach the glaciers.

Families with preschoolers may either bring their own bike trailer or rent one in Stehekin. Older kids, from preschool to age ten, must supply their own bikes. (Parents will need to walk and push the younger ones.) Families with children age ten or younger will probably be satisfied with a round trip of 8.8 miles, or less, turning around where the pavement ends at Harlequin Bridge.

Once the kids are tall enough to ride a bike with 24-inch wheels, you may leave your bikes at home and rent them at Stehekin. Options abound; teenagers who are energetic and enthused about mountain bike riding will leave their parents in the dust and head to the end of the road, all for the thrill of racing back down. Others may prefer to ride the bus at least part way upvalley and cruise back, stopping to explore, or fish, as they go.

The following is a description of the Stehekin Valley Road. A couple words of warning: If you have never ridden a bicycle off the pavement before, carry some bandages for potential tumbles and scrapes. If you own a helmet, bring it. If you do not own a helmet, wear one supplied by the rental shop.

The road begins at the boat landing and heads through town, passing the post office, ranger station, picnic area, and several houses before reaching the bike rental shop at 0.1 mile. Use caution; traffic is heavy in this area. After passing Purple Point Campground the road clings to the rocky hillside just above the lake. Near the 1-mile point, pass another picnic area. Shortly after, the road bends west and heads through the marshes at the end of the lake.

After 1.9 miles of nearly level riding the road bends sharply north. On the left is Stehekin Pastry Company, a very popular stop. The climb begins here and the road starts a slow but steady ascent. Lower Rainbow Falls Trail is passed at 2.5 miles. The road descends then climbs a couple of times, passing first the modern Stehekin Valley School then the old, one-room Stehekin School at 3.3 miles. Stop and take a look inside before continuing.

Immediately after leaving the school the road crosses Rainbow Creek then passes a fascinating hiking trail (no bikes allowed) to Buckner Historic Orchard. Just beyond the trail, a dirt road to Rainbow Falls branches off to the left. Park your bike at the turnaround and walk the short trail to the falls.

Timber wolf, a rarely seen denizen of the Northwest forests

At 3.5 miles a dirt road descends to the right, offering wheeled access to the orchard area. Harlequin Bridge is on the left at 4.4 miles. Cross the bridge to reach the campground located on the river's edge. The area is covered with sand, great for playing in before and after the picnic.

Beyond the bridge the road is gravel surfaced; however, elevation gain is gradual and riding relatively easy.

If this is your first experience riding off the pavement, start out slowly. The easiest riding is found on solid surfaces; however, it is a good idea to take a few moments to experiment with riding through loose dirt or gravel. When descending, avoid using your brakes except on hard-packed surfaces. Braking on loose ground may result in loss of control and spills. Plan ahead; panic stops frequently end in tumbles.

Note: All trails in the Stehekin Valley are closed to bicycles. When doing any off-road exploring, always leave your bike at the trailhead.

At 8.6 miles pass Stehekin Valley Ranch and Cascade Corrals. If you have made arrangements ahead of time, you may stop by for a meal. Bullion Camp for hikers and horses is passed at 10.1 miles, and at 11.1 miles reach the very high, High Bridge where the road crosses the Stehekin River and begins a short section of serious climbing. The Pacific Crest Trail bisects the road here, and there are also trails leading to Agnes Gorge and Coon Lake.

At 11.8 miles, pass Tumwater Camp and shortly beyond recross the Stehekin River on another airy bridge. At 12.7 miles reach Dolly Varden Camp. Continuing upvalley, pass Shady Camp to reach Bridge Creek Camp at 15.8 miles. Beyond Bridge Creek the climb is gradual for the final 6 miles to the road's end at Cottonwood Camp. Enjoy the cruise back.

MORE ACTIVITIES
Map on page 75

Nature Talks: Daily talks are given at the Golden West Visitor Center by park interpreters during the *Lady of the Lake II*'s 90-minute layover in Stehekin. Check at the visitor center for times.

Imus Creek Nature Trail: Starting from the south side of the Golden West Visitor Center, this 0.4-mile loop climbs the hill behind town. After gaining 200 feet the trail descends to the road at Purple Point Campground. Go left for a pleasant stroll back to town. Trail guides may be purchased at the visitor center. Views are limited.

Purple Creek Trail: This is an extremely challenging hike which climbs 5,700 feet in just 7.5 miles. The views are exceptional and the meadows near Purple Pass make the trip rewarding. Water and campsites are located at Lake Juanita. This hike is recommended for college age and up.

Rainbow Loop Trail: Although it is called a loop, this is actually a 4.4-mile half-circle that climbs 1,000 feet to cross Rainbow Creek high above the waterfall then returns to the Stehekin Valley Road 0.7 mile above Harlequin Bridge. Views are moderate.

Buckner Orchard Trail: This 0.2-mile trail from the Stehekin Valley Road to the historic orchard is recommended for everyone. The numerous bridges over the irrigation channel will make it especially appealing to younger hikers. Once at the orchard you may wander and explore (only the house is private; please respect their rights). Many old farm machines have been left out for visitors to look at. The trail begins 3.3 miles from the boat landing. Walk across Rainbow Creek and go left.

Stehekin River Trail: This trail begins at the airport, which is accessed from Harlequin Bridge 4.4 miles from the boat landing. The hike is 3.8 miles each way, unless you are lucky enough to finagle a ride on a private boat from Weaver Point Campground back to Stehekin. The trail is nearly level and forested for the entire distance. Some signs of beaver activity can be seen.

Agnes Gorge Trail: The gorge is beautiful, exciting, and potentially very dangerous. If you slipped into the churning waters of Agnes Creek, no rescue would be possible. If the family understands the dangers before starting, the 2.5 nearly level miles from High Bridge to the gorge make an enjoyable day hike.

Coon Lake: This area is laced with trails for hikers and separate stock trails for horses. To avoid paying for a two-zone bus fare, start this easy hike at either Bullion or High Bridge Campgrounds. The lake is forested and marshy, a great place to view wildlife.

Black Warrior Mine: When the valley road is open all the way to the Cottonwood Camp, the challenging 3.5 miles to the old mine can be an exciting hike for anyone who can handle the 2,000-foot elevation gain. The route follows Cascade Pass Trail for 2 miles then heads right on Horseshoe Basin Trail. Climb steeply for 1.5 miles to the mine. Do not go inside without a flashlight. The basin beyond the mine is truly splendid, with open meadows, creeks cascading down the hillsides, and impressive glimpses of the glaciers above.

Note: In 1997, the road was closed at Bridge Creek and the final 6 miles to the Cottonwood Camp had to be walked or bicycled. The park hopes to have the road repair completed by 1999. Check at the visitor center in Stehekin for updates.

Holden Village: The village is a Lutheran camp, located on the site of an old copper mine. It is a friendly place to visit even if you are not a Lutheran. To reach the village, ride *Lady of the Lake II* to Lucerne. From the dock it is an 8-mile hike or relatively inexpensive bus ride up to the village. A nearby campground offers an alternative place to stay. Once at the village, you may take day hikes to waterfalls or alpine lakes. There is even a nature loop through the old mining area. For more information write to: Registrar, Holden Village, Chelan, Washington 98816.

Domke Lake: From the boat landing at Lucerne it is a moderate 3-mile climb to forested Domke Lake. This is a great backpacking location for families with young children. Additional campsites are located at Lucerne.

Backpack Trips

Cascade Pass

ROUND TRIP: 8 miles
TRAIL DIFFICULTY: moderate
ELEVATION GAIN: 1,800 feet
ACTIVITIES: hiking, backpacking, photography
BEST: mid-July to mid-October
MAP: Green Trails: Cascade Pass
Map on page 81

This relatively short hike takes you to the alpine meadows, wind-sculptured trees, rugged mountains, and living glaciers that are the heart and soul of North Cascades National Park. On a clear day the beauty of this area has been known to move chemical engineers to write poetry. In fact, the view is so striking, even young children may look at the scenery.

The hike to Cascade Pass is on a wide, well-graded trail and can easily be done in a single day. But to really see this area, you need at least 2 days, allowing time to hike part or all the way up Sahale Arm to the Sahale Glacier, walk the trail over to Doubtful Lake and count waterfalls, or meander up the climber's route on Mixup.

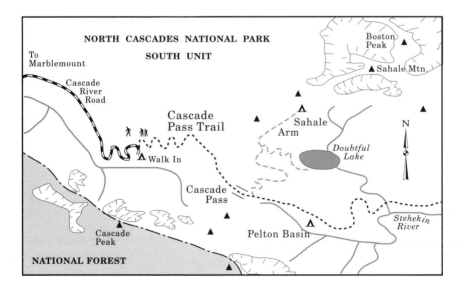

Small tarn at Cascade Pass

Due to the fragile nature of Cascade Pass, camping is limited to a few sites in the trees at Pelton Basin and a few more sites on the rocky slope below Sahale Glacier. If your family is strong enough to deal with the 4,000-foot elevation gain to the base of the glacier, then that should be the preferred area. Families with younger hikers will enjoy Pelton Basin, which lacks the grand views but does have a marvelous nature-made jungle gym of huge rocks, where kids will quickly forget their exhaustion. Because this is a popular area, plan to arrive as early as possible at the backcountry office in Marblemount to pick up your camping permit. If possible, arrange for your permit the day before the hike and spend that night at the spectacular walk-in camp area at the trailhead.

Drive Highway 20 to milepost 105 at Marblemount. At the west end of town, take a detour to pick up your backcountry permit at the ranger station then continue on to the center of town. When Highway 20 turns, leave it and go straight across the Skagit River on the Cascade River Road. Head upvalley for 25 miles, mostly on gravel, to the road-end parking lot (3,600 feet). The view of Johannesburg Mountain directly across the valley is a real adjective stealer. Walk-in campsites are located at the far end of the loop. Bring your own water or be prepared to boil and filter water from the nearby creek.

The trail switchbacks up the hillside from the parking lot then heads into the forest where it continues up with more leisurely switchbacks. It is a good thing the trail remains in the forest for the first couple miles, because when you finally leave the trees, the view is hazardously distracting. The glaciated crest of Eldorado Peak seems out of place in this temperate land, while avalanches roar down Johannesburg at the rate of about one every hour.

After a long, gradual traverse the trail reaches the 5,400-foot summit of Cascade Pass at the 4-mile point. A park volunteer hangs out there on weekends to remind you not to walk, sit, or even set your pack on the meadows. A small pit toilet is located on the south side of the pass on the way trail to Mixup.

If spending the night in Pelton Basin, head over the pass and descend 0.5 mile to the well-marked turnoff. Campers should try to limit the number of trips to the creek to avoid trampling the meadow. However, you may want to cook and certainly to play in the shadow of the big rocks below the camp.

The trail to Sahale Glacier and Doubtful Lake Trail branches off from the main route 100 feet east of the pass. If you are staying in Pelton Basin, you should drop your overnight packs and hike the first steep mile, which gains 800 feet while ascending to a broad bench with a grandstand view of the pass and Mixup. If time allows, wander as far along the gradually rising Sahale Arm as energy will allow. If you have an extra day, consider descending to Doubtful Lake, which lies 800 feet below Sahale Arm. Doubtful Lake is named not for the scenery but for all the old mines that bore into the surrounding cliffs.

Chelan Lakeshore Trail

ONE WAY: 17.5 miles
TRAIL DIFFICULTY: moderate
ELEVATION GAIN: 1,500 feet
ACTIVITIES: backpacking, fishing
BEST: April to June and September
MAP: Green Trails: Prince Creek, Lucerne, and Stehekin
Map on page 84

Lake Chelan is majestic. It is one of the deepest, bluest, and certainly purest lakes in North America. The lake lies in a narrow, glacier-carved trough, surrounded at the upper end by mighty summits and nationally protected wilderness areas. Due to that 21-foot rise in elevation from the dam there is little shore, and getting close to the lake waters without a boat is not possible. However, the Chelan Lakeshore Trail is the next best thing. It cruises along the shore when possible then climbs to rocky points with grand vistas when the shore is too cliffy. The result is an enchantingly varied trail that will keep the entire family interested as it tunnels through dark forests of giant ponderosa pines one moment then skims over grassy meadows speckled with wildflowers the next.

One of the most popular aspects of this hike, at least with the younger walkers, is its inaccessibility. The trail can only be reached by boat, or by long overland marches from the Methow Valley. Most hikers arrive by way of the *Lady of the Lake II*, which drops them off at the Prince Creek trailhead. They then hike to Stehekin where they pick up the boat once again for the return trip.

Note: This is a rattlesnake area. The potential hazard from rattlesnakes must be well understood before you begin. Adults must take extra precautions when arriving at camps to check for snakes before releasing children to play. In fact, it is best that younger children have an adult with them at all times when walking and recreating. Although the hike can be done the entire summer, the heat and snakes make it very unpleasant from mid-June on.

From Wenatchee, drive Alternate Highway 97 north toward Chelan. South of town, take the well-signed Lakeshore Road and follow it to Fields Landing. Arrive well before departure time, allowing at least half an hour to walk over to the kiosk and pay for parking, and to carry packs down to the boat dock.

Getting off the boat at Prince Creek is part of the adventure. The boat noses up to the shore and hikers descend a narrow ramp in full view of the other passengers, giving the feeling of being departing dignitaries.

The boat drops you off at around 11:00 A.M. and you have the choice of camping or, as most hikers do, continuing up the lake. Once on shore, head inland to an intersection with the Prince Creek Trail. Go left and hike along the lakeshore through the forest. Although campsites may be found in the nooks and

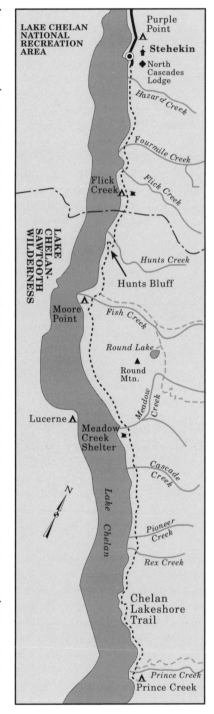

crannies around Rex, Pioneer, and Cascade Creeks, most hikers walk the 7 miles to Meadow Creek, a dark and gloomy place with an equally dark and gloomy shelter.

From Meadow Creek it is an easy 3 miles to the Moore Point Camp turn-off, located 0.4 mile below the trail at Fish Creek. Moore Point was once the location of a large resort and an afternoon can be spent exploring the old foundations and rock fences.

In the final 7 miles from Moore Point to Stehekin, the trail climbs to its 1,800-foot high point on Hunts Bluff. In the spring the bluff is a garden of colorful wildflowers and the view of the lake is unexcelled. Just 2.6 miles from Moore Camp turnoff is Flick Creek Camp and shelter. Campsites are few in number and small in size. The shelter is nice. The final 3.7 miles to Stehekin will go quickly as the trail parallels the lakeshore all the way to its end at the national park visitor center.

The boat departs by early afternoon; however, you may prefer to spend one or more nights at Purple Point Campground in Stehekin. See the Stehekin section for ideas. Some supplies may be purchased at the small store next to the lodge. (Meals may be purchased at the restaurant if you prefer.)

Winter

Summer ends all too quickly in the alpine world of the North Cascades. Flowers often wait as late as mid-July for the snow to melt. They bloom fast and brilliantly and by mid-August you will start to see the reds and yellows of fall creeping into the green leaves. Within just a couple of weeks the days suddenly become shorter, the frost gets thicker, and the rains turn to snow. There is no set date for the closing of the North Cascades Highway. Snow accumulation determines when the Highway Department feels that the danger of avalanches outweighs the advantages of keeping the road open. However, after the first of October it is best to call ahead if you are planning to drive over Highway 20.

Most winter activities take place around the periphery of the park. Skiing and snowmobiling are the most common; however, sight-seeing trips up Lake Chelan to Stehekin and bald-eagle viewing along, or on, the Skagit River are also popular pastimes.

For downhill skiers, Mount Baker offers world-class runs amidst excellent scenery. Lesser known, and definitely lower key, are the Echo Valley Ski Area near the town of Chelan and the Loup Loup Ski Area near Twisp. These small areas are very affordable and extremely family friendly.

Although the west side of the North Cascades offers skiers only limited cross-country opportunities, east of the mountains is famed for its groomed, skier-only trails. The Methow Valley area is a wonderful, family friendly place, with lots of easy trails for beginners, rolling terrain for the adventuresome, and miles of skating lanes. For families with older kids, there are backcountry huts in the Rendezvous area. Trail passes for the immaculately groomed trails are expensive; however, children under twelve ski for free.

The Echo Ridge SnoPark area above the town of Chelan is another great family area. Short trails loop around the scenic ridge crest providing fun skiing for all but rank beginners. Trail passes are not required; however, you will need a SnoPark permit.

Less scenic, but equally fun, are the trails at Echo Valley Ski Area. These cross-country ski trails are beautifully groomed and there is even one route suitable for first-time skiers. Skiers at Echo Valley do not need a SnoPark permit, but will need to buy a trail pass.

The most exotic cross-country ski resort is Stehekin at the head of Lake Chelan. The tempo of life at this isolated town is very quiet during the snowy months of winter. The cross-country trails are scenic and the snow is excellent. Families with active children may find Stehekin a little too quiet when confined to a small motel room on a long, cold winter night. This area is best enjoyed by adults who come with either a good book to read or a novel to write.

Early Winters

ROUND TRIP: 1 to 10.8 miles
TRAIL DIFFICULTY: easy to moderate
ELEVATION GAIN: up to 600 feet
ACTIVITY: cross-country skiing
BEST: late December to February
MAPS: MVSTA Mazama and Green Trails Mazama No. 51
Map on page 87

Rustic old farms, looping trails, rolling terrain, scenic vistas, and two warming huts make this a great area for skiers young, old, and in-between. Early Winters is part of the Methow Valley Ski Trails system and you'll need a trail pass to ski. Parking is free.

From Winthrop, drive west 16.6 miles on Highway 20 to the end of the open road at the Early Winters Campground (2,240 feet). You may also access these trails from the North Cascades Base Camp reached by driving 14.4 miles west from Winthrop then turning right on the Lost River Road. Cross the valley to Mazama then go left. After 2.2 miles go left on the Base Camp Road. Park in the day-use area.

Short loops or long loops, take your pick. For a short tour try skiing out on Methow Trail then returning on River Run. This loop is only 5.2 miles long and

Old barn along the cross-country ski trails at Early Winters

incorporates the best of the area. The easiest access is from North Cascades Base Camp. Descend from the parking area to cross the Methow River then go right and climb to an intersection of the River Run and Methow Trails. Go straight and ski upvalley on the Methow Trail. Glide or skate past old farms with dramatic views of ice-coated Goat Wall. Return to your starting point on River Run Trail. If you get cold, take a rest stop at the tiny Cow Beach warming hut.

For a longer loop combine Methow Trail and Jacks Trail. These two trails form a nearly level, 6.5-mile loop around the Early Winters area, which is ideal for beginning skaters. The warming hut at Cassal Ranch is a great place to stop and warm up. Warm drinks and snacks are available at this unique and very friendly place. The parking area at Early Winters provides the most convenient access for this loop.

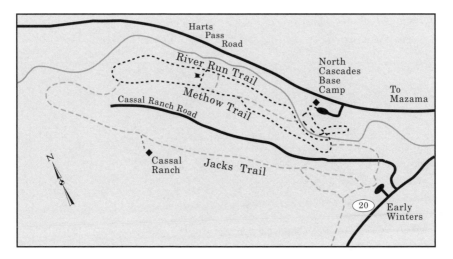

Heifer Hut

ROUND TRIP: 10 miles
TRAIL DIFFICULTY: challenging
ELEVATION GAIN: 1,365 feet
ACTIVITY: cross-country skiing to a hut
BEST: mid-December to mid-March
MAP: MVSTA Rendezvous
Map on page 88

An overnight stay at Heifer Hut is a true winter adventure. Kids will have a chance to learn the fun and work involved in spending a night in the snow and parents will appreciate the freedom of movement of a night in the hut rather than cramped in the tent.

Heifer Hut is the easiest of the six huts in the Rendezvous Hut system to reach. The hut itself is neither the biggest nor does it have the best view. If looking for something more exotic, but concerned about the family's ability to reach your chosen destination, or if you're in need of gear-hauling services, check with Rendezvous Outfitters Inc. at (800) 422-3048. These huts are popular so make your reservations several months in advance.

If you don't happen to be making an overnight stay, the Heifer Hut is a great destination for a day trip. Hut courtesy requires that you do not enter the hut when another party is already inside. If you light up the wood stove, leave a donation for the wood you used.

The well-signed trail to the hut is groomed for diagonal striding and skating. A Methow Valley Ski Trail Association trail pass is required.

Drive Highway 20 to the west end of Winthrop. Turn right, opposite the Red Barn, and head up West Chewuch Road for 6.6 miles. At Cub Creek Road go left and climb steeply for another 2.1 miles to the end of the plowed road. Go right and find parking at a farm house (2,635 feet).

From the parking area, go back to Cub Creek Road. Ski upvalley for 0.2 mile

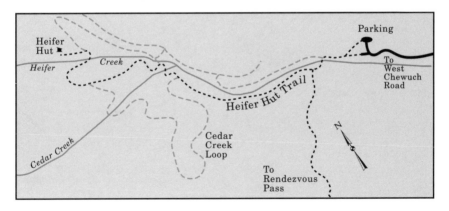

to a well-marked intersection and follow the groomed trail as it heads down and to the left. Immediately after crossing Cub Creek, the trail divides. Go right, following the signs to Heifer Hut and Cow Creek Trail.

The ascent is gradual as you glide through forest and clearcuts. However, just before everyone starts to get bored there are a couple of short descents followed by two very steep climbs.

At 3 miles, Heifer Hut Trail meets Cow Creek Trail (3,200 feet). Stay right. After another 0.2 mile you will ski past a sheep-loading ramp. At this point the trail makes a sharp bend and begins to climb steeply and steadily. Watch out for descending skiers and be sure to step out of their way.

The next junction is found at 4.2 miles (3,900 feet). The Cedar Creek Loop Trail on the left makes an interesting alternate return route. For now, stay right on a nearly level trail that meanders into the Heifer Creek drainage, crosses the creek, then wanders back out again. After another 0.5 mile, you will start the steepest climb of the tour. Tell everyone to rejoice—at the top is Heifer Hut.

Wolf Ridge

ROUND TRIP: as far as you can go
TRAIL DIFFICULTY: easy to moderate
ELEVATION GAIN: up to 400 feet
ACTIVITY: cross-country skiing
BEST: late December to February
MAP: MVSTA Rendezvous
Map on page 89

Welcoming and very friendly, Wolf Ridge is a great place for skiers young and old. The owners of the hotel at Wolf Ridge have built a beautiful warming hut. Skiers are free to come and go as they please, buy a snack or a warm drink

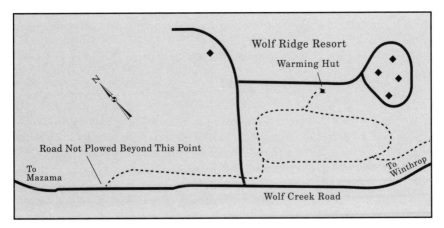

from the self-service table, or eat their own sack lunch. There is even a pool table if you want to shoot a few balls.

Before you develop any misconceptions, Wolf Ridge is located on a nearly level section of Methow River valley. All the ridges are elsewhere.

To reach Wolf Ridge Resort, turn left on Twin Lakes Road just before Highway 20 crosses the Methow River to enter Winthrop. After 1.3 miles go right on Wolf Creek Road and follow it for 4.4 miles to the entrance of the Wolf Ridge Resort. A Methow Valley Ski Trail Association trail pass is required to ski.

Just outside the warming hut is a big, flat loop around an open field. When the field is not busy with lessons, this is a great place for preschoolers to test out the new skis. Older kids can try racing each other or their parents. Beyond the practice loop, trails head both north and south. To the north the terrain is rolling and the skiing can be challenging. If you head south on Edward's Outback, you will have one initial hill followed by miles of nearly level skiing over snow-covered fields. Take your pick.

Echo Ridge

ROUND TRIP: 4.5 miles
TRAIL DIFFICULTY: moderate
ELEVATION GAIN: 150 feet
ACTIVITY: cross-country skiing
BEST: mid-December to February
MAP: U.S. Forest Service Chelan Ranger District
Map on page 91

The problem with placing a cross-country ski area on the top of an open ridge is the scenery. It is hard to take your eyes off the magnificent vistas long enough to look for the kids' sunglasses, help them tie their boots, or look for misplaced mittens.

Echo Ridge is a SnoPark area designed by the Lake Chelan Nordic Club and the forest service. This SnoPark provides skiers with a machine-free oasis in the center of a snowmobile playground.

The trip outlined here is just one of many possibilities. Families with teenagers may enjoy venturing beyond the described destination and trying their hand at some of the more challenging trails.

From the center of downtown Chelan, drive west on Highway 150 (North Shore Road) toward Manson. After 4 miles go right on Boyd Road following the signs to Echo Valley Ski Area. After 3.4 miles turn right on Boyd Loop Road, and after another 1.2 miles go right again on Cooper Gulch Road. At 7.4 miles from Highway 150 the paved road ends at the downhill ski area. Pass the resort and a snowmobile SnoPark then continue up on a steep, narrow forest road for 2.6 miles to its end at Echo Ridge SnoPark (3,400 feet). The final section can be very hazardous when icy. Drive cautiously and always carry chains.

Skier on the hillcrest above Echo Ridge SnoPark

Begin by skiing up Chickadee Trail. The initial steep climb soon turns into an easy traverse. Pass the Upsy Daisy Trail then continue on for 1 mile. At Grand Junction (3,550 feet) go right on Windsinger Trail and traverse southeast 0.7 mile to Chaos Corner. Once again take the trail on the right and ski Alley Oop Trail for 0.5 mile. At 2.2 miles, leave the groomed trail and head right on the Purte View Trail. Ascend a low, open hill for 0.1 mile to a viewpoint at the crest (3,425 feet).

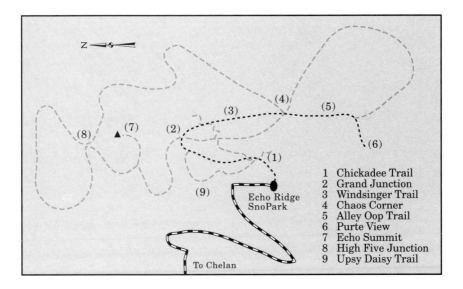

1 Chickadee Trail
2 Grand Junction
3 Windsinger Trail
4 Chaos Corner
5 Alley Oop Trail
6 Purte View
7 Echo Summit
8 High Five Junction
9 Upsy Daisy Trail

Echo Ridge SnoPark

To Chelan

2

Mount Rainier National Park

At 14,411 feet, Mount Rainier is the tallest in a string of volcanoes that dominate the Cascade Range from northern California to southern British Columbia. At less than one million years old, the Cascade volcanoes are young, and Mount Rainier, although it has not erupted since the 1820s, is still considered active. The word used to describe a volcano in this phase is "dormant." In other words, the mountain is napping, but could awake at any time.

While the basic shape of Mount Rainier is the result of volcanic activity, the dramatic sculpturing is the ongoing work of its massive glaciers. Today, there are twenty-seven active glaciers on the mountain and fifty permanent snowfields, most of which were active at one time.

Although just one of five active volcanoes in the state, Mount Rainier has claimed the hearts of Washingtonians in a way that none of the others has. Its picture is everywhere, most frequently seen in blue and white on car license plates. Perhaps most telling of all is the mixture of respect and reverence used when people talk about "The Mountain."

Not only is Mount Rainier famous for its classical shape, it is equally well known for its spectacular alpine meadows. These exquisitely delicate fields of wildflowers thrive in areas where the snow covers the ground for nine months of the year, which means the proper conditions for these meadows exist only between 5,000 and 6,000 feet. With such a short growing season and a narrow window of adaptability, the meadows are extremely fragile. Once damaged, alpine plants take decades to regrow. As a result, park rangers and volunteers are obsessed with their protection.

With the Paradise area of the park alone receiving 1.5 million visitors

Edith Creek Basin near Paradise in Mount Rainier National Park

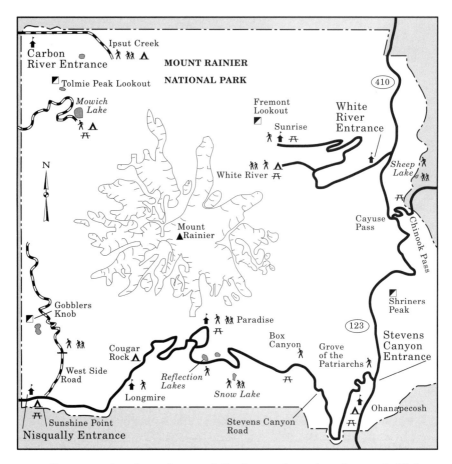

Carbon River Entrance
Ipsut Creek
Tolmie Peak Lookout
MOUNT RAINIER
NATIONAL PARK
410
Mowich Lake
Fremont Lookout
Sunrise
White River Entrance
N
White River
Sheep Lake
Cayuse Pass
Chinook Pass
Mount Rainier
Gobblers Knob
Shriners Peak
Paradise
Box Canyon
123
Stevens Canyon Entrance
Cougar Rock
Grove of the Patriarchs
West Side Road
Reflection Lakes
Snow Lake
Longmire
Ohanapecosh
Sunshine Point
Stevens Canyon Road
Nisqually Entrance

annually, preserving the park, especially the meadows, is a giant task. Visitors are expected to stay on the trails. No walking on the meadows is allowed. Plants are to be left alone; no poking or prying and positively no picking is allowed. Young children have the hardest time trying to conform to all the rules and regulations. Their tactile natures scream to touch and feel. They love to pick flowers because they are pretty or to pull them apart to see what is inside. As these kinds of activities result in unpleasant reprimands, it is best to discuss park ethics before you arrive. For the youngest walkers, try giving them something to hold in their hands, like food or a small toy, so they will be less tempted to grab at the flowers.

Children, and adults, too, have trouble staying exclusively on the trails. It may be hard to see what damage you are doing by stepping carefully off the trail; however, the tedious lecture you will receive for doing so is best avoided.

If all the restrictions give you the feeling that this is not a child-friendly place, you are partially correct. Not only are the rules very restrictive, but many of the trails are difficult for short legs. Most trails at Mount Rainier take the

Trail of Shadows at Longmire

straightest possible route to their destination. As a result, the trails are steep and often have large steps to clamber over.

Despite all the negatives, Mount Rainier is simply too great to ignore. If you are a Washington resident, you may want to wait until the kids are at least pre-teens before planning anything longer then a weekend at the park. If you live far from The Mountain and cannot arrange annual pilgrimages, then do not pass up the chance for a visit. Just come prepared to be flexible in your plans.

Paradise is the most popular place to visit at Mount Rainier: The views of The Mountain are unexcelled and the flower fields are famous for their rich and colorful displays. The south side of The Mountain, where Paradise is located, has the largest concentration of visitor services.

Sunrise is the second most popular destination at Mount Rainier. The road to Sunrise ends at the edge of high alpine meadows. On a clear day it is an awe-inspiring location, but when the weather is bad, it is a cold, wet, and miserable place.

Chinook Pass is a family-friendly area. Located at the edge of the park, many of the trails lead into national forest lands where you can take the family pet. Ohanapecosh is a lowland area and an ideal destination for families. Activities center around the sprawling campground and visitor center.

Mowich Lake and Carbon River are very low-key accesses on the northwest side of the park. Mowich Lake, which has a primitive, walk-in campground and no running water, is a popular trailhead for hikes to Spray Park, Eunice Lake, and Tolmie Peak. The Carbon River entrance is a rain forest area with opportunities for fishing and hiking.

Lodging in Mount Rainier National Park is limited to the Inn at Longmire and another one at Paradise. No gasoline is available in the park.

Camping is a popular activity here. Arrive early and secure your site before noon. For overflow, there are forest service campgrounds nearby. Ask at the park entrance stations for recommendations.

Permits: A fee is charged at all park entrances except Mowich Lake. Backcountry permits are required for all backpack trips; they were free in 1997 but may be issued on a fee basis in the future.

Paradise

Backpacking, food service, hiking, lodging, ranger-led walks, visitor center, wildflower viewing

No ethereal contemplation is needed to appreciate the incredible beauty of Paradise; it is a scene painted in bold colors. The deep, rich green of the meadows serves as nature's perfect backdrop for a kaleidoscopic mix of wildflowers. Above, the blindingly white mass of Mount Rainier lords over the meadows. On days when the sun does not shine and The Mountain is enveloped in its own personal cloud, the intense colors of the flowers create an almost other-worldly glow.

Paradise is a must-see place that should be on every park visitor's itinerary. Unfortunately, younger members of the party may not be as enthralled as their parents by the carefully guarded meadows.

Rules are just part of the problem. Paradise is a popular area and the trails that climb through the wildflower-colored meadows to the high alpine world of snow and ice above are busy, often clogged with eager hikers and mountain climbers. The trails are steep, some are paved, and all have steps to limit erosion. Short legs are at a great disadvantage on the high steps and small bodies may quickly feel the oppression of masses of humanity. Families with small walkers will have the best luck on the Nisqually Vista and Edith Basin Trails. Mazama Ridge is a great destination for the four- to seven-year-olds. Strong hikers can tackle Panorama Point.

Snow often blankets the meadows until mid-July, so early summer visitors should be prepared with sturdy, waterproof footwear. The brightest flower displays occur in early August and are followed quickly by a brief flash of fall color in early September. Snow returns to Paradise by mid-October and the meadows become a mecca for cross-country skiers, snowshoers, and snow boarders.

A visit to Paradise begins with an extremely scenic drive. Unfortunately, if you linger at the numerous viewpoints or attractions along the way, you may

Family descending from Skyline Ridge on Golden Gate Trail

have difficulties finding a parking place. The upper and lower parking lots fill to capacity as early as 10:00 A.M. on summer weekends. Alternative parking is found along Valley Road below Paradise Inn; however, you may descend a mile or more before finding a spot. For a stress-free visit, arrive early.

Once parked, plan at least one hike to sample the views and enjoy the incredible wildflower display. Ranger-led walks are an option. The 3-mile round-trip ranger walk to Glacier Vista is a chance for visitors to learn about the volcanic forces that created the mountain and the erosional forces that sculptured the shape it wears today. The creation of the mountain is a story that kids can usually relate to very well. The 1.4-mile Flower Walk is an easier hike and naturalists are careful to gear the discussion to the average citizen. This walk will appeal to some kids, those whose interest in natural history is strong enough to bear with the would-be experts who make a game out of trying to stump the ranger. If the Flower Walk is deemed unsuitable for the kids, send an adult who can explain the interesting facts later.

After a hike through the meadows, head to the visitor center for a look at the displays and the park movie. If time allows, visit the stately old Paradise Inn then check out the climbers at the Guide House. A large picnic area is located just below the visitor center so you may have a picnic lunch or dinner before heading back.

Paradise Inn offers meadow-side lodging for visitors wishing to overnight in this scenic location. The inn has 126 rooms and is open summers only. Breakfast, lunch, and dinner are served in the dining room. No television. The National Park Inn, at Longmire, has only twenty-five rooms, and offers full meal service. Book far ahead of your visit at (360) 569-2275. The visitor center at Paradise has a snack bar. Beverages and ice cream can be purchased at Longmire. For lodging outside the park, contact Mount Rainier/Saint Helens Chamber of Commerce at (360) 569-2339.

No camping is allowed at Paradise. Cougar Rock campground, 9.4 miles below, is the closest facility and has 200 sites. Evening programs are held in the amphitheater. Nature walks to Carter Falls depart here. No reservations are accepted, so arrive by noon to assure a site.

Sunshine Point Campground, 0.3 mile from the Nisqually Entrance, is the only camp area open all year. This camp has eighteen forested sites at the edge of the Nisqually River.

From the east, there is easy access to Paradise from the 205-site Ohanapecosh Campground, which features evening campfire programs, a visitor center, trails, and ranger-led walks. The campground fills by noon in the summer.

Comet Falls

ROUND TRIP: 3.5 miles
TRAIL DIFFICULTY: moderate
ELEVATION GAIN: 1,330 feet
ACTIVITY: hiking
BEST: mid-July to September
MAP: Green Trails: Mt. Rainier, West
Map on page 100

The scenery along the hike to Comet Falls is packed full of gushing water. Almost from the start, water is seen dancing down rocky slopes and thundering through deep canyons. Water is the lifeblood of Mount Rainier and here you will see it streaming through its arteries and rushing through its veins.

Rangers lead daily walks to Comet Falls during the summer. If interested, check at Cougar Rock Campground or at Longmire Museum for times.

The Comet Falls trailhead is located on the road to Paradise, 5.7 miles above Longmire, and 0.2 mile below Christine Falls. The parking lot often fills in the afternoon so arrive early (3,677 feet).

The trail starts off with a stiff climb. At the top of the first pitch, cross Van Trump Creek just above Christine Falls. Below the bridge, the water thunders, churning pools and carving niches in solid rock.

Before long, you will enter a narrow valley where the climb is steady but never severe. Above are the steep slopes of Cushman Crest. Below is Van Trump

Comet Falls

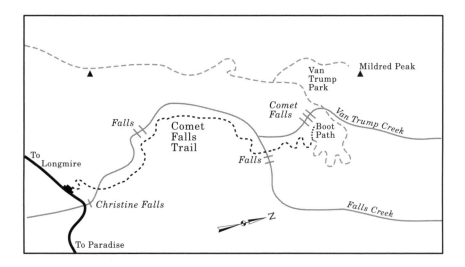

Creek, tumbling and tripping, racing itself, trying to be the first droplet to reach Puget Sound.

At 1.5 miles the trail crosses Van Trump Creek below an impressive double waterfall. If you have party members who are aching for a chance to touch the water, promise a stop here on the way back. For now, continue over the next rise where Comet Falls explodes into view. On a busy day, there is a traffic jam on the trail as hikers stop to gaze at the water plummeting 320 feet off the cliff. For a closer view, continue to the second switchback (a boot path will take you right into the spray of the falls; however, the rocks are dangerously slippery.)

If you are still energized, continue on to lower Van Trump Park, gaining 600 feet in the next mile. The meadows are not as rich as those at Paradise but they do have the advantage of seeing fewer visitors.

Nisqually Vista

ROUND TRIP: 1.2 miles
TRAIL DIFFICULTY: easy
ELEVATION GAIN: 300 feet
ACTIVITIES: hiking, photography, nature study
BEST: mid-July to September
MAP: Green Trails: Mt. Rainier, East
Map on page 101

Although not a truly easy walk, the trail to Nisqually Vista is one of the best for youngsters in the Paradise area. (The other easy walk is to Edith Creek Basin.) Popular features of the trail include a rock with a child-sized hole, a creek, benches at the viewpoints, and a loop. For the lovers of excellent scenery (the adults), the vistas are excellent, the flower fields brilliant in season, and the glacier view very interesting. Except for the steps at the start, strollers will have no difficulty.

The Nisqually Vista Trail starts on the lower (west) side of the Paradise Visitor Center. Follow the sidewalk along the upper side of the parking area to the stairs. Go up. At the top is an intersection; take the trail on the left and descend to Dead Horse Creek. The trail then skirts a meadow and passes a rock that begs to be climbed. Just over the crest of a small hill is the rock with the hole. A bench has been placed opposite the rock for parents who are waiting for their children to come back out.

Once away from the rock, descend, steeply, to a flower-filled meadow with an excellent view of Mount Rainier. Here, at 0.3 mile, the loop portion of the walk begins. For the best views, stay right and keep The Mountain ahead.

At 0.6 mile, the trail begins to skirt a cliff. Stay away from the edge except at the two fenced vistas. Below is the mud- and rock-covered terminus of the Nisqually Glacier. A sign points out the position of the ice about thirty years ago. The change is astounding.

Beyond the vistas, the trail climbs, switchbacking through the forest back to the start.

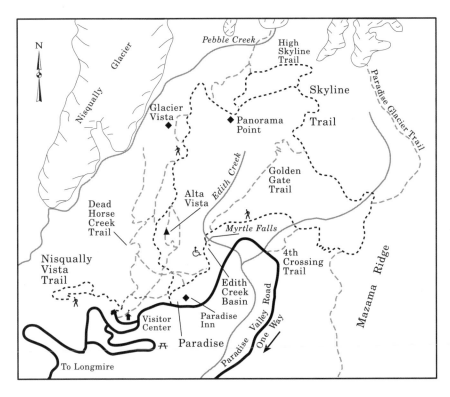

Mazama Ridge

EDITH CREEK BASIN
ROUND TRIP: 0.8 mile
TRAIL DIFFICULTY: easy
ELEVATION GAIN: 120 feet
ACTIVITIES: walking, photography
BEST: mid-July to September
MAP: Green Trails: Mt. Rainier, East
Map on page 101

MAZAMA RIDGE
ROUND TRIP: 2.2 miles
TRAIL DIFFICULTY: moderate
ELEVATION GAIN: 440 feet
ACTIVITIES: hiking, photography
BEST: mid-July to September
MAP: Green Trails: Mt. Rainier, East

On this hike, the views and luxuriant flower-covered meadows claim the attention of most adults. However, sharped-eyed youngsters may prefer to look for the marmots that make the meadows their home. With an abundance of succulent plants nearby, the adult marmots have plenty of time for relaxing on sun-warmed boulders. Younger marmots spend their time chasing their siblings and engaging in lively sparring matches.

This is the easiest walk in the Paradise area. The trail is paved to Myrtle Falls in Edith Creek Basin. Once the pavement ends, there is a gradual descent followed by a moderate climb to the flower fields at the crest of Mazama Ridge. Early season hikers will find lingering snowfields, ideal for sliding and slipping.

Start the hike opposite Paradise Inn by heading up some stone steps. When the trail divides, go right and follow the pavement on a gradual ascent through rich flower fields. The trail divides again as it rounds the shoulder of Alta Vista. Continue straight and enter Edith Creek Basin. Just before descending to the creek, a spur trail branches right to a view of Myrtle Falls. If you choose to walk the 100 feet to the viewpoint, leave strollers up top and hang on to the younger children and their grandmothers; the trail is extremely steep.

Beyond the side trail to Myrtle Falls, descend to Edith Creek. Don't be surprised if you have to weave your way through a group of enthusiastic photographers in order to cross the creek; the view here is a classic. Continuing on, the trail divides again. Stay right. You may return to this point by the Golden Gate Trail if you choose.

The trail to Mazama Ridge climbs briefly then descends into another meadow-filled basin. Cross a bubbly creek and then Paradise River. When the 4th Crossing Trail splits off to the right, continue straight. A final climb leads to the crest of Mazama Ridge, at 1.1 miles. The trail immediately divides; for easy explorations, go right and descend through fields of lupin and paintbrush about 0.2 mile.

If the group can handle some more climbing, head left up the Skyline Trail. You do not have to go far before you enter an area recently covered by glacier. Vegetation is short and stunted. Shortly after passing the Steven Van Trump climbing memorial, the trail divides. Stay left and continue up. Often a large snowfield lingers here, ideal for older kids (that is, parents) to do some fast dives and slides. At 6,380 feet, 0.9 mile after

Camp robber

reaching Mazama Ridge, the trail divides again. Go left and descend Golden Gate Trail to Edith Creek Basin to close the loop.

Skyline Trail

GLACIER VISTA
    LOOP TRIP: 2 miles
    TRAIL DIFFICULTY: moderate
    ELEVATION GAIN: 964 feet
    ACTIVITIES: hiking, photography
    BEST: mid-July to September
    MAP: Green Trails: Mt. Rainier, East
    Map on page 101

PANORAMA POINT
    LOOP TRIP: 5 miles
    TRAIL DIFFICULTY: challenging
    ELEVATION GAIN: 1,640 feet
    ACTIVITIES: hiking, photography
    BEST: late July to September
    MAP: Green Trails: Mt. Rainier, East

Despite the lack of appeal for younger children, this hike is a must for families that can pull, push, march, or bribe the kids to tackle the steep, busy trails to Glacier Vista. For adults, there is a feast of almost overwhelming beauty: meadows coated with wildflowers, views of Mount Rainier, the Tatoosh Range, the Goat Rocks, Mount Adams, and Mount St. Helens. Then there is the Nisqually Glacier, with its steep headwall, thundering avalanches, and deep blue crevasses. Climbers lumber past, laden with outrageously huge and heavy packs, their eyes filled with purpose, their minds determined. Squirrels and camp robbers (Steller's jays) swoop by to take advantage of the crush of humanity to steal a crumb or two of food. Marmots sit in the shade and watch the parade.

If the children have attained the status of pre-teens or older, consider the scenic loop over Panorama Point, which crosses a barren, high alpine desert then returns to the start on the Skyline Trail. The loop is steep and difficult and only for those who enjoy challenges.

Start the hike at the large sign near the restrooms in the upper parking lot at Paradise. Climb steeply on a paved trail, passing several intersections. Your goal is up and to the left. Stay on the west side of Alta Vista to reach the end of the pavement and an intersection. Go left and head toward Glacier Vista. All subsequent intersections are well signed. In early summer patches of snow offer considerable diversion. If turning around at the vista, consider descending the lesser-used Dead Horse Creek Trail through more flower fields.

Guided climbing party on their way to Camp Muir

For Panorama Point, head up from Glacier Vista along the ridge crest. Before long your trail will merge with the Skyline Trail. At the upper end of the ridge the trail turns and tackles the steep slopes of Panorama Point. The first switchback is often snow-covered until early August. Use caution and turn back if the snow is too hard or slippery to provide safe footing. The trail is narrow and steps have been built to aid the ascent. The throngs of climbers take the turnoff to Pebble Creek; hikers should continue straight ahead. At 7,100 feet, a large platform with rocks for seats is a great place to relax and study the giant panorama that includes Mount Adams and the steaming caldera of Mount St. Helens. The trail divides here. The Skyline Trail continues straight. Unfortunately, for much of the summer this section of the trail is closed due to a dangerous snowslope.

When closed, continue up the rocky slope on a rocky trail, passing an outhouse improbably perched on the steep hillside. Shortly after passing a second trail to Pebble Creek, cross a 7,300-foot high point and begin a rapid descent. A snowfield often lingers here; cross with caution. At the Golden Gate Trail you may leave the Skyline Trail and head directly back to Paradise via Edith Creek Basin. The alternative is to continue down another mile to the Mazama Ridge intersection.

Pinnacle Saddle

ROUND TRIP: 3 miles
TRAIL DIFFICULTY: challenging
ELEVATION GAIN: 1,100 feet
ACTIVITIES: hiking, photography
BEST: August to September
MAP: Green Trails: Mt. Rainier, East
Map on page 106

Although the trail is very steep, Pinnacle Saddle is an enticing destination. Meandering through the meadows beyond the saddle and investigating the snow patches or small tarns beyond the end of the trail can become the highlight of anyone's vacation.

Drive to the Pinnacle Saddle trailhead located on Stevens Canyon Road, 1.4 miles east of the intersection with Paradise Road or 18.4 miles west of the Stevens Canyon Entrance Station (4,867 feet). Parking is often crowded.

The trail starts off with steps. As soon as you are above the road, the trail heads into a moderately steep switchback through lush, subalpine meadows. At 5,275 feet reach a ridge crest where the trail levels for a few, blessed feet before resuming its climb through alternating bands of trees and meadows. Several small and nameless creeks are crossed as well as a couple of steep avalanche chutes. When the ridge crest becomes steep, the trail traverses south

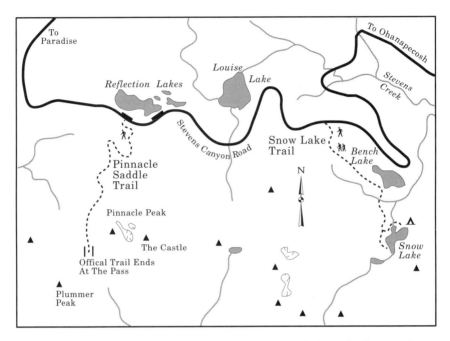

around the rubble-strewn west flank of Pinnacle Peak then climbs steeply toward the cliffs above. The going gets rough and the afternoon sun is unmerciful. Luckily, the saddle is close.

When the trail finally brushes the cliffs, look for a short path to a small cave. No gold or hidden passageways here—I already checked several times. Shortly beyond is the 5,967-foot saddle and the official end of the maintained trail; however, looking around, it is somewhat less than obvious. To the left, an excellent trail heads up the side of Pinnacle Peak and ends abruptly at the base of a climbing route. Do not be fooled by the easy trail. This is a route for experienced rock climbers only!

From the saddle, let the view of Mount Adams and the Goat Rocks draw you straight ahead on another excellent trail. This route skirts along a wide bench below Plummer Peak for 0.3 mile before ending at a rock slide. Meadows, streams, patches of snow, and even a couple of tent sites make this an enticing destination.

Experienced hikers, with some scrambling experience, may make Plummer Peak their goal. The peak is to the southwest of the saddle. The unofficial trail fractures at several points; the group leader must choose the safest path. At the top of the first hill is a broad alpine meadow with, depending on snowmelt, one or more tarns, a stream or two, a couple of snow patches, and a magnificent view of The Mountain, from Paradise to the Columbia Crest. If continuing, stay on the boot trail. Near the summit, the trail ducks into the trees, where roots and branches can be used as climbing aids. Use caution at the 6,370-foot summit; it is a narrow wedge surrounded by cliffs.

Snow Lake

ROUND TRIP: 2.6 miles
TRAIL DIFFICULTY: moderate
ELEVATION GAIN: 500 feet
ACTIVITIES: hiking, backpacking, swimming, fishing
BEST: July to September
MAP: Green Trails: Mt. Rainier, East
Map on page 106

Snow Lake is the best destination for families with young children in the entire Paradise area. Admittedly, Mount Rainier can barely be seen (and only from the north end of the lake), and the meadows are shabby compared to Paradise, but the lake is wonderful for wading, swimming, and fishing.

The trail appears easy on the map, but it is not. Young children usually can handle the distance, but short legs are often defeated by the tall steps designed to hold the trail together. If you bring a small hiker, be ready to lend a hand or a boost on the steps. The camp area is small, only two sites, right by the lakeshore, and is reached by crossing a shaky logjam over the outlet.

Drive the Stevens Canyon Road 3 miles east from the Longmire Road or west 12.8 miles from Highway 123. The parking area is located on the south side of the road (4,530 feet).

The trail starts with a steep climb to a broad, open area known as The Bench. Remnants of an old forest can be seen in the few silver trees still standing above the dense brush of huckleberries and mountain ash. Just when the going seems easy, the trail plunges down to cross a creek then climbs nearly straight back up the opposite hillside. Once back on The Bench, the trail turns into a boardwalk, crossing several marshy areas. At 0.7 mile, descend to the Bench Lake turnoff. The lake, surrounded by brush and marsh, is located a few feet off the trail.

Snow Lake

Continuing on, climb over a steep ridge then drop to cross a small creek, which is then followed to an intersection at 1.2 miles. Campsites are located 0.2 mile to the left. For the day-use area, stay right. Follow the trail until it crosses a creek then head through the trees to reach the best swimming hole. Be sure to wash off all insect repellent and sunscreen before you enter the water; the fish don't need sunscreen and they want to attract, not repel, bugs.

Unicorn Peak towers above; however, the real show is to the west where a herd of mountain goats may occasionally be spotted grazing on the steep hillside. If you follow the trail on another 0.2 mile, you will find another, smaller lake at the same elevation.

MORE ACTIVITIES
Map on page 108

West Side Road: Mountain bike or hike the old dirt road along the west side of the mountain for 9.2 miles to Klapatche Point. Elevation gain for the entire trip is 1,680 feet. Pass several viewpoints of Mount Rainier as well as trails to Lake George and Gobblers Knob, Emerald Ridge, Klapatche Park, and Golden Lakes. Difficulty level for this trip is challenging on a mountain bike.

Longmire Historic Buildings Walk: Pick up a map at the museum for a

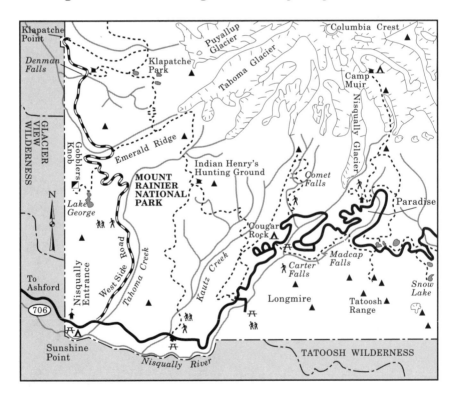

1.5-mile stroll around the historic structures at Longmire. Fascinating for architecture buffs, the uniformly brown buildings are less than exciting for everyone else. Rated easiest.

Longmire Trail of Shadows: Mountain views, soda springs, iron springs, an old cabin, an old beaver lodge, marshes, an old growth forest, and several creeks help keep the interest level high on this 0.7-mile loop. Rated easiest. Trail begins across the road from the Longmire Inn.

The River Trail: This 1.6-mile trail parallels the Nisqually River between Cougar Rock and Longmire. The trail is wide, relatively level, and rated easiest for walking. Although lacking in scenery, it is a great place for stretching out kinks in legs after a long car ride. The trailhead is located at the corner of the road just below the campground entrance. The trail ends at Longmire next to the ranger station.

Cougar Rock Campground—Carter Falls: Rangers lead daily nature walks to this falls, discussing the ecology of the lowland forest along the way. From the campground it is only 1.1 miles to the falls with an elevation gain of 560 feet. Some sections of the trail are steep. The trailhead is located on the opposite side of the road from the campground at the corner below the entrance. Carter Falls lies in a gorge below the trail and is hard to see. Continue on to the more visible upper falls before heading back.

Christine Falls: Located on the road to Paradise, 5.9 miles above Longmire, this attractive falls is a must-see for all first-time park visitors. The viewing area is reached by a 100-foot trail.

Nisqually River Bridge: Seven miles above Longmire is a large parking area just before the Nisqually River bridge. No stopping is allowed on the bridge or in the slide area just beyond, so if you are interested in viewing the old Nisqually Glacier moraine, park here. No trails lead you up the river; however, you can walk on the gravel bars for 0.3 mile.

Narada Falls: This is one of many spectacular falls in the park. The parking area is located 9.3 miles above Longmire.

Ice Caves: Although there are still references to the Ice Caves on signs and maps, the caves no longer exist. The Stevens and Paradise Glaciers have receded and the caves have collapsed.

Camp Muir: This 9-mile round-trip hike to the climbers' camp has a difficulty rating that is off the scale for this book. The hike, which involves an elevation gain of 4,500 feet, is made doubly difficult by the noticeable lack of oxygen found at the 10,000-foot Camp Muir. There are also the dangers of route-finding and walking on snow, which by September may be rock-hard, making a slip potentially fatal. Because The Mountain makes its own weather, clouds can obscure the route at any time. Hikers caught in a whiteout have been known to walk off cliffs! If considering the trip, check weather and snow conditions with a ranger before starting. Carry lots of water, food, sunglasses, sunscreen, and plenty of spare clothes. Waterproof boots are a must. From the upper Paradise parking lot, head up to Glacier Vista then climb over Panorama Point to Pebble

Creek where you will reach the base of the Muir Snowfield. Stay to the right of the middle of the snowfield until you reach Camp Muir. The view is glorious.

NEARBY ATTRACTIONS

Northwest Trek: Located 17 miles south of Puyallup on Highway 161, this wildlife park is an ideal stop on the way to or from Mount Rainier. Here you can actually see the animals talked about in the park. Beavers, otters, cougars, bears, deer, and elk are viewed in natural-like settings. A visit to Northwest Trek requires a minimum of 3 hours, 50 minutes of which are spent riding a tram to view the larger herbivores. In addition to the animals, the park features a Discovery Center for kids, a movie theater, and a picnic area. There are 5 miles of trails for forest exploration, including a Nature Quest Trail where you must match descriptions with numbered posts. Call (360) 832-6117 for more information.

Pioneer Farm Museum and Ohop Indian Village: Located 3 miles north of Eatonville in Ohop Valley between Highways 161 and 7, this outdoor museum is a wonderful introduction to the life and times of the early settlers in Western Washington. The activities are designed with children in mind. Basic tour lasts 90 minutes. Call (360) 832-6300 for more information.

Mount Rainier Scenic Railroad: For anyone who finds the crowded parking areas and trails at Paradise to be a bit overwhelming, this delightful steam train offers a pleasing alternative. From the railroad station in Elbe, on Highway 7, the trains travel to Mineral and back, a 90-minute trip.

Beaver pond overlook at Northwest Trek

Ohanapecosh and Stevens Canyon

Camping, fishing, hiking, nature walks, visitor center

Mount Rainier: the name conjures up visions of snow, ice, glaciers, and flower-filled meadows. It is easy to overlook the ancient forests and surging rivers that are also an integral part of the park.

Ohanapecosh is located in a deep valley, at the center of a venerable forest. This environment is much more resilient than the delicate alpine world above, making it a family-friendly location at which to base your park explorations.

The area is full of the unexpected, with the hot springs being perhaps its most surprising feature. At one time, people made arduous journeys to soak in these thermal waters and relax at a nearby resort. The resort is gone, and the thermal benefits of the waters are seriously in question. Today, doctors make faces when they look at the bubbling pools and discourage their children from even touching the water. Here, contemporary hot spring users tend to have four legs and sport antlers. These elk and deer meander around, soaking up the warmth and eating grasses that thrive near the springs.

Silver Falls is one of the most popular features of the Ohanapecosh area. This handsome fall is located on the Ohanapecosh River and is reached by trail. It is common to spend the better part of a day on the short and easy loop hike to the falls and fishing the quiet pools beyond. The stately Grove of the Patriarchs is another popular walk. The giant old trees are located on an island

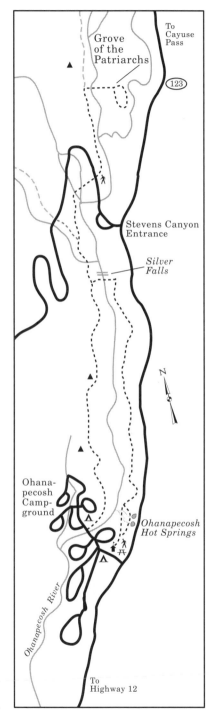

Checking out the cross-section of a giant tree at Ohanapecosh Visitor Center

in the Ohanapecosh River and attract visitors (of the human variety) from around the world, as well as a large number of locals (elk and deer). One of the most stunning spectacles of the area is Box Canyon, where a nature trail leads to an overlook of a narrow gorge carved by the Muddy Fork Cowlitz River.

The campground, picnic area, and visitor center are the nucleus of the Ohanapecosh area. The campground, which has 205 sites, some suitable for motor homes, fills nearly every night during the summer. Additional campsites are found in forest service campgrounds on Highway 12. Evening programs are offered in July and August.

Ohanapecosh Visitor Center is a friendly place where you may study the displays or just sit and do a puzzle while waiting out a rain shower. Park personnel are available to answer questions. Outside is a cross section of an old tree. Young children may be interested to see how their age compares with that of the tree. If your teenagers think their parents are awfully old, it may make you feel better to compare your age with the tree's, also.

Silver Falls

LOOP TRIP: 3 miles
TRAIL DIFFICULTY: easy
ELEVATION GAIN: 480 feet
ACTIVITIES: hiking and fishing
BEST: May to October
MAP: Mount Rainier National Park: Official Map and Guide
Map on page 111

Rolling, rumbling, racing, sprinting, sparkling, twisting, turning (you get the idea), the Ohanapecosh River rushes out of the mountains. Fed by numerous small creeks, the river is deep, powerful, and amazingly clear. No major glacier, with accompanying fine silts and sediments, contributes its waters to the Ohanapecosh, and the result is refreshingly clean and invigorating when you stand in the misty spray of Silver Falls.

To reach the trailhead, drive Highway 123 to Ohanapecosh Campground, located 3 miles north of Highway 12. If not staying at the campground, look for parking at the visitor center or at the trailhead in Loop A (1,900 feet).

The hike begins in Loop A or in conjunction with the Hot Springs Nature Walk, which starts behind the visitor center. The Silver Falls Trail heads upvalley, passing the hot springs and the location of the long-gone resort. After an initial climb, begin a long traverse on a trail that is wide enough for strollers. The moss-dotted forest floor and trees are the main attractions. The river is below, heard but not seen. At 0.9 mile cross Laughingwater Creek and shortly beyond reach a junction.

Go left and head into a narrow gorge to see the falls and cross the river on a wooden bridge. Expect to linger here, to look at the falls and feel the spray on hands and face. At this point, those with strollers and young walkers may wish to head back. The second half of the loop is a little rougher and a bit steeper.

A native resident of Ohanapecosh

Beyond the bridge, the trail continues upvalley, passing a second view of the falls. At 1.2 miles reach an intersection. Fishermen and ambitious hikers may want to continue on to the pools and the Grove of the Patriarchs. Loop hikers should go left and begin their downvalley trek with a climb. At 1.4 miles pass the Cowlitz Divide intersection. Continue straight, climbing the hillside to the base of some overhanging rocks that younger hikers may want to crawl under. Don't worry, they can be easily lured out with a snack. The woods get darker and deeper as you go, and when the trail finally dips back toward the campground, you are definitely in forest primeval.

At 2.8 miles the trail ends in Loop C. Go left and follow the pavement out to the main road. Head left again, crossing the Ohanapecosh River and returning to the start at 3 miles.

Grove of the Patriarchs

ROUND TRIP: 1.5 miles
TRAIL DIFFICULTY: easy
ELEVATION GAIN: 20 feet
ACTIVITIES: hiking, information signs, fishing
BEST: May to October
MAP: Mount Rainier National Park: Official Map and Guide
Map on page 111

On a small island in the center of the Ohanapecosh River lives a remarkable grove of Douglas-fir, western red cedar, and western hemlock. The trees in this grove are survivors. They have survived floods, beetle and bug infestations, and fires. And, perhaps the greatest survival feat of all, they remain untouched by saw or axe.

This stately grove of trees, giants among the spindly alders and vine maples, have massive girths, with one tree measuring over 35 feet in diameter. Take time to sit and look. Many of these trees have waited 1,000 years for your visit.

This popular walk begins 0.3 mile east of the Stevens Canyon Entrance. The large parking lot, located on the north side of the road, has restrooms and running water (2,200 feet). During the months of July and August, rangers lead daily walks through the grove. Check at the entrance station or at the Ohanapecosh Visitor Center for times.

The trail begins near the restroom and descends into the forest. It is a wide trail, allowing parents to walk with children or push a stroller. Observant hikers will find interesting fungi and swirling life rings on tree stumps as they go. Before long, the trail brushes the banks of the Ohanapecosh River then turns to parallel it upvalley. By midsummer the water level recedes, exposing a small gravel bar ideal for rock skipping.

At the 0.5-mile point, the trail divides. Go left and descend a tight

A true patriarch

switchback to a springy suspension bridge over the Ohanapecosh River. Once on the island, the trail passes through some brushy young trees then divides. Take either spur to enter the grove. Look and enjoy the trees, but please do not climb or clamber around them. Feet trampling their roots are creating damage that floods, fires, and diseases did not.

MORE ACTIVITIES
Map on page 116

Ohanapecosh Hot Springs Nature Trail: Starting behind the visitor center, this trail leads through forest to a series of pools. The first pools are cool, becoming progressively warmer as you go. At the 0.2-mile point, the nature trail intercepts the Silver Falls Trail. Go left for a short trip upvalley to see the site

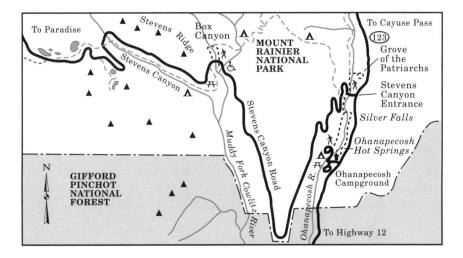

of the health spa, then turn around and follow the Silver Falls Trail back to Loop A of the campground. Walk the road back to the visitor center. If no pamphlets are available at the trailhead, ask at the visitor center. The nature trail is an easy 0.5-mile loop, but is not suitable for strollers.

Box Canyon: Nature has some tremendous erosional forces in her repertoire. At Box Canyon you can see a graphic display of these forces in an extremely scenic setting. Even if the family is not into having a learning experience, the features are impressive. Drive Stevens Canyon Road 10 miles from the entrance station to find the large Box Canyon parking area just before a bridge and a tunnel (not to be confused with Box Canyon Picnic Area, located 1 mile up the road). Follow the paved trail along a bench above the Muddy Fork Cowlitz River. When the trail divides, go straight. On the right, note the smooth, moss-covered rock marred by long scratches, called striations, which were caused by rocks pulled along the base of the Cowlitz Glacier centuries ago.

On the parking lot side of the road, walk down to a viewpoint of the canyon and the cascades below.

Chinook Pass

Backpacking, hiking, picnicking, wildflowers

Chinook Pass is a 5,432-foot low point along the eastern border of Mount Rainier National Park. Hikes starting from the pass cross from the national park, Wenatchee National Forest, to William O. Douglas Wilderness. In addition, the Pacific Crest Trail traverses through the area on its journey from Mexico to Canada.

The combination of meadows, wildflowers, subalpine lakes, and sweeping vistas bring visitors here by the hundreds to look, to picnic, to walk, and to enjoy the scenery. Excellent destinations such as Sheep Lake, Dewey Lakes, and the Naches Peak Loop are easy half-day hikes.

Because of its location on the eastern border of the park, the atmosphere is more relaxed than that of Paradise or Sunrise. In the national forest, children may step on the way trails to reach an overlook or climb an inviting rock. Dogs are allowed on the east side of the pass, making the area a mecca for anyone traveling with a canine companion. Horses are occasionally encountered on the Pacific Crest Trail and parents should be sure to warn their children about the dangers involved with these huge animals. If passed by horses, get the entire family together then move off the trail. If you are not sure what to do, talk to the riders and ask for suggestions.

No campgrounds or accommodations are located at Chinook Pass; however, the pass is an easy and scenic drive from either White River or Ohanapecosh. Lodging is available at Packwood, Crystal Mountain Resort, and Enumclaw.

Sheep Lake

Sheep Lake

ROUND TRIP: 4.2 miles
TRAIL DIFFICULTY: easy
ELEVATION GAIN: 320 feet
ACTIVITIES: hiking, backpacking, and fishing
BEST: mid-July to September
MAP: Green Trails: Mt. Rainier, East
Map on page 118

Like a serving of cool dressing in the center of a salad, Sheep Lake lies in the middle of a rocky bowl filled with green grass, brilliantly colored flowers, tall evergreens, and a variety of animals. The lake and the Pacific Crest Trail (PCT) which leads to it are in Wenatchee National Forest rather than Mount Rainier National Park, so dogs and horses are allowed. Backpackers do not need

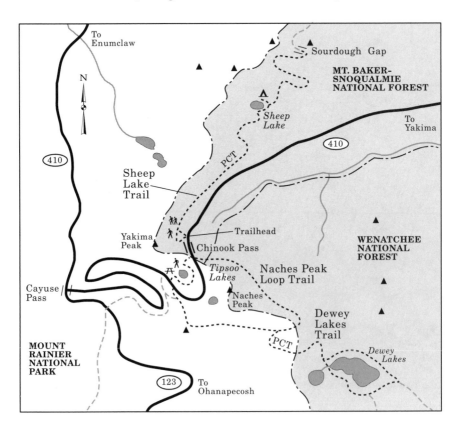

reservations; however, cars parked on the east side of the pass should have a forest service parking permit.

Drive Highway 410 to Chinook Pass. The trailhead is located just east of the summit. Park on either side of the road.

From the stone restroom on the west side of the highway, head uphill to the Pacific Crest Trail. Turn right and walk north on a nearly level traverse across the open hillside. Just below your feet is busy Highway 410, which gradually drops away. Games, such as "who can spot the first motorcycle," or "how many cars will there be following the next motorhome," can be played as you walk.

After the first mile, the trail bends away from the highway and enters a quiet forest where a gradual, but continuous, climb begins. The climb ends near 2.1 miles where the trail reaches Sheep Lake. Excellent campsites are located along the south and west sides of the lake. Picnic sites are everywhere. Swimming or wading is a popular diversion on warm days; on cool days fishing is a better pastime. Look for deer, chipmunks, and numerous Steller's jays (the infamous camp robbers) around the lake, and guard your food.

If spending the night, or if you still have energy to burn, head up to Sourdough Gap. Reached by a steep climb, the gap is 1 mile from the lake and 1,000 feet higher. Early risers may see deer grazing in the meadows and marmots patrolling their territory from atop rocky outcroppings. From the gap, the view extends south over Mount Adams and Mount St. Helens to Oregon's Mount Hood.

Naches Peak Loop and Dewey Lakes

NACHES PEAK LOOP
LOOP TRIP: 3.2 miles
TRAIL DIFFICULTY: moderate
ELEVATION GAIN: 500 feet
ACTIVITIES: hiking, scenic views
BEST: mid-July to September
MAP: Green Trails: Mt. Rainier, East
Map on page 118

DEWEY LAKES
ROUND TRIP: 5.5 miles
TRAIL DIFFICULTY: challenging
ELEVATION GAIN: 300 feet in; 600 feet out
ACTIVITIES: hiking, backpacking, fishing
BEST: mid-July to September
MAP: Green Trails: Mt. Rainier, East

It is hard to find a better place for a short hike than through the beautiful flower fields around Naches Peak. The views and vistas are outstanding, with ice-clad Mount Rainier domineering over all. By September, the huckleberries

A small tarn on the east side of the Naches Peak

ripen and the blue mouths of the hikers offer testimony to the popularity of this little fruit. The meadows take on a beautiful glow as the greens change to yellow, orange, and red. For the hikers who could care less about scenery, there are two lakes, two tarns, and a couple of streams to play in. Snowfields, which may linger through mid-August, can also be a source of great glee for the fun-loving.

Dewey Lakes are a destination preferred by fishermen young and old. The lakes also offer the nearest campsites to the peak loop. The trip to the lakes can be incorporated into the Naches Peak Loop or treated as a separate entity.

From Enumclaw, drive 43 miles south on Highway 410 to the summit of Chinook Pass. Go under the hikers' overpass then continue down 300 feet to find the parking area on the left. If that area is full, park on the right. If that area is full, start your loop at Tipsoo Lakes.

From the stone restroom at the hikers' parking area, head left, uphill, to the Pacific Crest Trail, paralleling Highway 410 to the summit of the pass. Cross the road on the overpass then climb steadily around the eastern flanks of Naches Peak. Snow lingers here and one or more small patches may be crossed before the trail reaches open meadows at 0.3 mile.

After passing an inviting tarn, the trail switchbacks up to the crest of a ridge with an excellent view of Dewey Lakes and Mount Adams. This is the highest point of the loop; from here it is downhill to Tipsoo Lakes.

Shortly after beginning the descent, the trail divides. The Pacific Crest Trail goes left, heading down 1.3 miles to Dewey Lakes. If spending the night at the lakes, stop at the self-registration box and fill in the required backcountry camping permit.

Loop hikers stay right at the intersection and follow the trail over the next low ridge and into Mount Rainier National Park. Dogs are not allowed. Continuing on, the trail crosses a low rise then enters a small tableland covered with a luxuriant cloth of flowers. Mount Rainier looms above like a domineering father checking on your table manners.

Beyond a small tarn, the trail descends rapidly. Just before crossing Highway 410, look left for a short trail leading to the upper Tipsoo Lake. When you are ready, cautiously cross the highway then veer left slightly to find a parking lot with trail access to lower Tipsoo Lake. Stay right at the next intersection and descend to the well-manicured lake loop trail. Keep to the west side of the lake and walk to the edge of the picnic area where you will find a trail up the hillside to the hikers' overpass and the end of the loop.

MORE ACTIVITIES

Tipsoo Lake Loop: From the Tipsoo Picnic area, located 0.2 mile west of Chinook Pass, walk the nearly level trail from the upper end of the picnic area parking lot around Tipsoo Lake. This 0.1-mile stroll is popular with flower lovers.

Sunrise and White River

Backpacking, camping, food service, hiking, ranger-led talks and walks, scenic drive, self-guided nature walks, visitor center, vistas, wildlife viewing

At 6,400 feet, Sunrise is the highest spot in the state of Washington accessible by a paved road. At road's end, visitors step out of the car into a high alpine world of small hardy plants and short, weather- and wind-sculptured trees. However, it is Mount Rainier that dominates the scene. On sunny days the glaciers and snowfields blaze with a nearly blinding intensity. Grandest is the Emmons Glacier, which starts at the summit and flows down 5.5 miles, descending over 9,000 feet in elevation before reaching its terminus at the head of

Mount Rainier viewed from the Sourdough Ridge Trail near Dege Peak

the White River. It is the largest glacier in the United States outside of Alaska.

The Sunrise/White River area is ideal for families. The east side of the park receives less visitation than Paradise and parking is easier, even on summer weekends. Short hikes here are as scenic and rewarding as the longer ones and wildlife—deer, elk, mountain goats, marmots, chipmunks, and squirrels—is common.

The buildings at Sunrise were built in Old Western style and the visitor center looks like a stockade. The history and reasoning behind this architectural blunder is obscure, but obviously somebody in Washington, D.C., circa 1930, thought that Mount Rainier was the wild west. As you stand in the parking lot, try to imagine what the area looked like seventy years ago, when the meadows were blighted with 250 cabins. Or think back even further to the days when the Native Americans came to pick berries and race horses across the meadows. Take time on the drive up to explain to the family why they cannot run over the meadow, pick flowers, or move rocks around. You may wish to have them consider the implications of the very short growing season here. The snow lingers on the meadows until mid-July and returns in early October. Compare that with the growing season at your own home. (When all else fails, you can explain that rangers will lecture all transgressors at great length.)

The drive up to Sunrise is an attraction in itself. From the dark forest and giant trees of the White River valley, the road climbs for 10 miles to reach the mountain tops. A stop at Sunrise Point is a must for views over the White River valley to Crystal Mountain and Norse Peak. From this point, the road cruises along the ridge, entering the high meadows. Early morning and evening visitors may spot grazing deer or elk. Before long Mount Rainier comes into view. The first glints are muted by green trees, but soon The Mountain boldly domineers and everyone will be squinting or scrambling to find their sunglasses.

Families wishing to spend the night at Sunrise must backpack 1.3 miles to the walk-in camp at Shadow Lake. White River Campground, the nearest car-accessible facility, is located in the valley. It has 117 sites (no group sites). Evening campfire talks, weekends only, are interlaced with songs, poems, and amusing anecdotes. The White River Campground fills up almost every night, so arrive by early afternoon to grab a spot. When the campground is full, sites may be available at Silver Springs Forest Service Campground, located 6 miles north of the White River turnoff on Highway 410.

White River Campground is a staging point for climbers ascending the mountain via the Camp Sherman and Emmons Glacier Route. Throughout the day, and often throughout the night, climbers can be seen walking through the campground with huge packs heading for the mountain or returning exhausted from a day that probably started at 1:00 A.M. The climbers' trail is also a popular hikers' access to a view of the Emmons Glacier and to the mining ruins in Glacier Basin.

Lodging is nonexistent at or near Sunrise. The closest motels and hotels are located around Crystal Mountain Ski Resort, north of the park. The nearest cities with lodging are Packwood, to the south, and Enumclaw, to the north.

Basic food service is available at Sunrise Lodge. For families who would prefer to eat at the large walk-in picnic area (wheelchair access is available) or on the trail, sack lunches may be purchased.

Note: The elevation of the Sunrise area gives rise to special concerns. The sun can be extremely bright and hard on unprotected eyes and skin. All visitors are advised to wear sunglasses and a hat. Generous and frequent applications of sunscreen are essential. Babies should be constantly shaded by an umbrella. When the sun is not shining, the weather can be extremely inclement, and coats, warm hats, mittens, and rain gear are required (snowfall in July and August is not uncommon).

Burroughs Mountain

LOOP TRIP: 5.2 miles
TRAIL DIFFICULTY: moderate
ELEVATION GAIN: 900 feet
ACTIVITIES: hiking, photography
BEST: August to September
MAP: Green Trails: Mt. Rainier, East
Map on page 124

Burroughs Mountain may just be the most scenic of all the trails at Sunrise. The trail climbs from the alpine environment at the visitor center, to the high alpine, and finally into the delicate high tundra—an incredible experience. Amazingly, this trail to the top of the world is excellent, wide, and well graded—and often crowded, with a mass of humanity that ranges in age from a couple weeks old to octogenarians.

Snow, in this high alpine environment, has a tendency to linger. By mid-July a path is generally dug across the steep slopes. However, a slip would be very dangerous, so check with a ranger concerning the status of the trail before setting out. Fremont Lookout and Dege Peak are great alternatives; remember, all trails are scenic here.

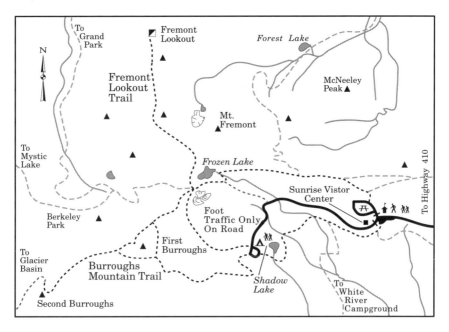

A father and son on the summit of the First Burroughs

Start your hike by walking up the paved road next to the restroom. After a few feet take a right on a wide gravel trail that leads to an orientation map and a box containing the Sourdough Ridge Nature Trail self-guiding pamphlet. Head up the hill to the first intersection and go right. After climbing for 0.3 mile, a chore for everyone at this elevation, the trail gains the crest of the ridge and an intersection. Stay left, following the trail as it surges up another rise then divides again. Keep to the left and begin a traverse with views of Shadow Lake, the Emmons Glacier, Goat Island Mountain, and, of course, Mount Rainier.

As you walk, watch for marmots and listen for their distinctive whistles warning their friends of approaching humans. Squirrels are everywhere; if you cannot find one, just stop and pull some food out of your pack.

At 1.5 miles, after passing Frozen Lake (a reservoir that supplies water for the Sunrise area), the trail reaches a five-way intersection (6,773 feet). To the right is Fremont Lookout. Straight ahead, the Wonderland Trail continues its round-the-mountain journey by heading north toward Mystic Lake. Left is Burroughs Mountain Trail, your objective. To the far left is a trail to Sunrise Camp and Shadow Lake, an excellent bailout trail if the weather sours.

Burroughs Mountain Trail heads steadily up rocky slopes where snowfields linger. Push on, the top is in sight. At 2.2 miles the trail crests the summit of the First Burroughs, a broad volcanic plain dwarfed by Mount Rainier. At 7,200 feet, vegetation is miniaturized, stunted by the long winters and harsh winds.

The lava soil offers only poor nutrition for the struggling plants. If stepped on, these delicate beauties may take more than 100 years to recover. Stay on the trail! Leave rocks in place. A moved rock will expose fragile root systems.

The trail crosses the First Burroughs then divides. If you wish to turn your hike into a loop, go left and begin the descent. At this point, many hikers are completely under The Mountain's spell and find it impossible to head back. If everyone is willing, continue on another 0.4 mile to the top of the Second Burroughs (7,400 feet).

The loop route contours around the First Burroughs then descends to the Emmons Glacier Overlook. Continue down to a walk-in campground. Go right and walk around the paved camp circle to find the trail to Shadow Lake on the right at 4.9 miles. The lake is a popular gathering point for families, and children often splash in the chilly waters. Beyond the lake, the trail crosses several grassy meadows then ascends gradually back to the visitor center.

Fremont Lookout

ROUND TRIP: 5.6 miles
TRAIL DIFFICULTY: moderate
ELEVATION GAIN: 1,000 feet
ACTIVITIES: hiking, wildlife viewing
BEST: mid-July to September
MAP: Green Trails: Mt. Rainier, East
Map on page 124

Don't forget the binoculars.

Mountain goats roam the open slopes around the old lookout and binoculars are essential when trying to distinguish the woolly white coats of the goats from the white snow patches they love to nap on. On summer weekends, a park naturalist carries a spotting scope to the lookout to help locate these denizens of the high alpine world.

Even if the mountain goats are hiding, there are plenty of other sights for visitors. The lookout itself is fascinating. You can walk up the steps of the tower and peer in the windows. The centerpiece of the room is a large, round fire-finder, an essential piece of equipment that helped the vigilant lookout determine the exact locations of fires. Imagine what it must have been like for the lookouts, perched on glass-footed chairs, plotting lightning strikes as a storm raged around them.

The view from the lookout is an incredible panorama where Mount Rainier reigns over a host of lesser dignitaries of the central Cascades. Mount Stuart, the Snoqualmie Peaks, Three Fingers, Glacier Peak, and Mount Baker can be seen on clear days. To the northwest lies the Puget Sound basin, waterways and cities, as well as the Olympic Mountains.

Fremont Lookout

From the parking lot at Sunrise, walk up the paved road next to the restrooms. Where the road divides, stay right for 200 feet then go right again to the hiker's orientation board. Head up hill, climbing steeply to an intersection. Go left and continue climbing. Do not let this initial war with gravity disturb you; the trail soon levels. At the ridge crest, pass a bench and go left. The trail divides again at the 0.3-mile point; stay left and begin a traverse overlooking Shadow Lake basin, Goat Island Mountain, and the very rugged Sarvent Glacier. The trail sweeps back into the open meadows as it traverses around Frozen Lake to arrive, at 1.5 miles, at a busy five-way intersection (6,773 feet).

The trail to Mount Fremont Lookout is to the right; however, most people find this a convenient stop for a snack break. The squirrels, chipmunks, and marmots expect it and come popping out of their hiding places to sit on their front porches and watch.

Beyond the intersection, the trail descends then climbs an open slope. Start looking for mountain goats on the hills above or below. The trail climbs to 7,250 feet then descends and climbs again to the lookout. You do not need to climb the tower for the grand view; it is spread out around the mountain. Watch out for voracious squirrels and chipmunks when you are ready to picnic.

Dege Peak–Sourdough Ridge

ROUND TRIP: 3.8 miles
TRAIL DIFFICULTY: moderate
ELEVATION GAIN: 600 feet
ACTIVITIES: hiking, photography, wildlife, wildflower viewing
BEST: mid-July to September
MAP: Green Trails: Mt. Rainier, East
Map on page 128

Dege Peak offers a classic view of the mountain with meadows in the foreground. Early morning is best for pictures; however, any time of day is ideal for views.

The trail is wide enough for two people to walk side by side the entire distance. Only the final pitch could be considered difficult, where the trail is steep with some loose rock, and younger hikers may require a little assistance. The top is very precipitous on three sides, so warn the kids to stay away from the edges, then keep an eye on them. Carry quarts of water and gallons of bug repellent.

Starting at the Sunrise parking area, follow the paved road around the back side of the restrooms. When the road divides, stay right. After 100 feet, go right again, this time on a gravel trail that leads to the hikers' orientation board. You may want to take this opportunity to walk all or part of the Sourdough Ridge Nature Trail on your way to and from Dege Peak, in which case you'll want to pick up a trail guide.

Follow the trail as it climbs steeply for a couple hundred feet to a well-signed Y intersection. Go right and continue to follow the nature trail. If you have a booklet you will be too busy looking for the next numbered post to notice the steep pitch of the trail. The views are exhilarating and the meadows, delicately beautiful.

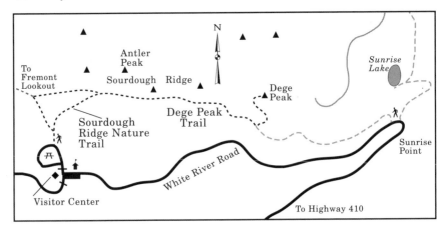

At the 0.7-mile point, the trail divides again. Stay right, leaving the nature trail, and walk east along the ridge crest through a forest of wind-sculptured trees. The trail remains level for 0.1 mile then rolls with the ridge, descending then climbing toward the peak. At 1.7 miles the trail divides again. The main trail continues along the ridge another 1.2 miles to Sunrise Point. Dege Peak is to the left, reached by a steady 0.3-mile climb. The view is a 360-degree masterpiece—a great place to watch a sunrise or sunset!

On the way back, finish the nature walk or just head straight down to the lodge for an ice-cream cone (or hot chocolate).

Emmons Moraine Trail

ROUND TRIP: 3 miles
TRAIL DIFFICULTY: moderate
ELEVATION GAIN: 700 feet
ACTIVITIES: hiking, glacier viewing
BEST: July to October
MAP: Green Trails: Mt. Rainier, East
Map on page 130

This hike to the crest of the moraine overlooking the Emmons Glacier is ideal for anyone staying at White River Campground. The trail offers an opportunity to study the dynamics of a mighty glacier as well as a place to relax and enjoy the area's truly excellent scenery. Along the way you will pass parties of climbers going to or returning from their assault on The Mountain. Loaded down with gear, the climbers are easily distinguished from the backpackers heading up for an overnight stay in Glacier Basin. Wildflowers abound, providing interest for budding botanists, and several bubbling creeks and one roaring river offer distractions for the less studious hikers.

The trail begins at the upper end of the White River Campground (4,300 feet). If you do not have a site, park in the combined picnickers' and climbers' parking area then walk to the upper end of Loop C.

Playing hide and seek around giant boulders

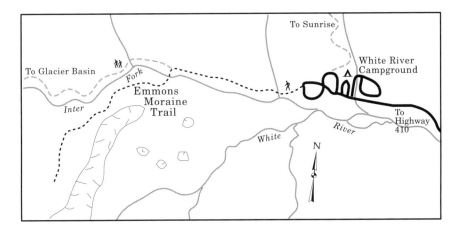

The trail leaves the campground and tunnels its way through the dense forest. Shadows are deep and the thin shafts of sunlight, by contrast, blinding. After an initial easy 0.2 mile, the trail begins a steady ascent, soon crossing the first creek. The forest thins and is replaced by brush as the climb steepens.

At the 1-mile point, the trail divides. Go left and descend to cross the roaring Inter Fork River on a single-log bridge. Hold on to the younger children to ensure that no one is accidentally launched into the raging torrent.

Once across the river, the trail passes a tempting bench and heads up the steep moraine. The ground below your feet is a loose jumble of rocks, boulders, and fine sand all pushed together by a river of ice. The dirt and rocks are tenuously held together by the bushes and trees that are slowly taking root on the barren ground. Pass several viewpoints overlooking the small tarns (ponds) below the glacier terminus before, at 1.5 miles, the trail officially ends in a 5,200-foot saddle. A rough path continues on along the crest of the moraine for another 0.2 mile.

From your chosen vantage point, look out over the mighty mass of 11,138-foot Little Tahoma which, in years past, has been a major contributor to the masses of mud and rock that cover the lower, terminus end of the glacier. Look closely at the brown mounds to discover the walls of mud-covered ice, impressive once you realize what they are.

Many people descend the moraine and walk out to the glacier. If you choose to do so, stay well back from the ice. Rock- and ice-falls are common.

SHORT WALKS AROUND SUNRISE

Map on page 131

The following three hikes are short and hikeable for the entire extended family.

Emmons Vista: This 0.5-mile round trip leads to a viewpoint of Mount Rainier, the White River valley, and Emmons Glacier. Stop at the first vista

Sunrise Visitor Center

or continue on to the second; both are excellent. From the second vista you may continue on the Silver Forest Trail through flower-covered meadows for more views. This is an easy hike.

Sourdough Ridge Nature Trail: Although this steep trail has a difficulty rating of moderate, self-guiding nature walks are a popular activity for all ages. The booklet covers the ecology of the alpine meadow, identifies some of the key plants, and points out many of the physical alterations man has made to the landscape. The trail is 1.5 miles long.

Sunrise Rim Trail: Although lacking in some of the spectacular scenery that keynotes the other trails in this area, this 3-mile round-trip hike has very

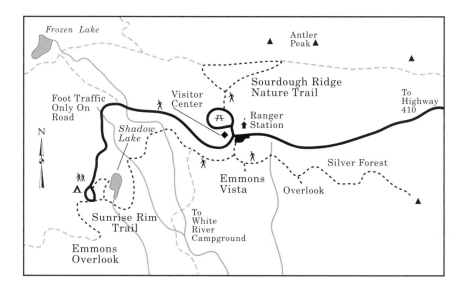

strong kid appeal. The loop is a combination of trail and old road and is doable with strollers. The most popular feature of the hike is Shadow Lake, a great place for a splash and a picnic. The trail begins at the south side of the parking lot and follows the Emmons Vista Trail for a short distance before branching right. From Shadow Lake, continue on to Sunrise Backcountry Camp then follow the road back. An extension of the hike can be made by heading 0.2 mile up from the backcountry camp to the Emmons Glacier Overlook.

MORE ACTIVITIES
Map on page 133

Ranger Walks: In July and August take your pick of several informative walks designed to move at a speed that fits the needs of slower walkers. The shortest of these walks departs twice daily from the Sunrise Visitor Center and offers an excellent introduction to the area. On weekends, a ranger-led walk along the Emmons Moraine Trail is a great way to learn about geology. Ranger-led walks vary with trail conditions so check information boards or at the ranger stations for updated schedules.

Junior Rangers: This program provides environmentally sensitive activities for kids ages six to eleven. Most activities, such as kids' walks, are done on weekends. Ask a ranger for information about this great program.

Palisades Lakes: This is a great area to explore on a warm afternoon. The first lake, Sunrise, is only a 0.3-mile walk from the Sunrise Point trailhead. Clover Lake is 1.5 miles from the road and Palisades Lakes are 3.5 miles. No views of Mount Rainier, just good lakeshore fun.

Sunrise to White River Campground: For the hyperactive, the 3-mile trail between Sunrise and White River Campground can be an energetic way to spend an hour descending or 2 hours climbing. The elevation loss, or gain, of 2,000 feet is covered by a seemingly endless series of switchbacks through the forest.

Pet Exercise Loop: Pets are not allowed on park trails, except on this

Ranger-led walk at Emmons Vista

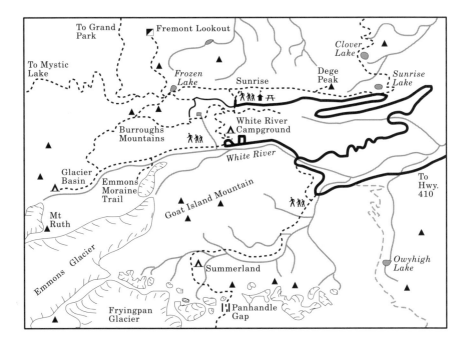

Map labels:
To Grand Park · Fremont Lookout · Clover Lake · To Mystic Lake · Frozen Lake · Sunrise · Dege Peak · Sunrise Lake · Burroughs Mountains · White River Campground · White River · To Hwy. 410 · Glacier Basin · Emmons Moraine Trail · Goat Island Mountain · Mt Ruth · Emmons Glacier · Summerland · Owyhigh Lake · Fryingpan Glacier · Panhandle Gap

special 1-mile loop. Pets must be on leash. The trail begins at the Sunrise parking area near the restroom.

Crystal Mountain Resort: This very popular ski area is also an excellent place for summer fun. The stables offer daily horseback rides. The chairlift runs visitors up to the mountain top for views and meals at the restaurant. You may then ride the lift back, hike, or mountain bike ride down. (Mountain bike rentals are available; however, this activity is very challenging and appropriate only for high school age and up.)

Carbon River and Mowich Lake

Backpacking, camping, fishing, hiking, swimming

Carbon River and Mowich Lake Entrances are located on the northwest side of Mount Rainier. First-time visitors to the park are often lured to these two areas because of their proximity to the Puget Sound metropolitan area. Unfortunately, neither entrance offers visitor facilities or even views of the mountain. However, with proper preparation, both Carbon River and Mowich Lake can make great destinations for family camping trips.

The Carbon River area is reached by a narrow road along the sides of the very deep Carbon River canyon. The pavement ends near the park boundary and the final 5 miles to road's end are on a well-graded gravel and clay road.

A small tarn in Spray Park

Once in the park, visitors are tempted from their cars for a short, self-guiding nature loop through the rain forest, a walk to a forested lake, and a couple of short jaunts to waterfalls. The road ends near Ipsut Creek Campground, a twenty-nine-site area, which fills up early during the summer. The main activity for campers is hiking or backpacking. Most hikers head up the relatively level trail to the base of the Carbon Glacier.

Note: The Carbon River Road washed out in 1997 and had not been replaced at time of publication. Please call the park for updates.

Mowich Lake is reached by a nerve-racking drive up the narrow canyon followed by a stint on a moderately well-maintained dirt road. The road ends at the lake, where visitors are treated to a frankly putrid toilet and a small walk-in campground. If planning to overnight at the campground, stop at the ranger station in Wilkeson (a red caboose at the end of town) and obtain a backcountry camping permit. *No drinking water is available at Mowich Lake!* Bring your own water or the means to purify water from the nearby stream. NO fires are allowed at the camp area, so bring your stove. Campers may drive their vehicles to the end of the road and unload before finding a parking spot.

Once at the lake, there is a lot to do. Stroll around the shore for a glimpse of Mount Rainier, wade in the cool, clear water, fish from the shore, or bring your own small craft (it must be hand-carried several hundred feet from the road to the shore) and fish from the water. Hiking is the most popular activity at Mowich. Just 1.9 miles to the north is Eunice Lake and a magnificent view of The Mountain. To the south, 3 miles from Mowich Lake, is Spray Park, famous for its outstanding floral displays.

For hikers on the Wonderland Trail, Mowich Lake is an obvious overnight stop and resupply point. The Wonderland Trail, for those who have not heard of it, is a 99-mile loop around The Mountain. Due to the steepness of the trail and the potential for difficult snow crossings, this a hike best for families where the majority of the members have reached their teens.

Eunice Lake

ROUND TRIP: 3.8 miles
TRAIL DIFFICULTY: moderate
ELEVATION GAIN: 720 feet
ACTIVITIES: hiking, swimming, fishing
BEST: July to September
MAP: Green Trails: Mt. Rainier, West
Map on page 136

This small, gem-like lake set in alpine meadows is almost overwhelmed by the sublime view of Mount Rainier. For the peak-baggers, the trail continues on from the lake to an old lookout at the summit of 5,939-foot Tolmie Peak. If you bring some good flashlights for the return trip, the lookout is a great place to watch the sunset.

Drive Highway 410 to the town of Buckley, located between Sumner and Enumclaw. At the south end of Buckley, turn east then take an immediate right and follow signs to Wilkeson and Mount Rainier National Park. At Wilkeson, pass the ranger station then continue upvalley on Highway 165. Shortly after crossing Fairfax Bridge (a single-laner), the road divides. Go right and head uphill. At the crest of the hill the pavement turns to gravel and remains that way to Mowich Lake. On busy weekends you may have to park a half-mile or more down the road.

Begin your hike by descending to Mowich Lake. The trail rounds the forested shore of the lake, with occasional glimpses of Mount Rainier through the trees, then climbs, gradually at first, then with increasing determination until reaching Ipsut Pass (5,200 feet) where it divides. Stay left and descend, drop-

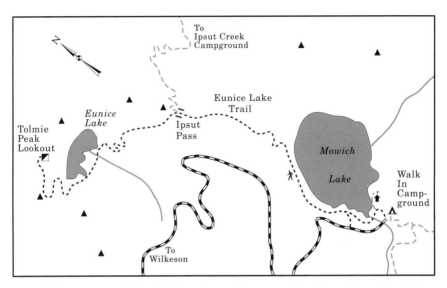

ping below some mighty cliffs and crossing a couple of small creeks before making a sudden charge back up the hill to 5,354-foot Eunice Lake, 1.9 miles from the start.

The main trail never touches the lake. To reach the shore, take one of several spur trails over the open meadows. In midsummer the water at the northwest corner is literally alive with salamanders.

To continue up to the lookout, return to the main trail for a steep, switchbacking climb. Several large steps, designed to prevent erosion, may be a cause of consternation for short-legged hikers. The lookout is 1 mile above the lake and well worth the effort.

Spray Park

ROUND TRIP: 6 miles
TRAIL DIFFICULTY: challenging
ELEVATION GAIN: 1,200 feet
ACTIVITIES: hiking, flower viewing
BEST: mid-July to September
MAP: Green Trails: Mt. Rainier, West
Map on page 137

Even before the snow melts, determined avalanche lilies and glacier lilies push their way up through the snow and start to coat the meadows with mats of color. By August, the white and yellows of the lilies give way to the blues and reds of lupines and paintbrush, colorful and joyful. In fall the flowers fade and are soon replaced by the reds and yellows of the frost-tinted leaves.

Spray Park is one of those special places where, by the thousands, people come back to visit year after year. The enthusiasm generated by this area has led the park to initiate some very restrictive rules, making it much like visiting an art museum: Look but don't touch. No camping is allowed in Spray Park. Most way trails have been closed, limiting access into the meadows. Even the main trail has been reshaped into a nearly straight line to minimize impact.

All these restrictions tend to put a crimp on fun for younger family members. To help them enjoy the trip, you might want to consider bringing along a special "fun bag" filled with a coveted snack and a favorite toy.

Following directions to Eunice Lake, drive to Mowich Lake. Walk into the campground and take an immediate right to find the trailhead. Descend into the forest, dropping down a series of steps to cross Crater Creek on a log bridge. The trail then heads south, contouring around the steep hillside, sometimes climbing over low ridges, sometimes descending, but generally staying level. At 0.4 mile, the Wonderland Trail departs to the right for a long descent to the North and South Mowich Rivers.

After crossing several more small creeks, the trail divides again at 1.7 miles where a short side trail descends to Eagle Cliff. This rocky point overlooks the North Mowich River valley and the North Mowich Glacier. A bare 0.2 mile beyond, a second trail heads down the hill, this one to the cliff-hanging Eagle's Roost backcountry campsite.

The trail crosses a stream-laced hillside then divides again just before Grant Creek. If you continue straight for 0.3 mile you will reach Spray Creek

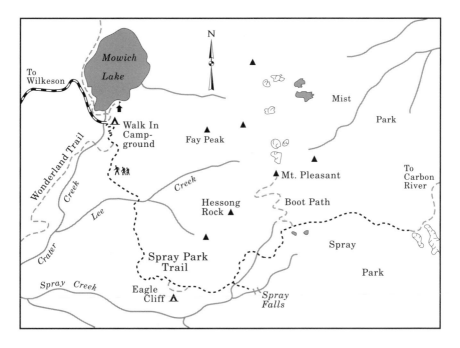

and a view of Spray Falls. The hillside is steep and composed of loose boulders, making it a poor choice for younger children. Instead, pull a few sugar-coated energy pills out of the pack and prepare for the 0.8-mile ascent to the meadows. The initial flying leap up from the intersection is steep, with rocks and roots to crawl over. Occasionally one of the nearby streams jumps its banks then shoots down the trail for 10 feet or more.

After a couple of switchbacks, the going improves and the flower fields begin. Before long you will know why you persevered, as the meadows get larger and the trees fewer and farther between. After crossing Grant Creek, the trail makes a final surge up to Spray Park (5,600 feet). At this point, look for a path on the left which crosses over the meadow to a small pond and climbs a ridge to the summit of 6,454-foot Mount Pleasant for a more than pleasant view. A short distance beyond, find another spur trail on the right leading to a couple of small tarns where Mount Rainier reflects photogenically in the shallow waters. The main trail continues to the top of a 6,100-foot ridge then ascends some more, climbing to the high alpine tundra before descending to Seattle Park and the Carbon River.

Backpack Trips

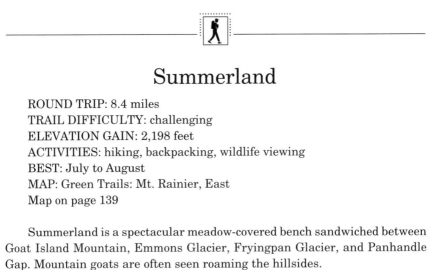

Summerland

ROUND TRIP: 8.4 miles
TRAIL DIFFICULTY: challenging
ELEVATION GAIN: 2,198 feet
ACTIVITIES: hiking, backpacking, wildlife viewing
BEST: July to August
MAP: Green Trails: Mt. Rainier, East
Map on page 139

Summerland is a spectacular meadow-covered bench sandwiched between Goat Island Mountain, Emmons Glacier, Fryingpan Glacier, and Panhandle Gap. Mountain goats are often seen roaming the hillsides.

Note: This is a very popular destination and the campsites usually fill up on the weekends. Arrive a day ahead of your hike to avoid disappointment. If the children are strong hikers, you may continue above Summerland and camp off-trail.

Drive Highway 410 to the White River Entrance of Mount Rainier National Park. Pick up your backcountry permit at the entrance office then continue on

Father and daughter hiking the Wonderland Trail at Summerland

3 miles. Look for the trailhead and parking immediately after crossing Fryingpan Creek (3,800 feet).

The hike begins as a gentle stroll through a forest of tall trees which have seen many years and countless hikers go by. After 0.1 mile, join the Wonderland Trail and continue upvalley. The climb does not get serious until the 1.3-mile point where the trail starts a series of zig-zagging switchbacks that take you high above the roaring of Fryingpan Creek. Views are still limited with just a few teasers of what is to come.

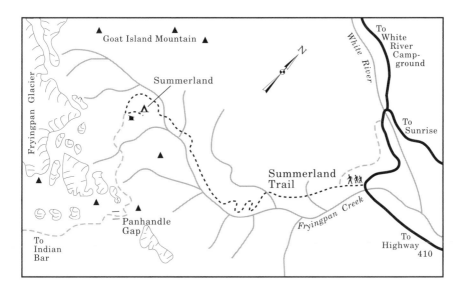

At 3 miles, the crossing of Fryingpan Creek on a log bridge signals the beginning of the final climb to Summerland. The trail heads across several winter avalanche areas where the tread nearly disappears under masses of flowers.

The Summerland Meadows and stone shelter (part of the group camp area) are reached at 4.2 miles. Campsites and a solar toilet lie east of the shelter.

Once camp is set, pull out the binoculars and start looking for mountain goats. In late August, when the snow has melted off Panhandle Gap, take an evening walk up to the ridge crest for an even better chance at wildlife viewing.

Glacier Basin

ROUND TRIP: 7 miles
TRAIL DIFFICULTY: moderate
ELEVATION GAIN: 1,400 feet
ACTIVITIES: backpacking, hiking, views, wildlife
BEST: July to September
MAP: Green Trails: Mt. Rainier, East
Map on page 141

Old mining machinery along the trail to Glacier Basin

Glacier Basin is an oasis of green meadows between the rock and stone ramparts of Burroughs Mountain and Mount Ruth and the steep, icy expanse of the Inter Glacier. The views of Mount Rainier are limited to summit regions, but the younger members of the group won't care anyway . . . there is old machinery and strange pieces of rusting iron lying around to explore.

From the late 1800s to the 1930s, Glacier Basin was the scene of a major mining operation. It was not until after a mineral survey in the late 1950s failed to find the supposedly rich deposits of silver and copper that all operations ended. When the miners left, they abandoned massive amounts of machinery, much of which was destroyed in a fire set by an anti-mining group in the 1960s.

The old miners' road to the basin makes an easy-to-walk trail that can be successfully negotiated by all but the shortest legs. The scenery is compelling for the adults, while the old machinery and the promise of plenty of trail treats keeps the kids moving. This is a popular first backpack trip for families and there are frequently other kids around for company. The group site makes it possible for several families to join together for moral support.

The Glacier Basin Trail begins at the upper end of Loop C of the White River Campground (4,300 feet). Unless you are day hiking out of the campground, your car must be left in the picnickers' and hikers' parking lot. Backpackers need a permit which can be issued in Enumclaw at the White River Ranger Station, from the ranger's office opposite the White River entrance booth, or at any other backcountry office in the park. Space at Glacier Basin Camp is limited to six sites and permits can be hard to get. On weekends it is best to secure the permit the day before the hike.

The trail begins in forest shade, but soon heads out across flower-brightened meadows. Stream crossings are frequent, and younger children will require assistance with some of the longer jumps.

After 1 mile, the trail to the Emmons Glacier viewpoint branches off to the left. Shortly beyond, a section of washed-out old road is bypassed by a steep trail. After 0.3 mile, the trail returns to the old road, passing the first of many old machine parts.

The trail to Burroughs Mountain and Sunrise heads off to the right at 2.6 miles. At 2.8 miles, opposite the site of the miners' sawmill and power plant, the trail leaves the old road and begins a steady climb to the basin. The final 0.3 mile is the steepest of the hike. At 3.1 miles the trail arrives at Glacier Basin

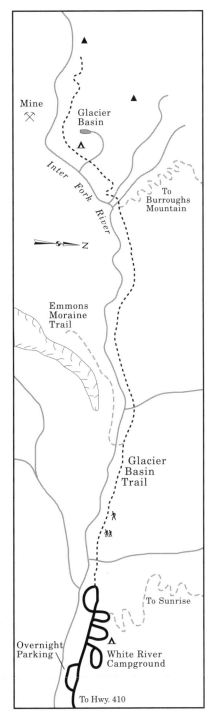

Elk

Camp (5,690 feet). Old mining ruins are located in camp and splattered around the hillsides above. A major mining site lies across the White River and is inaccessible until early fall.

The trail officially ends at the campsite, but you would never know it. A wide path continues out into the meadow then on up a moraine to end at the edge of the Inter Glacier. The hundred or so people each day who continue on are climbers on their way to the summit of Mount Rainier.

The meadow area offers great animal viewing opportunities. Marmots roam the green areas, picking flowers and laying them out to dry on any convenient rock. Occasionally, they even meander through the campsite. Deer and an occasional elk wander through, and bands of mountain goats are commonly spotted in the early mornings and evenings roaming the hillsides above. The nearby pond and outlet stream are filled with an amazing number of frogs sunbathing in the mud.

If spending more than one night at the basin, motivated hikers can find excellent views on the challenging hike up to the summit of the 7,400-foot Second Burroughs.

Winter

Winter is a very special time at Mount Rainier. Storms blow over the mountain with great force, shrouding the meadows and entombing the trees beneath massive overcoats. This is a great place to enjoy a family outing in the snow. Bring plenty of warm clothes, enthusiasm, a sled, skis or snowshoes, and take some time to explore. In winter you may trample right across the meadows (safe under a cover of 12 feet of snow).

The Nisqually Entrance is the only one that remains open throughout the winter. The road to Paradise is often icy. Tire chains or four-wheel-drive is a requirement. In mid-winter the road is gated at Longmire by 4:00 P.M. The road usually opens between 9:00 A.M. and 10:00 A.M. unless the avalanche hazard is too high for safety.

Cross-country ski rentals are available at Longmire and limited food service can be found on weekends at Paradise and Longmire. Longmire Inn is open throughout the winter, as is Sunshine Point Campground near the park entrance.

Just outside the park is the Tahoma Ski Trails network. This is a public area with three huts and a yurt. Skiers are required to have a SnoPark permit on their cars. If desiring to stay at one of the huts or the yurt, contact Mt. Tahoma Trails Association, Attn: Hut Reservation Program, P.O. Box 206, Ashford, WA 98304. These huts are popular, so plan several months ahead.

Skiing with Dad's help

Paradise Valley

ROUND TRIP: 3 miles
TRAIL DIFFICULTY: moderate
ELEVATION GAIN: 538 feet
ACTIVITIES: skiing, snowshoeing, winter exploration
BEST: mid-December to March
MAP: Green Trails: Mt. Rainier, East
Map on page 144

During the summer, the marshy valley below Paradise is generally ignored in favor of the richer meadows and more flamboyant views above. The narrow one-way road into the valley offers summer visitors an alternate parking location when the lot at Paradise is full, if they are willing to walk the mile or more back up.

During the winter, this narrow roadway provides the only easy ski tour in the Paradise area. And the scenery is anything but second-rate. The view of the Tatoosh Range is extremely photogenic and the frozen streams and waterfalls have a strong appeal to all ages.

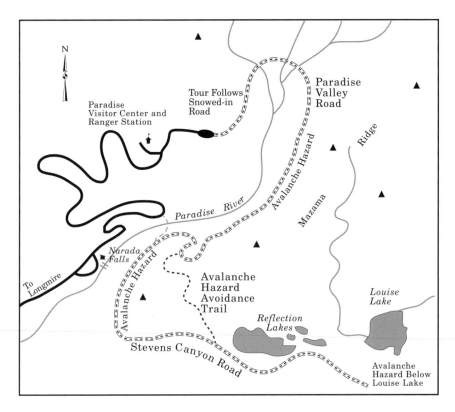

From the Nisqually Entrance to Mount Rainier National Park, follow the Paradise Road to the end of the plowing at Paradise Inn (5,450 feet). If unfamiliar with the winter hazards of the area, talk to a ranger before starting out for some general information and specific updates on that day's snow and avalanche conditions.

Start your tour at the southeast corner of the parking lot. Climb the bank to the top of the snow covering the Paradise Valley Road then put on the skis or snowshoes. As a common courtesy skiers, snowshoers, and hikers should each create their own set of tracks and not mess the tracks left by the other users.

Younger family members will like the start of the trip, as the road descends into the valley. However, if your family group includes novices on skis, they may soon change their minds. Descend to the third bridge below the parking lot then continue a few feet to a level area and evaluate how everyone is doing before continuing on down.

Near the 1.5-mile point, the road crosses the first of two avalanche chutes. If the snow has not taken its first slide for the season these slopes look just like the rest. This is where you will follow the ranger's recommendations. If the snowpack is stable you may continue on; if not, turn around here or descend to the valley floor for 0.1 mile then climb back to the road.

At the 2.3-mile point, a trail on the left climbs over a forested ridge and descends to Reflection Lakes, avoiding an avalanche hazard on the Stevens Canyon Road. Unless all the group are practiced skiers or snowshoers, this is a good place to turn around and begin the long trudge back to the parking lot. Of course, if you have a sled waiting at the car, the promise of some snow play will make the return trip go pretty fast.

Copper Creek Hut

ROUND TRIP: 6 miles
TRAIL DIFFICULTY: challenging
ELEVATION GAIN: 900 feet
ACTIVITIES: skiing, snowshoeing, snow play, visiting a hut
BEST: mid-December to mid-March
MAP: USGS: Ashford
Map on page 147

This rolling tour along forest roads is the least demanding of all the hut access routes in the Mt. Tahoma Trails system. Even if your family's skiing skills are not the greatest, you may sample the joys of skiing into an isolated, but comfortable, mountain hut. Young children find the destination very appealing and adults can pull extra gear on sleds. The tour is not considered difficult; however, first-time cross-country skiers, especially young, grade-school-aged children, may have a hard time on some of the hills. If you

Copper Creek Hut

do not own them, consider renting child-sized snowshoes for anyone whose balance is suspect on potentially icy descents.

Drive east from Elbe on Highway 706 for 6.5 miles, then go left on a narrow road signed 92 ROAD ACCESS, CENTRAL DISTRICT ACCESS, AND ELBE HILLS ATV. The road passes several houses then heads out for a long climb up DNR forest lands. The intersections are well signed and all forks to the right. After 6.3 steep and rough miles the road arrives at the ridge top SnoPark (3,300 feet). Note: Do not head up these steep and difficult roads without chains and a shovel in your car. If the snowfall has been heavy, the plowing may stop a mile or more below the top.

The most difficult section of the tour is the narrow trail from the parking lot to the forest roads. Follow the signed Champion Trail from the east end of the parking area up a short steep hill. Many skiers prefer to walk to the top. Once on the crest of the hill the trail begins an easy contouring ascent to the east.

After 0.5 mile the Champion Trail joins a wide forest road and descends to the right (east). Two short descents are followed by a gradual, but steady, climb. Routefinding is easy and intersections are well marked. You will pass several

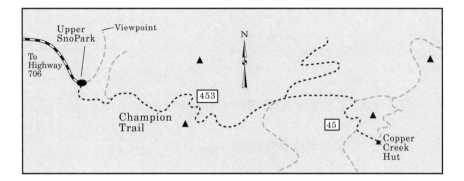

minor spur roads on the right and left as well as one major service road that branches right at 1.5 miles. Shortly after, the road divides. Stay right on Road 453 and continue to climb.

The route heads up and along a broad ridge crest to views of Mount St. Helens and Sawtooth Ridge then steepens for a climb to a forested saddle and the first views of Mount Rainier. The road continues its gradual ascent around the north side of the knoll to reach a second saddle and intersection at 2.6 miles. If the hut is your goal, go right and descend Road 45 for 500 feet then take the first left. This road descends briefly then climbs steeply up an exposed hillside to reach the hut at 3 miles (4,200 feet).

If the hut is not the goal, continue straight for another 0.3 mile up a steep and exposed road to excellent touring and views on the open ridges above.

Other Tours

Ohanapecosh: Once the snow falls, visitors can enjoy cross-country skiing or snowmobiling a 10-mile section of the Stevens Canyon Road from the entrance station to Box Canyon.

White River: During the winter months, Highway 410 is closed at Crystal Mountain turnoff. A SnoPark, located on the right directly after the turnoff, is the starting point for an easy tour on up the highway. Elk inhabit this area and may be spotted in the early or late hours of the day. Highway 410 may be skied for 4.5 miles to the White River Road, which can be followed for another 7 to the old growth forests at White River Campground.

Mount St. Helens in 1980, during an early phase of its eruption

3

Mount St. Helens National Volcanic Monument

Northwest natives tell many stories of the great volcanic peaks of Washington and Oregon. In one story, St. Helens was a beautiful girl desired by the warriors Adams, Rainier, and Hood. The warriors fought, throwing rocks at each other, heaving fire bolts, and stomping the ground with their great feet, destroying the countryside. Rainier lost the fight for the girl and went north. Hood was also defeated and went south. The maiden became the bride of Adams. Of course, one must wonder what Mount Adams thinks about his blushing bride now!

In the spring of 1980, Mount St. Helens awoke from a sleep that had lasted well over 100 years. During this quiet period, the mountain cloaked itself in a thick, luxuriant overcoat of glaciers and the hazards of this young, active volcano were forgotten. A fire lookout was built at the summit, but was determined to be impractical due to weather and was abandoned. Spirit Lake, on the north side of the mountain, became a popular recreation area with a campground, three youth camps, and two lodges. The beauty and symmetry of St. Helens was so famous that it was named sister mountain to Japan's famous Fujiyama.

The awakening and subsequent eruption of the volcano started quietly, announcing itself with a series of earthquakes. In March of 1980, a crater opened on the summit which steamed and sent out small ash emissaries to let the world know that St. Helens was active again. Initially, this phase of activity seemed to progress normally, following the pattern expected by geologists. But this was not going to be a normal eruption. When a bulge began to form on the north side of the mountain, expanding at the rate of about five feet per day, geologists could not believe it. They sent for new instruments before they could accept the truth. The bulge pushed out a full 300 feet until, on the morning of May 18, something let loose and the entire north side of the mountain blew out in an unprecedented lateral blast. Ash soared into the sky and, in massive

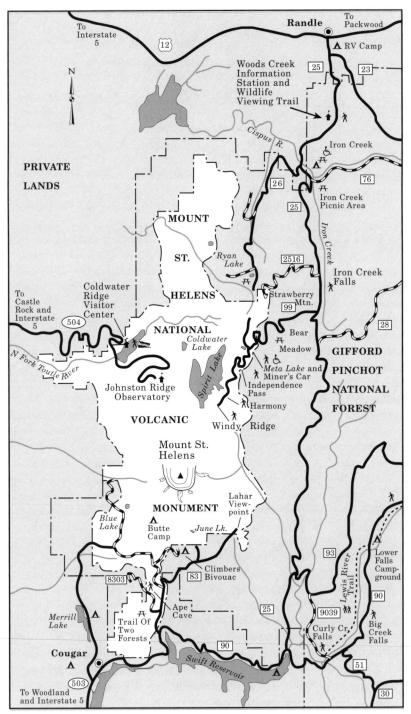

clouds, blew east, choking eastern Washington then continuing on into neigh-boring states, giving birth to the phrase, "Don't visit Washington, let Washington come to you."

But the spread of ash was only a minor inconvenience compared to the destruction caused by the incredible force of the eruption. Superheated air, filled with rocks, swept over the countryside leveling trees throughout 230 square miles of forest. This stone wind stripped the bark and branches off trees then laid them down in neat rows. The largest landslide in recorded history swept off the north side of the mountain and headed down the North Fork Toutle River, carrying massive chunks of the mountain with it. Huge mudflows (known to geologists as lahars) roared down the mountain. The mudflows were com-posed of debris from the mountain mixed with the melted snow and ice from its glaciers. In just a few minutes, one of the most beautiful spots in the world had been transformed into a wasteland.

The first biologists into the area came expecting to find a sterile landscape devoid of life, but once again Mount St. Helens had some surprises up her sleeve. Incredibly, small pockets of life were found. Buried under the unmelted snow were trees, grasses, flowers, huckleberries, insects, small animals, and even fish.

In 1982, the Mount St. Helens National Volcanic Monument was created. The monument's goal is to protect and preserve the devastated area so that scientists can study and learn from this unusual eruption and people can view the amazing forces that caused this mass devastation and are now creating such energetic regrowth.

Mount St. Helens National Volcanic Monument is a young park. Visitor services and trails are not yet fully established. Also, geologically speaking, since its eruption, the mountain and surrounding countryside being preserved are young. The land is undergoing constant change from slides of loose ash and soil, rapid regrowth of vegetation, and the return of the wildlife.

The devastation is the most visible feature of the area, with miles and miles of rolling hillsides covered with dead trees and a heavy blanket of ash. The landscape is dotted with pockets of life. These areas are small, and the nurtured life is also small: bees, flies, tadpoles, snakes. In some sites there are grasses and flowers and hardy blackberries and other forms of pokey vegetation. These small footholds of life are only exciting when visually contrasted with the miles of total devastation caused by the eruption.

The mountain can be approached on three sides: from the east by Road 99, Highway 504 from the west, and, on the south side, from Cougar. A minimum of one entire day is required to see the mountain from any of these three locations.

If walking is not a favorite family pastime, Highway 504 is the best intro-duction to the monument. The four visitor centers along the highway are full of modern audiovisual and interactive displays to touch and explore. Several nature walks provide introductions to the amazing destruction and regrowth. Highway 504 starts in Castle Rock and follows the North Fork Toutle River val-ley to Johnston Ridge. From the observatory at the end of the highway you may look straight into the crater where the new dome is slowly building and steam can be seen floating lazily to the sky.

Road 99, on the east side of Mount St. Helens, twists and winds its way across steep hillsides, heading straight through the heart of the devastation zone to end on the edge of the mountain at Windy Ridge. This is an area of high visual impact. Much can be seen without ever getting out of the car; however, with a bit of exploring, the trip can become an intensely memorable experience.

The southern access from Cougar leads to the Ape Cave and the Lahar area of the mountain. As most of the force of the 1980 blast went to the north, this portion of the mountain has retained much of its graceful beauty. Activities here are of a more varied nature and generally considered to be family pleasers. The most popular walk is a trek into an underground lava tube called the Ape Cave. Walks to lakes, waterfalls, and high alpine meadows are also popular. The south side is the only area from which the mountain may be climbed.

Accommodations are nonexistent in the monument; however, several large camp areas are located around its boundaries. On the south side of the mountain, open camping is allowed on spur roads and turnouts.

Food service is available at some visitor centers on Highway 504. However, you are advised to pack a large picnic lunch before heading into the monument on the south or east sides.

Spirit Lake in 1958

Permits: In 1997, the monument initiated a facilities fee. This fee must be paid if you are planning to visit any visitor center or walk a nature trail. The fee applies to everyone who is sixteen or older. Climbing permits are required for all who wish to go to the summit. These were a pricy $15 per person in 1997. Winter visitors will need a SnoPark permit.

West Side Access: Highway 504

Elk viewing, fishing, movies, nature walks, swimming, talks, visitor centers

When Mount St. Helens erupted on the morning of May 18, 1980, the north side of the mountain exploded outward and collapsed. The collapse created an avalanche of rock and glacier ice. As it hurled forward, the debris avalanche picked up the soil and the vegetation in its path and became the greatest landslide ever recorded.

Part of the landslide swept north into Spirit Lake, causing a giant tidal wave which surged 1,000 feet up the surrounding hillsides. However, the largest mass of debris headed west down the wide, heavily forested North Fork Toutle River valley.

Spirit Lake in 1990

As the avalanche swept down the valley, entire forests and logging camps were buried in mud and debris. The masses of dirt formed natural dams at the side valleys, stopping creeks and creating new lakes. The powerful flow of debris pushed the North Fork Toutle River ahead, creating a wall of water that swept away anything in its path, including trees and homes. Even after the heavier elements of the debris came to rest, the finer sediments continued to flow, suspended in and pushed along by the rush of water. These sediments flowed all the way to the Columbia River, filling the river channel and blocking shipping lanes.

After the eruption, Weyerhaeuser Timber Company began the largest salvage logging operation in history, then followed up with a massive replanting campaign. The company also donated large chunks of land to the new volcanic monument.

Much of the northwest side of the mountain was incorporated into a giant research area dedicated to studying the regrowth process. Today, almost twenty years after the eruption, textbooks are being rewritten because of what has been learned. Many animals have returned and the largest herd of elk in the state now resides in the North Fork Toutle River valley.

Because the northwest side of the monument lies entirely inside the research area, visitors are restricted as to where they can go and what they can do. Visitors may not wander across the barren landscape; instead they are required to stay on established trails.

Highway 504, which travels 51 miles east from Castle Rock to end at a lofty viewpoint on Johnston Ridge, has four

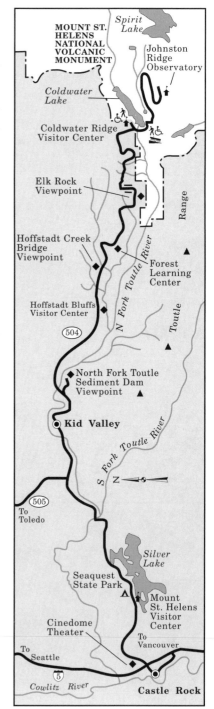

visitor centers designed to help you understand the eruption and the regrowth process. Each visitor center has fascinating displays and excellent movies. However, if you are traveling with young children, send an adult ahead to check out the movie first. (The live footage of the eruption, combined with intense sound, may be too much for some youngsters.)

The trip along Highway 504 from Castle Rock to Johnston Ridge Observatory can be driven in one day. But it takes two days to really see the visitor centers, watch the movies, attend an interpretive talk, and enjoy a few walks.

Hotel and motel accommodations as well as restaurants are located in Castle Rock. For camping, Seaquest State Park, directly across the road from the Mount St. Helens Visitor Center, is very convenient. The state park has seventy-four campsites, ten trailer sites, and four primitive hiker-biker sites. The group area is large enough for reunions of up to fifty people. Nearby Silver Lake also provides opportunities for swimming, fishing, and boating. Reservations are advised during the summer. Private trailer parks and campgrounds are located along the first 25 miles of Highway 504 from Castle Rock.

Highway 504 climbs to an elevation of 4,200 feet before ending at Johnston Ridge Observatory. The upper section of the road receives considerable snow in the winter and is closed from October to May.

ACTIVITIES
Map on page 154

Highway 504 starts at Exit 49 off Interstate 5. Once you leave the freeway, head east and drive uphill on the well-signed road.

Cinedome Theater: Just east of the freeway overpass is a Cinedome theater which features an Imax film of the eruption of Mount St. Helens. The sound and format make this movie inappropriate for preschoolers.

Mount St. Helens Visitor Center at Silver Lake: The visitor center is located 5.5 miles east of Interstate 5 on Highway 504, opposite Seaquest State Park. It is open from 9:00 A.M. to 6:00 P.M. throughout the year except Thanksgiving and Christmas.

Events leading up to the eruption and the eruption itself are highlighted. Displays give information of the volcanic history of the area, moving from the entire globe to the Cascade Range, then narrowing the focus to Mount St. Helens as you make your way around the room. The high point is a walk through a simulated volcano. Plan to spend at least an hour at the visitor center, and take in a movie at the theater.

A trail loops around outside of the building and, weather permitting, Mount St. Helens can be seen over Silver Lake. There is also a trail to Seaquest State Park.

Seaquest State Park: The park is located opposite the east entrance to the Mount St. Helens Visitor Center. Besides camping and picnicking, the park offers 8 miles of trails through the forest ranging from a 0.2-mile nature trail loop to a 4-mile trek up a ridge. Some of the trails follow old roads and are open to mountain bikes.

Kerr Road Boat Launch: Located 7.7 miles east of Highway 504, this small boat launch and fishing area is a great place to escape from the mosquitoes if you are staying at Seaquest State Park. Small boats, canoes, and kayaks are ideal for exploring the narrow channels through the lily pads at the east end of Silver Lake.

North Fork Toutle Sediment Dam Viewpoint: Drive Highway 504 southeast 21.3 miles from Interstate 5, then turn south on Sediment Dam Road for 1 mile to a parking lot with restrooms, picnic tables, and a gift shop. The viewing area is located 300 feet up a wide trail. The dam was built after the Mount St. Helens eruption to slow the Toutle River and force it to drop its load of sediment and ash before reaching the Columbia River. The information board at the head of the trail is interesting; the view of the earth dam is not. For a closer view, there is a 1-mile trail from the viewpoint to the dam.

Hoffstadt Bluffs Visitor Center: Cowlitz County erected a beautiful building, called it a visitor center, and filled it with gift shops. Several viewing platforms overlooking the Toutle River attempt to give this place some legitimacy as an elk-viewing area. Picnic tables, food service, and restrooms are found here. The Hoffstadt Bluffs Visitor Center is located 27 miles from Interstate 5.

Hoffstadt Creek Bridge Viewpoint: For inquiring minds-that-want-to-know, this stop has an excellent information sign explaining how this massive bridge was built. The bridge viewpoint is located on the left, 29.8 miles southeast of Interstate 5.

Forest Learning Center and Rest Stop: Located 33.8 miles southeast of Interstate 5, the Forest Learning Center is a must stop. This facility was built by the Weyerhaeuser Company and has some marvelous displays.

If traveling with children age eight or younger, you may want to head straight for the playground, an inspired work of art with slides that come out of a recreated Mount St. Helens, machines for digging in the dirt, and a climbing toy that looks like a forest.

When you are ready to go inside, open the door and step into a pre-eruption forest, complete with sounds. The next stop is a movie of the eruption followed by a tour through the Salvage, Recovery, and Reforestation Room—the only place where the economic aspects of the eruption are discussed. Next, enjoy a video tour of the land around Mount St. Helens as seen from the sky. The final section of the Forest Learning Center is devoted to the elk living in the North Fork Toutle River valley.

Outside the center, a short trail climbs to a viewpoint over the North Fork Toutle River valley and a longer trail drops steeply below the playground through a tree plantation to another valley view. Elk tracks are frequently seen on the gravel surface of the lower path.

The road is closed from October to May east of the Learning Center.

Elk Rock Viewpoint: This viewpoint of Mount St. Helens, located on the monument boundary, overlooks the upper section of the giant debris slide created by the avalanche that swept down the North Fork Toutle River. The large viewpoint parking area is located 41.7 miles from the Interstate 5 exit. This is just 0.5 mile before Highway 504 crosses a 3,080-foot high point and begins its descent to the Coldwater Ridge Visitor Center.

Coldwater Ridge Visitor Center: From the massive windows at the Coldwater Ridge Visitor Center, Mount St. Helens regally raises its cropped head over the debris-filled North Fork Toutle River valley. This visitor center, located 42 miles from Interstate 5, is full of wonderfully interactive displays, including computers that let you take a crack at reestablishing a species in the devastation zone. The movie runs nearly continuously. A restaurant offers a selection of sandwiches and salads. There is also a gift shop and a bookstore.

Park interpreters give talks several times each day on the deck. When the weather is poor the talks are held indoors. Allow about 20 minutes. Guided walks along the 0.2-mile Winds of Change Interpretive Trail start at the visitor center. Times for the talks and walks are posted at the center.

Winds of Change Interpretive Trail: This 0.2-mile long, barrier-free loop offers a quick look at the devastation caused by the incredibly powerful stone wind created by the eruption. All standing trees were knocked down or broken off. Vegetation was stoned, then covered with a thick layer of ash. The interpretive trail allows us to see the destruction, then moves on to look at the plants and animals that survived and the subsequent regrowth that has occurred.

Coldwater Lake: This 5-mile-long lake was created during the 1980 eruption of Mount St. Helens. Scientists are monitoring the lake with great care to learn how aquatic life emerges in an ecosystem that is nearly devoid of living organisms. To protect the lake and the surrounding shoreline, access is severely limited.

The lake is located just east of the Coldwater Ridge Visitor Center and can be reached by a 0.8-mile-long trail or by following Highway 504 another 2 miles beyond the visitor center to the lake turnoff. Facilities include restrooms, picnic tables, a public phone, a nature trail, a pet-walking trail, Discovery Trail, a lakeshore trail, and a boat launch.

Boating on Coldwater Lake is a popular activity. Electric-powered motorboats, canoes, and kayaks can easily explore the entire lake in one day. Many visitors come to fish. Rules change frequently, so check your Washington State fishing regulations before setting out. A fish-cleaning area is located near the boat launch. Fishing from the shore is allowed at three designated sites only: the boat launch and two lake access points located at 1 and 4.5 miles up the lakeshore trail.

Boaters may leave the water only at the boat launch and the two lake access points. Swimming is not allowed from the road end parking area. Swimmers must walk the shore trail to one of the two lake access points.

Birth of a Lake Interpretive Trail: This trail starts at the picnic area at Coldwater Lake and makes a 0.2-mile loop along the shoreline. The trail is

Ranger pointing out interesting features along Johnston Ridge

barrier-free for wheelchairs and strollers. Signs along the route explain how the lake was formed and how life has come to the lake. The final portion of the trail circles a large hummock composed of ash, sand, and a massive chunk of the old mountain. Younger members of the family may find the information signs a bit technical and may prefer running along the boardwalks and peering from the viewing platforms.

Discovery Trail: This very short trail starts at the upper end of the picnic area at Coldwater Lake. The trail follows the outlet stream for several hundred feet and was designed to allow a closer look at the area's natural features and vegetation. This is still part of the research area, so visitors are asked to avoid stepping on plants and to leave all rocks, bugs, and plants where they were found.

Hummocks Loop: From little ponds to massive chunks of the old Mount St. Helens, this 2.3-mile loop is the best way to explore the North Fork Toutle River valley. This brief tour takes hikers through an energetic environment where new life is sprouting around every turn. Views of the mountain are impressive. For children, uninterested in events that took place long before they were born, there are frogs and bugs to look for in the many little ponds. Also look for signs of elk. The loop begins 0.1 mile past the Coldwater Lake turnoff.

Loowit Viewpoint: Located 50.2 miles east of Castle Rock, this turnout provides an excellent preview of what you will see 0.8 mile above at the Johnston Ridge Observatory.

Johnston Ridge Observatory: Located within 5 miles of Mount St. Helens' steaming crater, the observatory looks straight across the flood plain of the North Fork Toutle River into the massive crater caused by the eruption. From the outside terrace or the massive observatory windows, visitors can watch smoke puff lazily from the darkly growing dome or view the massive plumes of ash and dust blowing off the crater rim. The observatory was named in honor of Dr. Dave Johnston, who died during the eruption. His natural exuberance and endless enthusiasm for volcanoes has served as inspiration to all who have studied the mountain since the eruption.

The observatory features a computer-generated movie simulation of the actual eruption that ranks with Hollywood's greatest disaster films. The movie does a remarkable job of illustrating the power and violence of the initial explosion. Parents will need to sit very close to the grade school age and younger children and be prepared to explain some of the sequences. The movie begins at a fever pitch, with the excited voice of Dave Johnston yelling, "Vancouver, this is it!" then sweeps you along until reaching a crescendo as the movie screen rises to reveal the actual mountain.

After viewing the movie, looking at the remainder of the displays will not take long, and you will be ready for an interpretive talk or walk. Check for posted times at the observatory entrance.

Lakes Trail

ROUND TRIP: 2 miles
TRAIL DIFFICULTY: easiest
ELEVATION GAIN: 50 feet
ACTIVITIES: hiking, swimming, fishing
BEST: June to September
MAP: Forest Service: Mount St. Helens National Volcanic Monument
Map on page 160

Barricaded by rules and regulations, it seems unduly difficult for a family to enjoy a day of recreation at Coldwater Lake. However, for anyone willing to walk, there are opportunities to explore and relax along the lakeshore and take a cooling dip in the lake.

There are two ways to reach the lakeshore access areas. You may descend from Coldwater Ridge Visitor Center on the Elk Bench Trail No. 211D, which has excellent views but is rather steep. And all who slip down the 0.8-mile trail to the lake must regain those 600 feet of elevation on the long, dry, and very steep hike back up. If starting from the visitor center, look for the trailhead near the exit of the parking lot, next to a maintenance road.

The second, recommended way to reach the lakeshore access area is by walking the nearly level Lakes Trail No. 211 along the west shore of Coldwater Lake. Views of the lake and surrounding peaks are excellent.

To reach the Lakes Trail, drive Highway 504 east 43 miles from Interstate 5 to the Coldwater Lake turnoff. Park at the boat launch area (2,490 feet). Walk down to the dock then head left to find the trailhead. The trail follows the lakeshore just a few feet above the water. Stay on the trail at all times; the minimum fine for wandering is $100.

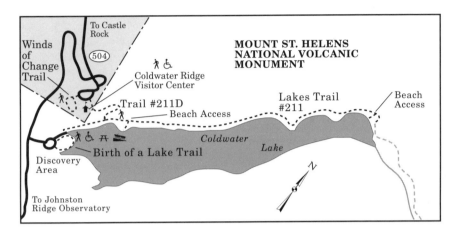

The trail curves with the rolls of the hillside, passing small seeps where vegetation is growing richly. By the time your children have children, the hillsides around the lake will be recovered with green trees and the view obscured by their branches. For now, the jagged crest of Minnie Peak and the steep sides of Coldwater Peak and Johnston Ridge look sharp and foreboding as their open slopes pierce the skyline.

At 0.7 mile, the Elk Bench Trail from Coldwater Ridge Visitor Center intercepts the Lakes Trail and ends. Continue on for a short, stiff climb followed by a quick descent around a small point to reach the first shore access at 1 mile. The area is small and a restroom is the only facility.

Descend to the lake on a designated trail then prepare for some real beach

Canoeing on Coldwater Lake

enjoyment. The water near the shore is shallow and, by midsummer, warm enough to entice swimmers in for a full body dip. The shore is sandy, great for use in the building of roads and other engineering exploits. For those who do not wish to get fully immersed, crawling around on the logs near the shore is a good way to enjoy the water and still remain separated from it. You may also wish to explore the access area. In the midst of the devastation, it is teeming with life. The vegetation is dense, with blackberries currently claiming more than their share of space. Ants are active, as are garter snakes and honey bees.

If you would like to continue hiking, at 4.5 miles is a second day-use lake access.

Boundary Trail No. 1

RIDGE WALK
> ROUND TRIP: up to 5 miles
> TRAIL DIFFICULTY: moderate
> ELEVATION GAIN: up to 600 feet
> ACTIVITY: views
> BEST: mid-June to September
> MAP: Green Trails: Spirit Lake
> Map on page 162

ARCH
> ROUND TRIP: 9.2 miles
> TRAIL DIFFICULTY: challenging
> ELEVATION GAIN: 1,800 feet
> ACTIVITY: goal-oriented walk to arch
> BEST: July to September
> MAP: Green Trails: Spirit Lake

The crest of Johnston Ridge is incredibly barren and surprisingly scenic. Without trees or vegetation to obstruct the view, hikers get an incredible feeling of freedom and openness that usually is only experienced at much higher elevations.

This is a landscape in its most infant stage of life. Before long you may start appreciating the random placement of boulders and stones in this garden of rocks. Small plants, struggling to gain a toehold, may remind you of weeds. Resist the urge to remove them and remain strictly on the trail; this is a study area and leaving the trail can result in a stiff fine.

Weather permitting, the hike along the ridge from Johnston Observatory should be on every visitor's itinerary. How far you choose to walk is a factor to be determined by the ages and desires of the members of the group. Families with very young children may prefer the 0.2-mile paved loop. Sturdy walkers will be able to continue on for 1.5 miles before turning back. Goal-oriented teen-agers and adults may be inspired to hike the entire 9.2 miles round trip to the arch just for the opportunity of walking through it.

From the terrace outside the Johnston Ridge Observatory, the trail begins with a paved, barrier-free swoosh up the neighboring knoll. The climb is mod-erate but wheelchairs may need a helping push. On top of the first knoll the view is excellent, as good as it gets for the next couple miles. Continue east and descend to the intersection where you can either go left and return to the park-ing lot or continue straight on a dirt trail.

Once you leave the pavement, follow the Boundary Trail No. 1 east along the rolling crest of the ridge. Use caution on the descents; the loose soil tends to be slippery. The trail is wide, with grand vistas of the mountain.

At 1.5 miles the trail leaves the crest of the ridge and bends south to traverse the Devil's Elbow. This section is narrow, horribly exposed, and not for everyone. Walkers on this part of the trail must keep their mind entirely focused on their feet. Families should end discussions and everyone should concentrate on walking carefully: A slip would probably end 1,000 feet below on the flood plain.

For those who choose to traverse the Devil's Elbow, the rewards are more magnificent views, including a grand vista over the upper section of Spirit Lake to Windy Ridge and Mount Adams. At 2.4 miles, Trail 207 branches off to the right. Continue straight, climbing barren ground to a barren ridge. The trail divides again at 3.5 miles with a spur trail branching right to Harry's Ridge. Continue straight and start up a steep, open hillside. After climbing to the 5,000-foot level the trail begins to descend steeply down a slippery slope,

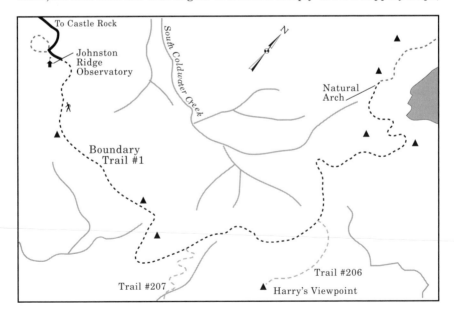

Family exploring the Boundary Trail on Johnston Ridge

crossing to the opposite side of the ridge. Head around a dome. The trail goes right through the arch and Mount Adams is scenically framed in the center. On the opposite side of the arch, take some time to study the three life zones as spread out before you, ranging from complete devastation to standing forest. On warm days, nearby St. Helens Lake seems to beckon, inviting swimmers to come and cool off. The lake may be looking for company, but you will have to ignore it, as it lies in the research area and there is no trail. If you are still looking for some way to wear out those teenagers, continue on for another 2 miles to the summit of 5,727-foot Coldwater Peak.

East Access: Road 99

Backpacking, hiking, picnicking, ranger talks, scenic drive, walks

Entering the blast zone is dramatic. Miles of blown-down forest with the trees laid out in neat rows command attention. While the entire area is fascinating, the aftermath of the raw power of nature is awesome and even a little fearsome. Some family members may need to be reassured that the volcano is not planning to erupt on the day they are visiting, followed by a discussion of

Visitors at Windy Ridge heading up the steep trail to a hilltop viewpoint

the early warning signs of an awakening volcano. Earthquakes are the most common announcement made by a volcano before it erupts, and scientists monitor the mountain continually. At the first sign of renewed activity, access to the mountain will be closed.

If you have never visited the north side of Mount St. Helens, stop at the Woods Creek Information Center located 5.6 miles east of Randle on Road 25, and ask if they are offering talks at Windy Ridge on that particular day. If they are, drive south from Randle 19 miles on Road 25 then go right on Road 99 and continue on another 17 miles to road's end at Windy Ridge. The talks are wonderfully informative, explaining what happened when the volcano erupted and how it changed the landscape. By the end of the talk you will understand why the trees in the devastation zone were laid out in parallel rows, how Spirit Lake was affected, and how some trees, vegetation, and small animals survived the blast and stone-filled winds that traveled at over 650 miles an hour, with temperatures of over 600 degrees. It is a remarkable story of destruction and regrowth that will put everything you see inside the blast zone in perspective.

After attending a talk at Windy Ridge, climb the steep trail to the top of the hill next to the restroom for a view into the crater and over Spirit Lake. If time is limited, spend the remainder of it exploring the Independence Pass Trail for views of the destruction, and take the short walk to Meta Lake to observe a miracle of survival. If you have time for a moderate-length hike, follow the

Harmony Falls Trail to the shores of Spirit Lake. The best hiking in the area is found on the Boundary Trail, where views of everything from miles of devastation, to Spirit Lake and the new crater on Mount St. Helens, as well as flower-covered meadows and panoramic looks across the Cascade Range are found. On your way out of the monument, you may want to plan a stop at Iron Creek to revitalize yourselves with the sights and sounds of a mature forest.

The closest accommodations to Road 99 are found in the small towns of Randle, Morton, and Packwood. For information, contact the Mount Rainier/ Saint Helens Chamber of Commerce at (360) 569-2339. Camping is somewhat limited. Iron Creek Campground, located 9.5 miles south of Randle on Road 25, provides ninety-eight sites, pit toilets, and running water. Campfire programs are given on weekends. This campground fills up early in the summer. Tower Rock Campground, off Road 76, is an alternative.

Private campgrounds may be found in Randle, just 0.1 mile up Road 25 after its turnoff from Highway 12, and on Road 76 near Tower Rock. Pick up a Gifford Pinchot National Forest map for the location of other forest campgrounds in the area.

Harmony Falls Trail

ROUND TRIP: 2 miles
TRAIL DIFFICULTY: moderate
ELEVATION GAIN: 660 feet
ACTIVITY: hiking
BEST: July to mid-October
MAP: Green Trails: Spirit Lake
Map on page 166

Spirit Lake: The name brings warm, happy memories to those who visited before the 1980 eruption. The lake was picture perfect, surrounded by an intensely green forest, with the graceful image of Mount St. Helens reflecting in its still waters. Of course, those who knew the lake will remember that it was not always a calm or quiet place; with a Boy Scout Camp, a Girl Scout Camp, and a YMCA Camp on its shores, as well as a couple of lodges and a nearby forest service campground, the air often rang with shouts and laughter.

Currently, the only access to the lake is a trail that descends from Road 99 to the location of the old Harmony Lodge.

Drive south from Randle on combined Roads 23 and 25 for 0.9 mile to a Y intersection. Stay right on Road 25 for 18 more miles before heading right on Road 99 for 13.1 miles to the Harmony Viewpoint and trailhead (4,100 feet).

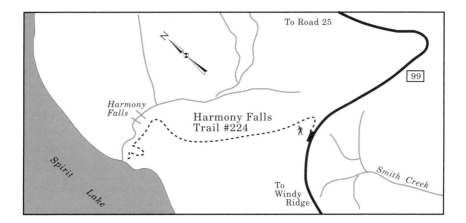

The trail starts on the right-hand side of the viewpoint and immediately heads downhill. In fact, it is all downhill from the parking area to the lakeshore, so save some energy food for the grind back up. Along the way, there are various indications of the vast destruction that occurred here in 1980. Near the lake, the trail crosses a flood plain created by the debris from the exploding mountain. To the right, note the hillside that was swept bare by the giant tidal wave that surged across the lake during the blast.

While looking at signs of destruction, do not forget to look for regrowth. Trees and plants are sprouting up everywhere. Watch the trail for tracks of deer and elk, and look for birds and squirrels.

The trail ends at 1 mile on the shore of Spirit Lake (3,440 feet). While the younger members of the party try to determine how to get past the logs that form a barrier between the beach and the water, contemplative party members can look south into the mountain that dumped more then two cubic miles of earth and rock into the lake.

Independence Pass Trail

ROUND TRIP: 3 miles to viewpoint
TRAIL DIFFICULTY: moderate
ELEVATION GAIN: 600 feet
ACTIVITY: hiking
BEST: July to mid-October
MAP: Green Trails: Spirit Lake
Map on page 167

This trail tours a scenic ridge that is ideally situated for appreciating the grandeur of Mount St. Helens and the new, improved version of Spirit Lake. It is not necessary to walk far to enjoy the views; however, with a little perseverance, the trail will take you across open hillsides covered with wildflowers to an outstanding viewpoint.

Drive south from Randle 19 miles on Road 25. Go right on Road 99 and follow it for 11.9 more twisty and very scenic miles to the small Independence Pass trailhead (4,000 feet).

The initial climb is steep, reaching in 0.2 mile a viewpoint and an interpretive sign. The sign shows the location of past and present landmarks and will strike poignant memories in all who knew the area before the 1980 eruption.

The trail then heads north, descending briefly in preparation for the second steep climb. Once the switchback is completed the climb moderates and the trail heads through an area of stone-wind-flattened forest. A quick bit of speculation will allow everyone to correctly guess the direction of the wind.

Due in part to the fragile nature of the barren hillsides, some of the trail was washed out in the floods of 1996. The current trail includes several narrow sections and everyone should use caution when traversing the steeper slopes. At 1 mile the Independence Ridge Trail No. 227A branches off to the

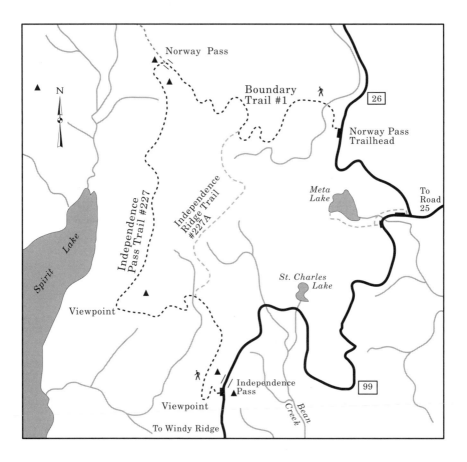

Independence Pass Trail crossing a hillside where the timber was blown down by the stone-wind during the 1980 eruption

right and heads around the east side of the ridge 1.3 miles to intersect the Boundary Trail. Stay left and continue the gradual ascent.

After passing excellent views of the mountain and lake for 1.5 miles, the trail arrives at the official Spirit Lake Viewpoint (4,500 feet) where both mountain and lake may be contemplated at the same time. It takes a giant stretch of the imagination to visualize the blast that tore the mountain apart and sent a tidal wave across the lake, scouring hillsides of vegetation and even dirt. It is said that this massive blast, which left the lake almost entirely covered with logs, was not even heard by people who were close to the mountain.

The viewpoint is steep and exposed, so if you are looking for a good spot to relax and enjoy lunch, head back to the Independence Ridge Trail junction. If relaxing is not on your agenda and you would like to see more, continue on up the trail for another 1.7 miles to Norway Pass. From there you can loop back to the start by descending 1.2 miles then going right on Independence Ridge Trail.

Boundary Trail

NORWAY PASS
    ROUND TRIP: 4.5 miles
    TRAIL DIFFICULTY: moderate
    ELEVATION GAIN: 900 feet
    ACTIVITY: hiking
    BEST: July to September
    MAP: Green Trails: Spirit Lake
    Map on page 167

MOUNT MARGARET
    ROUND TRIP: 11.5 miles
    TRAIL DIFFICULTY: challenging
    ELEVATION GAIN: 2,300 feet
    ACTIVITIES: hiking, backpacking
    BEST: August to September
    MAP: Green Trails: Spirit Lake

From nature's finest flower gardens to nature's grandstand display of raw power, the Boundary Trail offers one of the best opportunities to study the most fascinating features of Mount St. Helens National Volcanic Monument. The view over the miles of timber laid out in parallel lines is humbling. The view over Spirit Lake to the steaming dome at the center of the crater is thrilling, and from Mount Margaret, the panorama of the nearby volcanic summits of Rainier, Adams, and Hood is as beautiful to behold as it is sobering to contemplate.

The Boundary Trail is completely dry. Because there is no drinking water available along the trail, all water must be carried, although in early summer there may be snow to melt. As no large trees survived the eruption, all shade must be carried too, in the form of a hat. Backpackers should haul about one gallon of water per person; however, if you plan no-cook cheese-and-cracker-type dinners and breakfasts, the amount of water can be reduced to near-manageable levels. Camping is allowed on the north side of the Boundary Trail starting about 1 mile beyond Norway Pass.

Drive south from Randle toward Mount St. Helens on Forest Road 25. After 19 miles turn right on Road 99 and head west 8.9 miles. Go left on Road 26 for a final mile to the large Boundary Trail parking area (3,700 feet), which has a water pump and outhouses.

The poorly marked trail begins at the northern end of the parking area. It crosses a basin then begins a steady climb on a traversing and switchbacking path that tunnels through a jumble of fallen trees. To the south, Meta Lake comes into view. Note the young trees growing on the north side of the lake, which survived because they were still covered with snow during the eruption. As you continue, you will pass other small pockets of vegetation.

View from Boundary Trail of miles of timber blown down by the stone-wind during the 1980 eruption

At 1.2 miles (4,300 feet), the Independence Ridge Trail No. 227A intersection marks the end of the serious climbing. Shortly after, the trail rounds the shoulder of the hill and heads west. Stop here and take a long look down the valley to get a feeling of the massive scope of the blow-down area. As you continue, watch for wildflowers, like glacier and avalanche lilies, showing an unusual number of multiple florets, attesting to the rich growing environment.

At 2.2 miles the trail reaches Norway Pass (4,600 feet) and an intersection with the Independence Pass Trail No. 227. (A loop can be made using the Independence Pass and Independence Ridge Trails which will return you to your car in 7.5 miles.) To best enjoy the view, either descend a few feet beyond the pass or climb a short distance on the Independence Pass Trail. At one time logs nearly covered the entire surface of Spirit Lake; now large expanses of water can be seen.

Beyond Norway Pass, the Boundary Trail switchbacks up to reach a meadow-covered ridge crest at 3.3 miles. The trail then heads west along the ridge with several noticeable ups and downs. At 5.5 miles a short spur trail branches off the Boundary Trail and climbs to within a few feet of the 5,858-foot summit of Mount Margaret.

MORE ACTIVITIES
Map on page 172

Picnic Areas: Good sites for picnics are scarce in the monument. The north side of Mount St. Helens is a designated research area and visitors are not allowed to step off the trails or roads for a leisurely meal. The best areas for large groups, with picnic shelters and tables, are located on Road 25 just 5 miles south of Randle opposite the Woods Creek Information Center, and 10 miles south of Randle at the Iron Creek Picnic Area. A few picnic tables are found along Road 99 at Bear Meadow Viewpoint and at Smith Creek Viewpoint.

Woods Creek Watchable Wildlife Interpretive Trail: Although a typically boisterous family may not see wildlife on this extremely walkable loop, they will see abundant signs of the wildlife that lives in this marshy plain. And, although swamps and forest may not be on your agenda for a Mount St. Helens visit, this is an ideal walk when the weather conditions require a quick reformation of plans.

The trail is located on Road 25, just 5.7 miles south of Randle opposite the Woods Creek Information Center. The loops are rated as easiest for walking. Young children can look for benches to sit on and interpretive signs with animal track imprints on them. Older kids and parents can look for signs of beaver, such as chewed sticks and trees, prints, and lodges, along the turgid waters of Woods Creek. Also watch for prints of deer and elk.

Iron Creek Campground Loop: A walk around this 1.5-mile loop will revitalize your senses after a day spent in the shadeless devastation around Mount St. Helens. This easy-to-walk loop is great for the entire family, with 600-year-old trees, a fern-cloaked forest floor, access to the Cispus River, and an interpretive loop.

Interpretive sign along the Woods Creek Watchable Wildlife Trail

The loop can be accessed from each of the four lobes of the Iron Creek Campground located on Road 25, just 10 miles south of Randle. A short interpretive loop starts at the picnic area.

Strawberry Mountain Viewpoint: Strawberry Mountain Viewpoint is set on a ridge at the edge of the devastation zone. On the west side of the ridge, the trees were blown over by the stone wind. Just a few feet east, protected by Strawberry Mountain, the forest survived. Drive south from Randle 17.3 miles on Road 25 then go right for a 7-mile climb, mostly on gravel road, to the viewpoint.

Iron Creek Falls: This is an often-overlooked beauty spot. The waterfall is located 500 feet off Road 25 in a pleasant little basin. Once the spring flooding is over, there is ample room to walk on the gravel bar at the edge of the creek. The trail to the falls has only one small sign to mark its location and is easy to miss as you are rushing toward Mount St. Helens. Look for a turnout on the left side of the road at milepost 18.5.

Bear Meadow Viewpoint: An ideal stopping point for a first look into the monument. The viewpoint has an outhouse and picnic tables and is reached by driving 19 miles south from Randle on Road 25 then 4.7 miles west on Road 99.

Monument Boundary Viewpoint: Located on the south side of Road 99 at milepost 6.7, this viewpoint lies at the edge of the devastation. Of equal interest is the view over the Clearwater Creek valley. After the eruption, the valley was salvage logged and replanted. Before it was completely stabilized, the severe storms of 1996 caused giant slides.

Miner's Car: Many people stop here

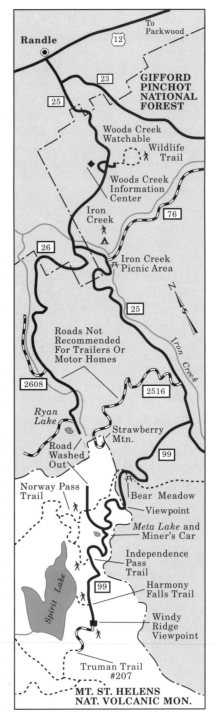

Mature forest on the Iron Creek Campground Loop

to look at the flattened and now very rusty miner's car. The car belonged to a family that talked their way into the closed zone before the blast and died in the eruption. Why was the car left there and why do people stop to see it? If you have young children, you may want to think about how to answer all the inevitable questions before you stop. The Miner's Car is located 9 miles from Road 25 on the north side of Road 99 right after its intersection with Road 26.

Meta Lake: At the time of the 1980 eruption, the lake and surrounding hillsides were covered with snow that protected some of the low-lying vegetation and aquatic life. Today, the 500-foot walk to the lake, on a barrier-free trail, passes under the shade of a grove of Pacific firs. The lake itself is a giant nursery to a teeming population of frogs and strikingly blue dragonflies.

Donny Brook View: Located on Road 99, 14.3 miles west of the Road 25 turnoff, this is one of the best views of Spirit Lake. An information board discusses the logs that nearly covered the lake after the eruption and their subsequent disappearance.

Smith Creek Viewpoint: A breathtaking view, a restroom, and several picnic tables make this a very popular stop; located on Road 99, 14.6 miles from the Road 25 turnoff.

Windy Ridge Viewpoint: At 16 miles from the Road 25 turnoff, this is the end of Road 99 and as close as you can drive to the mountain. The name fits the location, so have jackets handy. Ranger talks last thirty minutes and are extremely informative. The hike up a pumice-covered hill from the south side of the parking lot on an extremely steep trail leads to a better view of the mountain.

Truman Trail No. 207: Starting from the Windy Ridge parking area at the end of Road 99, the Truman Trail follows an old, washed-out road for 2 easy-walking miles to the base of the mountain and the very edge of the debris plain. Although this walk offers very little for younger children, older family members may enjoy continuing on from the end of the road for another 2.3 miles to Loowit Falls or 3 miles to the Plains of Abraham.

South Side

Backpacking, camping, climbing, fishing, hiking, picnicking, sightseeing

The south side of Mount St. Helens was the least affected by the 1980 eruption. Many of the well-known features, such as the Ape Cave and the Trail of Two Forests, existed long before this recent event. However, this area was not entirely bypassed by the eruption. The giant lahar flow at the end of Road 83 was the derivative of the mountain's once-beautiful overcoat of snow and glacier ice, mixed with material that exploded from the mountain. The resulting flood poured down the mountain, ripping out entire forests and burying them in an oozy mass with the consistency of cement.

Despite the flooding, the overall damage on the south side was minor compared to other parts of the mountain, and visitors have a chance to see the remnants of older eruptions as well as enjoy the sights and sounds of a mature forest environment.

Because the southern flanks of the mountain are not part of the recovery study area, visitors are freer to enjoy, recreate, roam, and camp where they please. Anyone wishing to hike to the new top of the mountain may do so on this side of the mountain only.

Activities on the south side of the mountain are ideal for the young and the young at heart. When planning your trip, budget plenty of time for a walk through the Ape Cave. The Trail of Two Forests, which wanders through the remnants of an ancient forest and features a 50-foot crawl through the casts of a couple of old trees, is another child pleaser. Finally, as a grand finale, walk the spectacular Lava Canyon Trail for views of impressive waterfalls.

If you have more than one day, try a hike to Butte Camp or toward the Plains of Abraham. If looking for an easy walk, take the trail to June Lake, explore the waterfalls along the Lewis River, or ramble through an old-growth forest at Cedar Flats.

Nearby accommodations are limited. Motels are found 10 miles southwest of the monument at Cougar; however, your best bet for rooms is on the

Trail crossing an ancient lava flow on route to Butte Camp

Interstate 5 corridor at Woodland, Vancouver, or Kelso. Restaurants may be found in Cougar.

The nearest campgrounds with facilities are located on Swift and Yale Reservoirs and are run by Pacific Power and Light. These campgrounds are oriented toward boaters and fishermen. The ninety-three-site Swift Campground offers running water, restrooms, and a boat launch. Beaver Bay has sixty-three sites, running water, restrooms with showers, and a boat ramp. Cougar Camp provides forty-five sites, running water, restrooms with showers, and a boat ramp. Cresap Bay Campground has sixty-two sites, restrooms with showers, running water, and a boat ramp. Evening programs are offered on weekends at Cougar Campground, located on Highway 503 just 0.5 mile east of Cougar, and at Cresap Bay on the road to Amboy. Cougar has a private RV park.

A little farther from the mountain is Lower Fall Recreation Area Campground, which has forty-seven sites, outhouses, and a water pump. This scenic forest service facility is located next to the Lewis River, with access to trails and the falls.

Less structured camping can be found at the Climbers' Bivouac and Kalama Horse Camp, which have outhouses but no running water. Dispersed camping is also allowed in the forest on spur roads and turnouts, as long as you do not block traffic.

Trail of Two Forests

ROUND TRIP: 0.2 miles
TRAIL DIFFICULTY: easy
ELEVATION GAIN: 10 feet
ACTIVITIES: walking, exploring underground
BEST: June to October
MAP: Green Trails: Mount St. Helens
Map on page 177

Two forests: an ancient one that is long gone, and one that is growing today. Both forests are amazing, but it is the forest of the past that will capture your attention and fire the imaginations of the children. The ancient forest was in the path of a lava flow that spilled from Mount St. Helens 1,900 years ago. The weight of the advancing flow knocked over many of the trees in its path, then buried them in the lava. A few trees withstood the pressure and remained standing as the fiery molten liquid rolled around them. The heat of the lava caused the trees to burn and, over the years, even the ashes disappeared. All that remains of the once mighty forest are molds and impressions of trees in the hardened lava. Looking into the deep holes left by the trees you can see the finely detailed texture of the bark.

The most popular feature of this trail is an underground tunnel formed by the lava casts of two large trees that were pushed over by the lava. These casts are known as The Crawl. Carry a flashlight for this adventure. Long pants are recommended for adult-sized explorers: the lava mold of the tree bark is rough on hands and knees. Younger kids will scamper right through: adults will follow slowly on all fours. Most kids will go through a couple of times; for adults, once will probably do it.

Despite the distractions, take time to admire the tenacity of the current forest. How the roots find a hold on the hard lava and eke out an existence from the small pockets of soil is one of nature's biggest miracles.

This is a barrier-free trail, designed for wheelchairs and strollers. A restroom and picnic tables are available at the parking area, but there is no running water.

Drive Highway 503 east from Woodland 29.5 miles to Cougar, then continue along Swift Reservoir for another 6.8 miles. At the next intersection, go left and head up Road 83. After 1.8 mile go left on Road 8303 for 300 feet then turn left again to the Trail of Two Forests parking area.

The trail starts at the upper east side of the parking lot and heads into a sparse forest, descending gradually. After a couple hundred feet the trail divides; go right, and save the best for last. The trail loops over the old lava flow then around to the tree casts. Information boards point out the features. Once you have had a chance to identify the casts and impressions of the bark, you are ready for The Crawl. This is a one-way affair. Imagine a big tree growing straight and tall and you will understand that there is no place to pass inside.

Beyond The Crawl the trail heads back to the start.

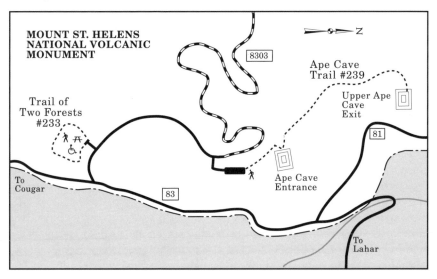

Ape Cave

LOWER CAVE
> ROUND TRIP: 1.5 miles
> TRAIL DIFFICULTY: easy
> ELEVATION GAIN: 200 feet
> ACTIVITIES: walking, exploring
> BEST: mid-May to October
> MAP: Green Trails: Mount St. Helens
> Map on page 177

UPPER CAVE
> ROUND TRIP: 2.8 miles
> TRAIL DIFFICULTY: challenging
> ELEVATION GAIN: 400 feet
> ACTIVITIES: walking, exploring
> BEST: mid-May to October
> MAP: Green Trails: Mount St. Helens

Imagine the great flow of lava that poured off Mount St. Helens like a river some 1,900 years ago. This great river was composed of superheated molten rock. The top of the lava-river cooled first, creating a shell over the molten rock still flowing beneath it. Slowly, the outer edges of the flow slowed and then cooled, creating a shell over the channel. Inside the shell the lava continued moving. The flow diminished and eventually stopped. The lava ran out, leaving behind the empty shell. The result was a cave, with an open channel where once the lava flowed inside.

The Ape Cave is the largest lava tube in the continental United States. No apes ever lived here; the cave was named for the group that first explored it. It is approximately 2 miles long, with high caverns and narrow passages. The cave is divided into two sections. Anyone who enjoys this kind of exploration may want to do both. The Lower Cave is 0.7 mile long. Although there is some rubble on the floor, most of the lower section is easy to walk and recommended for families with young children. Rubble-coated floors and a five-foot ascent of a vertical wall makes negotiating the upper section of the cave very difficult and best left to the sure-footed who enjoy the dark, age ten or older.

When exploring either the Upper or Lower Cave, dress warmly. Temperatures in the caves remain in the 40s throughout the year. During the summer, when the temperature gradient is the greatest, a chilly wind howls through the remote sections of the cave, making it feel even cooler. Long pants, a windproof jacket, and mittens are the suggested attire.

Once in the cave you will need a light. Ideally, everyone should have their own. Young children, who generally do not care for the dark anyway, should definitely have a flashlight to hold. A Coleman lantern is very useful and can be rented near the entrance. Lanterns must be returned by 5:00 P.M.

Lower Ape Cave

If you would like to know more about the cave, or just have company while you explore, join a ranger-led walk. There are usually four walks per day on weekdays and five on weekends from late June through September. The walks last about 30 minutes.

Drive to Road 8303, following the directions given for the Trail of Two Forests. Continue up the road for 1.1 miles then go right (2,115 feet). The lot is often full and you may need to go back down the road to find a space. There are restrooms but no running water at the trailhead.

The trail to the caves starts next to the ranger kiosk. Books, postcards, maps, and lantern rentals, as well as answers to any questions you may have concerning the monument or surrounding forest may be found here.

The trail heads through the forest for a couple hundred feet to the cave entrance. Descend the concrete steps then stop to put on extra clothes and get lights out before continuing down the steep metal steps to the cave floor.

A large, glow-in-the-dark sign directs visitors toward the Upper and Lower Caves. If heading down into the Lower Cave, look for the giant lava balls suspended above your head in a narrow portion of the cave about 0.5 mile from the entrance. Large accumulations of sand at 0.7 mile let you know when you have reached the end of the cave.

The Upper Cave trail heads directly into the largest chamber of the cave. At one point, the roof of the cave has collapsed and you will see the light of day. Shortly beyond is a difficult climb over a five-foot-high wall. At the upper end a 1.3-mile trail through clearcuts returns you to the start.

June Lake

ROUND TRIP: 2.8 miles
TRAIL DIFFICULTY: moderate
ELEVATION GAIN: 500 feet
ACTIVITIES: hiking, wading, backpacking
BEST: July to October
MAP: Green Trails: Mount St. Helens
Map on page 180

June Lake is an ideal playground for children of all ages. The east shore of the lake has a wide beach composed of the finest quality sand, perfect for would-be engineers to build roads or castles, or equally perfect for some high-quality sun ray collecting. The lake itself is shallow with a sandy bottom for wading, splashing, or impromptu boat racing.

Note: This is a great hike for family fun, but not a trail for mountain viewing.

Drive west from the town of Cougar 6.8 miles to the intersection of Forest Roads 83 and 90. Go left and head uphill on Road 83 for 7 miles. The well-signed turnoff to June Lake is found on the left shortly after crossing an unnamed creek. Head uphill for a final 0.2 mile to the trailhead (2,740 feet).

From the parking lot, follow June Lake Trail No. 216B into the forest. The trees along the trail are shy of full growth and provide only partial shade on sunny days. There is little to distract or entertain the younger hikers. The few side trails lead to less than exciting views of the roaring creek below.

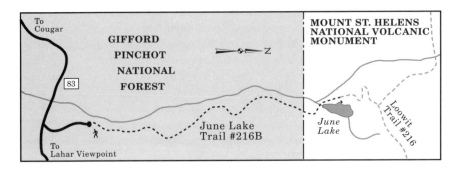

Waterfall on the hillside above June Lake

At 1.4 miles the trail crosses the lake outlet on a wooden bridge and passes the best view. If you look across the jumbled lava flow ahead, the truncated summit of Mount St. Helens can be seen. But you are here to recreate, not dwell on the shortcomings of Mount St. Helens, so continue on another 100 feet to the shore of June Lake.

The lake is tucked into a cove, sheltered on three sides by rock walls and trees. A waterfall tumbles off the cliff on the west side. Break out the sand toys and don your water shoes, it's time for play.

For further hiking, the trail continues on to a campsite and the Loowit Trail in 0.2 mile.

Lava Canyon Trail

ROUND TRIP: up to 5 miles
TRAIL DIFFICULTY: easy to challenging
ELEVATION GAIN: 300 feet to 1,360 feet
ACTIVITIES: hiking, bridges, ladders, views
BEST: July to mid-October
MAP: Green Trails: Mount St. Helens
Map on page 182

It is hard to believe that the same forces which created the broad and nearly featureless Lahar Plain are also responsible for this fantastic canyon. While the plain is a cerebral study in rock art, the canyon offers the raw excitement of a river crashing down a carnival-style ride, racing through narrow chutes, rolling over cascades, and diving over cliffs.

The Lava Canyon Trail has a touch of amusement park excitement to it, with viewing platforms, bridges, and even a ladder over a cliff. Unfortunately, not all of this trail is suitable for children, or some adults, either.

If you are unsure of your family's abilities, join a ranger walk into the canyon. Rangers lead groups from late June through September, twice a day during the week and three times a day on weekends. Check the monument handout, inquire at the Ape Cave kiosk, or look at the trailhead signboard for a current schedule.

Drive east from Woodland 29.5 miles on Highway 503 and Lewis River Road to Cougar, then continue on another 6.8 miles to the intersection of Forest Roads 83 and 90. Go left on Road 83 for 11.5 miles to its end at Lava Canyon trailhead (2,930 feet). Picnic tables and a restroom are found here, but no running water.

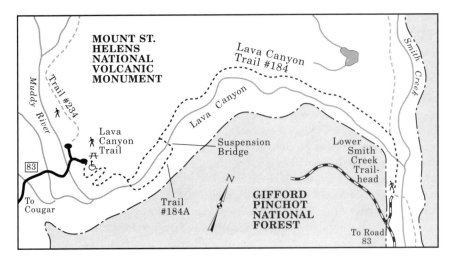

Bridge over the Muddy River in Lava Canyon

A barrier-free trail heads out from the parking area, descending gradually on pavement and boardwalk. This initial section ends at a viewing platform overlooking the canyon. From the vantage point, marks of the lahar flow can be seen.

The trail continues down, switchbacking to the edge of the Muddy River (yes, that is its real name) to view the canyon, the waterfall, and pillars of columnar basalt. The next 0.8 mile of trail is a loop. Cross the river on a wide bridge and descend. Several large outcrops of basalt are passed, and side trails lead to dramatic canyon views. At the base of this loop, the trail recrosses the Muddy River on a rollicking suspension bridge. At this point, most hikers should turn around and go back up the way they came, ignoring the return leg of the loop which is steep and exposed.

Beyond the suspension bridge the trail divides. The right fork descends rapidly into the bowels of the volcanic landscape. The trail is steep and narrow, with lots of exposure on the near-vertical hillsides. Good shoes are a must. For those who continue, the long ladder down a cliff face is a real thriller. Do not miss the side trail to an unparalleled view of the waterfall. Remember, the climb back up takes a lot longer than the descent.

Lewis River Trail

ROUND TRIP: up to 5 miles
TRAIL DIFFICULTY: moderate
ELEVATION GAIN: 200 feet
ACTIVITIES: hiking, waterfall viewing, fishing
BEST: June to October
MAP: Green Trails: Lone Butte
Map on page 184

The Lewis River Trail is not in Mount St. Helens National Volcanic Monument; in fact, it is not even really very close. However, the trail does go right by the most scenic campground on the south side of Mount St. Helens.

The section of this 10-mile-long trail described here starts at the Lower Falls Campground and passes four major falls on the Lewis River and one long, narrow ribbon of a falls on Copper Creek.

Drive to the intersection of Forest Road 90 (from Cougar) and Road 25 (from Randle), then head east on Road 90 for 15.5 miles to the Lower Falls Campground. Go right and descend into the campground and either find a site or park in the day-use/picnic area.

If starting from the day-use area, you will descend directly to a viewpoint of the Lower Falls. This spectacular falls cascades off a rocky tabletop created by an old lava flow. Several trails from the campground descend to the river's edge, and one goes right to the top of the falls. Use caution and keep out of the fast-moving water—it is dangerous!

Head upriver, following the trail along the edge of the campground then onto a bluff. At about the 0.5-mile point, pass a bridge standing in the middle of the Lewis River. Never completed, never connected to shore, this massive

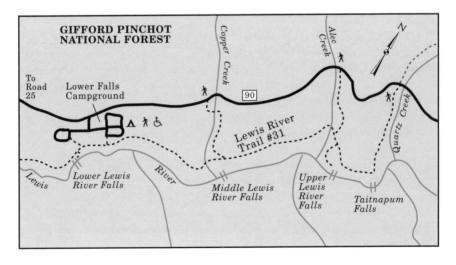

Lower Lewis River Falls

structure remains like a giant window box in the center of the rushing waters. At 1 mile, stay right at an intersection then descend to the Middle Falls at 1.2 miles. The small, rocky beach here offers the safest river access and makes an excellent picnic site.

Middle Falls was also created by an old lava flow. By late summer the water is low enough to disperse into several channels rather than the mighty blast of late spring. Although the flat rocks near the base of the falls appear to offer access to the water, they are amazingly slippery and best avoided.

The trail continues upriver through deepening forest. At 1.5 miles pass the Copper Creek Trail. An easy 0.2-mile side trip takes you to a view of ribbon-like Copper Falls. Upper Falls is reached at 2.5 miles where a short side trail leads to a viewpoint a few feet from the thundering wall of water, roaring through any conversation you were having and seeming to shake the ground you are standing on. Although, in reality, no more spectacular than the Lower or Middle Falls, Upper Falls may well be the most memorable.

If young, and older, legs are willing, continue on upvalley for another 0.2 mile to Taitnapum Falls overlook. Like the three falls below, Taitnapum rolls off a tabletop of lava, making a spectacular descent to the next level.

If you enjoyed these waterfalls and would like to see more, stop at Big Creek Falls and Curly Creek Falls on your way back to the monument.

MORE ACTIVITIES
Map on page 187

Lahar Viewpoint: For a detailed explanation of a lahar and its effects, or if you would just like a good view, put this stop on your agenda. Forest interpreters are on hand to give talks and answer questions three times a day on weekends and twice a day during the week from late June through September. The talks last 15 minutes. The viewpoint is located on Road 83, 10.5 miles northeast of the junction of Road 90 and Road 83.

Moss Springs Viewpoint: With so much to do and see around Mount St. Helens, there is little reason to stop and look at this overgrown stream. The viewpoint is located 10.8 miles northeast of the Road 90 and Road 83 intersection.

Stratigraphy Viewpoint: Located along the edge of the Muddy River in the center of the Lahar Plain, this stop offers a great view of Mount St. Helens. The stratigraphy aspect is interesting but vague, and there is no attempt to correlate the information with the exposed layers of rock viewed. The viewpoint is located on Road 83, 11 miles northeast of its intersection with Road 90.

Blue Lake: This lake was formed by a flow of mud that blocked Coldspring Creek. The resulting lake has no beach on the west side; however, by mid- to late summer the beach on the east side can be reached by descending a steep hillside then crossing the creek on a couple of shaky logs. Follow Road 81 from its origin just west of Cougar. Head north 12 miles, then leave Road 81 and continue north on Road 8123 for a final 3 miles to the Blue Lake trailhead. This 0.4-mile round trip is rated easiest.

Lahar plain and Mount St. Helens from Lahar Viewpoint

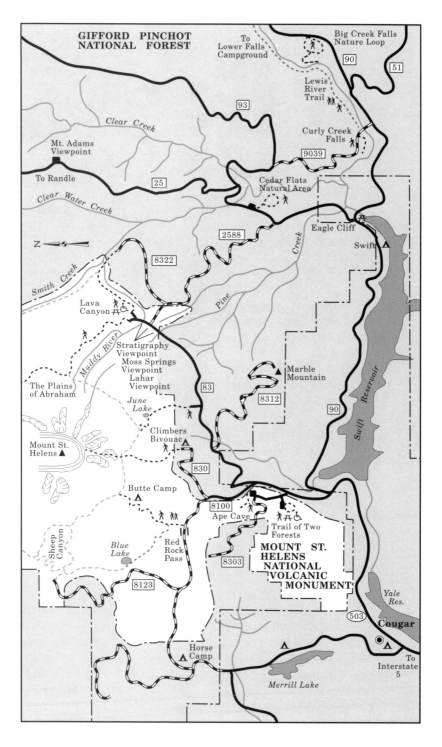

Curly Creek Falls

Cedar Flats Natural Area: This is an ideal family walk. The nearly level trail makes a 1-mile loop through a grove of large old cedars. Children can yell, shout, and play hide and seek or Robin Hood to their hearts' content. The trailhead is marked by a small, easy-to-miss sign, so watch carefully for the parking area on the east side of Road 25 at milepost 40.3, located 21 miles south of the Road 99 intersection, and 3.8 miles north of the Road 90 intersection.

Curly Creek Falls: This unusual falls is viewed through an arch. If you are driving Forest Road 90 to or from the Lewis River area, the falls view is worth the 1.1-mile side trip. The falls turnoff is located on Road 90, 5.2 miles east of its intersection with Road 25.

Big Creek Falls Nature Loop: A 0.2-mile, paved loop trail tours this impressive falls. For more exercise, follow a spur trail 0.7 mile to an overlook of the Lewis River. The falls parking area is located on the north side of Road 90, just 4 miles east of the Carson turnoff.

Backpack Trips

Climbing Mount St. Helens

ROUND TRIP: 9 miles
TRAIL DIFFICULTY: challenging
ELEVATION GAIN: 4,640 feet
ACTIVITY: hiking
BEST: August to September (after snowmelt)
MAP: Green Trails: Mount St. Helens
Map on page 190

What could be more exciting than sharing the experience of standing on the crater rim of a smoldering volcano with your family? For the kids, it is the kind of experience they will talk about and remember for years to come.

Early in the summer, there are several long and steep snowfields to be climbed on the way to the summit of Mount St. Helens, requiring an ice ax and crampons. Anyone who is not experienced in the use of climbing tools will need to be roped in between two people who are. Once the snowfields have melted, the climb turns into a long walk up steep slopes of loose pumice. By late summer, the ascent of Mount St. Helens is more of a hike than a true climb. However, the ascent can be exhausting and anyone who makes the attempt should be strong and equipped with sturdy boots. Climbers must be prepared for very adverse conditions such as low or no visibility, rain or snow, and violent dirt and grit storms.

Anyone going above the 4,800-foot-level on Mount St. Helens needs a permit. One hundred permits are issued per day at the cost of $15 per person. Advance reservations are strongly advised between May 15 and October 31. A minimum of forty unreserved permits are given out by lottery at 6:00 P.M. for the following day at the Climbers' Register.

If the mountain should show any signs of volcanic activity, it will be closed and climbing permits cancelled. Climbers are required to stop at the Climbers' Register and pick up their permit on the way to the mountain as well as check out posted warnings and closures.

A Mount St. Helens Climbing Information brochure is published by the Gifford Pinchot National Forest. If interested in climbing, obtain this brochure and study it thoroughly.

There are three main routes up the mountain. Described here is the approach from Climbers' Bivouac, the most popular route because it starts at 3,740 feet. The Butte Camp route starts nearly 1,000 feet lower and is a rigorous, two-day

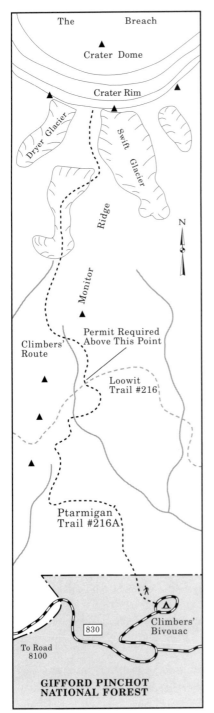

trip. The third route, via the Worm Flows, is used primarily in the winter by skiers.

Drive Interstate 5 to the Woodland Exit No. 21 and follow Highway 503 east 24 miles to the Climbers' Register at Jacks Country Store next to the Amboy turnoff. With permit and registration taken care of, continue east, passing through Cougar to reach the intersection of Roads 83 and 90 in 12 miles. Go left on Road 83 for 3.8 miles then go left again on Road 8100. Before long, the pavement ends. In 1.8 miles reach Spur Road 830 and go right. The road ends in 3 miles at the Climbers' Bivouac, a waterless car-camping area at 3,740 feet.

The trip up the mountain starts off on Ptarmigan Trail No. 216A. The trail is 2.1 miles long and spends most of its time in forest or in dense huckleberry thickets. After gaining 960 feet, the Ptarmigan Trail meets the Loowit Trail No. 216 and ends. Go straight, leaving the official trail for a well-trodden climbers' route. Head up to timberline, passing an outhouse on the way. At 4,800 feet leave the trees behind. From this point on, wooden posts mark the safest and easiest route along the steep and exposed slopes of Monitor Ridge. The route picks its way through the broken lava flows, often on unstable ground. When Monitor Ridge begins to blend into the surrounding slopes, the line of wooden posts ends. The route then heads up a slope composed of pumice and volcanic ash. Feet sink in and slip back with every step; the final 1,000 feet are the slowest of the climb.

At 4.5 miles reach the rim of the crater (8,130 feet). Use extreme caution when approaching the unstable edge. Look for a solid rock outcrop for the best viewing platform to peer into the crater and examine the slowly growing dome. On clear days, Mount Rainier is visible

Father and son team at edge of the crater on the summit of Mount St. Helens

to the north. To the east, Mount Adams exposes a cold shoulder to its one-time bride, and south, Mount Hood and Jefferson shine above the haze. The rim is not the actual summit. Dogmatic peak baggers will have to walk west around the crater rim almost 0.5 mile to reach the 8,365-foot true summit.

Note: To obtain information and an application for a climbing permit, contact: Mount St. Helens National Volcanic Monument, 42218 NE Yale Bridge Road, Amboy, Washington 98601; phone (360) 750-3961.

Butte Camp

ROUND TRIP: 5 miles
TRAIL DIFFICULTY: moderate
ELEVATION GAIN: 1,184 feet
ACTIVITIES: hiking, backpacking
BEST: mid-July to August
MAP: Green Trails: Mount St. Helens
Map on page 192

Butte Camp is one of the few destinations in the Mount St. Helens National Volcanic Monument where backpackers have a moderately reliable source of water. The camp is also an excellent base for timberline explorations along the

Loowit Trail, the around-the-mountain loop. Families with teenagers or soon-to-be teenagers can walk to the Loowit Trail and back in a comfortable day (providing the teenagers are willing). Families with younger children will have more fun if they make this a two-or-more-day adventure.

Drive to the intersection of Forest Roads 83 and 90, located 6.8 miles east of Cougar. Head left, up Road 83 for 3 miles, then take a right on Road 8100. The pavement soon ends; however, the road remains in good condition for the next 3 miles to the trailhead at Red Rock Pass (3,116 feet).

On the north side of the pass, follow the Toutle River Trail up a steep switchback. (Note: This trail is shared with mountain bikes and horses.)

In the first mile you will cross three very distinct life zones. Once above the pass, the trail heads into the first life zone, a broken and jumbled old lava bed. Most plant and animal life avoid this rocky area. Beyond the lava flow, cross a grassy plain with a scattering of hardy trees. In this life zone the soil is neither deep nor rich. Small animals can be seen scurrying through the grass and larger animals may be spotted at dawn and dusk. The third life zone is the forest, where tall trees provide shade and shelter for the larger mammals and nesting places for birds and squirrels.

At 1 mile, the trail arrives at a junction (3,450 feet). Go straight on Trail 238A (closed to horses and bicycles). The trail remains in forest for the next 1.5 miles as it climbs to 4,000-foot Butte Camp. Head left at the T junction for 100 feet to find the camping area. The campsites are scattered around the grassy meadow. The stream is nearly obscured by the deep grass and is often easier to find by listening for it than by looking.

To explore above Butte Camp, follow the trail from the camp, climbing 800 feet in the next 1.2 miles to timberline and the Loowit Trail. Views extend south over the large reservoirs that control the Lewis River to the glacier-white slopes of Mount Hood. To the north rise the barren slopes of Mount St. Helens, desolately open all the way to its crater rim.

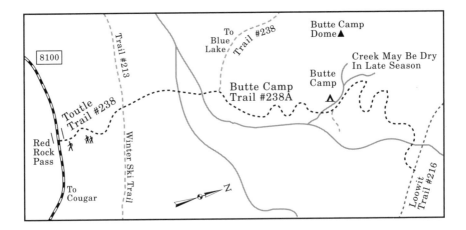

Plains of Abraham

ROUND TRIP: 12 miles
TRAIL DIFFICULTY: challenging
ELEVATION GAIN: 1,600 feet
ACTIVITIES: hiking, backpacking
BEST: July to September
MAP: Green Trails: Mount St. Helens
Map on page 193

Sheltered by a stand of old-growth trees, hikers on this trail are insulated from the devastation of the 1980 eruption by the soft colors and soft, muted sounds of giant, moss-covered trees. On the south side of the trail lies a massive lahar (a fancy term for mud flow); to the north lies Ape Canyon, a narrow gorge scoured clean of earth and vegetation by giant slides that occurred during the 1980 eruption.

The Ape Canyon Trail is one of the miracles of survival and regrowth that make Mount St. Helens fascinating. At the edge of the devastation zone, this trail tours an area that was impervious to the tumultuous eruption.

The forest is not the only remarkable feature found along this remarkable hike. The deep, dark cut that is Ape Canyon stretches to truly awesome lengths down the mountain. Equally remarkable are the alpine meadows found near the Loowit Trail junction, looking like colorful islands amidst the dark volcanic landscape. And perhaps most extraordinary of all are The Plains of Abraham, as delicate and beautiful as a carefully maintained Japanese rock garden.

Dispersed camping is allowed near the intersection of Loowit and Ape Canyon Trails. This is a very scenic area with excellent views and, after the spring snowmelt, absolutely no water. The nearest source of water (if you can

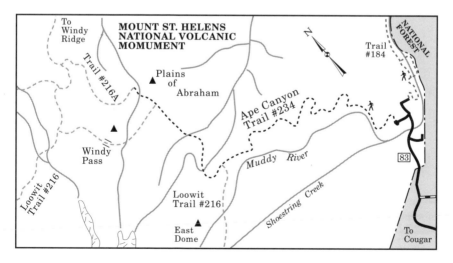

call it that) is the Muddy River, 0.6 miles to the south. If you intend to use water from the Muddy River, carry a handkerchief and pre-filter the chunks out before boiling.

From Interstate 5, drive east 35 miles on Highway 503 to the intersection of Forest Roads 90 and 83. Go left and head up Road 83 for 11.5 miles. Cross the Muddy River on a cement bridge then take an immediate left into the Ape Canyon Trail parking lot (2,860 feet).

The trail briefly parallels the Muddy River then begins its gradual climb. Views of Mount St. Helens are excellent, if she has not chosen to wrap her bald pate in a cloud. The trail heads through an old clearcut and passes tangles of huckleberries, which are very tasty in season.

After a rolling 1.2 miles, the trail leaves the clearcut and heads up a ridge in the shade of the giant trees. It is hard to imagine that only a few years ago, much of the countryside was covered with trees like these. The trail switchbacks, climbing steadily. At one point you will leave the trees and skirt along the top of an old clearcut. The ridge twists and rolls and the trail follows with parallel ups and downs.

The meadows are reached at 5.3 miles. To the right, an old volcanic dike with a V cut in the center forms a strainer-like top for the remarkable Ape Canyon. Just beyond is Mount Adams—its top may be rather flat but at least it's still there.

At 5.5 miles Ape Canyon Trail meets the Loowit Trail and ends (4,210 feet). Scenic campsites are found to the south, above and below the Loowit Trail. Remember, no fires.

To reach the Plains of Abraham, stay right and head north first over a flower-covered hillside then cross the rock-and-pumice fields. Despite signs warning of dire consequences should you stray off the trail, elk paths branch off in all directions. I wonder what currency the elk use to pay their fines.

Winter

A coat of winter white is very flattering on Mount St. Helens. Snow covers the bleak volcanic landscape, filling and softening her folds and wrinkles while brightening the uniformly dull grey color of the soil and rock.

Winter is a busy time on the southern flanks of the Mount St. Helens National Volcanic Monument, and cross-country skiers and snowmobilers flock to the massive Marble Mountain SnoPark on Road 83. Other winter activities include snow hikes to the Ape Cave and snow camping.

Cross-country skiers will find tours to fit all abilities. Snowshoers will have a harder time finding trips that are easy and that stay away from the snowmobile-dominated roads.

Campgrounds close in the winter and accommodations are located some distance from the mountain. Self-contained motor homes are allowed to overnight at the SnoPark.

Further opportunities for cross-country skiing, snowshoeing, and snowmobiling may be found at the Road 99 and Highway 504 accesses.

Cross-country skier crossing the bridge over the June Lake outlet stream

Wapiti Loops

LOOP TRIP: 1 mile and up
TRAIL DIFFICULTY: easy
ELEVATION GAIN: 50 feet
ACTIVITIES: cross-country skiing, winter play
BEST: January to February
MAP: Green Trails: Mount St. Helens No. 364
Map on page 196

The Wapiti Loops are fun. Loops within loops, on top of loops, keep everyone going to the next intersection. If everyone gets a chance to choose a trail and lead the way, you can go around in circles until you are dizzy.

It is fun that skiers search for on the Wapiti Loops, not scenery. These loops lie on a forested plain where the trees are interspersed with occasional snow-covered meadows and frozen ponds. The trees serve to buffer the noise of the

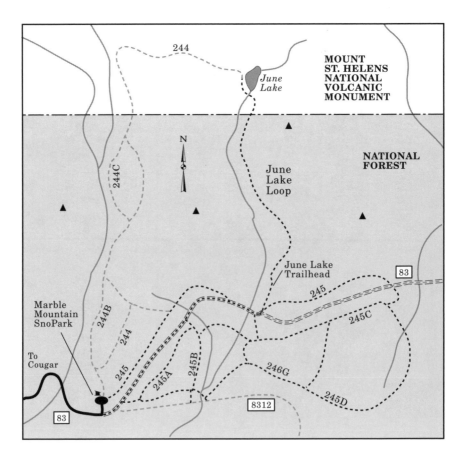

roaring snowmobiles on the nearby roads and give a feeling of wilderness without going very far. Note: Because these loops are in the forest, shaded and sheltered by the trees, snow accumulations will be less than on the nearby roads. Do not try to ski here in the early or late part of the season.

Drive State Route 503 east 28.8 miles from Woodland to Cougar. Go straight through town and continue east another 6.8 miles to an intersection. Head up Road 83 for 5.7 miles to the end of the plowing at the Marble Mountain SnoPark (2,640 feet). A valid SnoPark parking permit is required. Check maps and up-to-date trail information at the warming hut before you set out.

The Wapiti Loops are all part of the Trail 245 system. You may access the trails by following the Pine Martin Trail from the upper corner of the SnoPark or get away from the snowmobiles by walking down to the snow-covered Road 83 and finding a trailhead across from the SnoPark entrance. Once away from the road, the trails are well signed and getting lost or looped is a voluntary condition.

June Lake

ROUND TRIP: 4.5 miles
TRAIL DIFFICULTY: moderate
ELEVATION GAIN: 460 feet
ACTIVITIES: snowshoeing, cross-country skiing
BEST: January to February
MAP: Green Trails: Mount St. Helens NW No. 364S
Map on page 196

June Lake is an ideal destination. It is one of those rare trips that offers just enough challenge and scenic views to satisfy the experienced winter travelers yet is still fun for the less-confident members of the group.

The tour follows a summer hiking trail up a steady incline to the lake. The climb is fairly easy; however, the descent will be a challenge to inexperienced skiers and young children. If your group is not proficient at stopping cross-country skis on unpacked snow, consider trying this trip on snowshoes.

The tour starts at the Marble Mountain SnoPark on Road 83; see previous tour for details.

It is 0.7 mile from the SnoPark to the June Lake trailhead. This distance can be covered in three ways. The easiest is to join the snowmobiles and snowshoe or ski Road 83 to the turnoff. The road is accessed from the lower side of the parking area and is groomed for snowmobiles, which tend to race along at high speeds, creating feelings of envy in the hearts of our very practical children. Pine Martin Trail No. 245 starts at the northern end of the upper side of the parking loop then stays in the trees as it parallels Road 83 for 1 mile. This is a rolling route, fun but challenging. If snowshoeing on this ski route, please

Father and son exploring the cross-country ski trails radiating out from Marble Mountain SnoPark

make your own trail off to the side of the ski tracks. When the trail ends, go left and ski Road 83 over the Lake Creek bridge to find a large sign marking the June Lake trailhead on your left (2,700 feet). The third option is to follow the Wapiti Loops, located on the south side of Road 83, to the June Lake trailhead.

At the June Lake Trail turnoff, follow the road uphill 0.1 mile to the trailhead. Once on the trail, the route is well marked as it heads up an old clearcut. Ahead, Mount St. Helens is in full view. At 2.1 miles from the SnoPark, the trail makes a short, steep drop to an old logging platform. Bear with the short climb that follows and soon you will reach a bridge. Once across, head out onto an open bench. June Lake is to the right, bounded by steep cliffs (3,100 feet). The most amazing feature is a waterfall that streams off the hillside and drops into the lake. Stay back from the water, as it is difficult to determine where the lakeshore actually is.

The trail continues on, heading up the snow-covered lava flow. The route becomes steep and challenging, and is best left to experienced winter travelers or strong teenagers who are still immune to the laws of gravity.

Other Winter Accesses

Red Rock Pass: Road 81 to Red Rock Pass is less developed and a lot less popular than the Marble Mountain SnoPark. This lack of popularity translates into a calmer place for a ski or snowshoe outing. The road climbs at a very moderate pace, making it easy for beginners, with just enough slope to get an occasional glide. Scenery is generally poor. The SnoPark is located 3 miles up Road 83 at its intersection with Road 81.

Ape Cave: Exploring the Ape Cave is a family pleaser, and once in the caves the weather is not an issue. Winter visitors should come prepared to walk, ski, or snowshoe the mile from Road 83 to the cave entrance. Bring your own flashlights and lanterns as there are no rentals in the winter. Be extremely cautious descending into the caves. The steps and ladder may be covered with ice.

Coldwater Ridge (Highway 504): Highway 504 is gated in the winter, 38.7 miles east of Castle Rock. The road is open for skiing, snowshoeing, and snowmobiling. Depending on the winter you may have to hike up the road to the snow. Views on this tour are excellent. However, because much of the road lies in the research area, you are not allowed to do any off-road exploring.

Highway 99: The Wakepish SnoPark at the intersection of Roads 99 and 25 is the only reliable winter access on the north side of the monument. The SnoPark was designed for snowmobiles, so skiers and snowshoers must share the road with machines. Families, especially if the children are young, are advised to visit here mid-week only. If you head up Road 99 for 5 miles from the SnoPark you will reach Bear Meadow Viewpoint. Turn around here; the avalanche potential beyond the viewpoint is very high.

4

Olympic National Park

For the adventurous family, the marvelous diversity of Olympic National Park promises a real treat for everyone. A trip to the park means an opportunity to explore the high alpine meadows, wander through nature's richest garden in the temperate rain forest, swim in steaming hot springs, or explore tide pools and create sand castles on one of the last remaining stretches of wilderness beach in the continental United States.

Less known, but no less impressive, is the rich cultural heritage of the Olympic Peninsula. Before the arrival of European settlers, Native Americans lived along the coast in large homes built of cedar and hemlock. Most of their food was gathered in the spring and summer, leaving plenty of time during the fall and winter months for the women to weave baskets, mats, and clothing and for the men to carve canoes and ceremonial masks. With an abundant food supply right at their doorsteps, these people had time to create and acquire objects of art and value which they would give away in huge, and very prestigious, gatherings called potlatches.

Although the arrival of Europeans destroyed much of the native culture, the ruins of Ozette Village, buried in a landslide about 500 years ago, provide us with a valuable link to the past. The Makah Cultural and Research Center at Neah Bay houses the artifacts found at the old village site and offers powerful insights into the history of this area.

With 95 percent of Olympic National Park a designated wilderness, it might seem like an easy task to explore the remaining 5 percent in a single day. Not so. Olympic National Park lies at the heart of the Olympic Peninsula and is accessed only by a long drive or a time-consuming ferry trip across the Puget Sound. Once on the peninsula, driving times between the various park attractions range from one to several hours.

Rain forest of the Sol Duc River valley

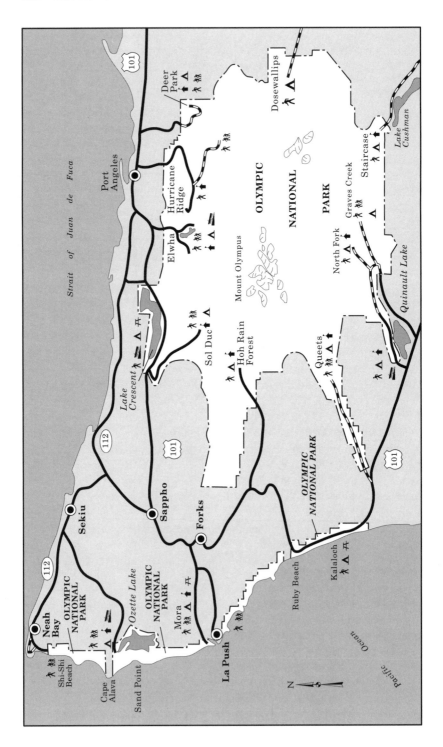

If you have only one day to spend in the park, make the experience enjoyable by limiting your explorations to a single area. From metropolitan Puget Sound, catch a cross-sound ferry (always a kid pleaser), then drive to Port Angeles and start your day in the park with a trip to the visitor center. Then, depending on the weather, drive up to Hurricane Ridge and devote the remainder of the day to exploring the high alpine world or, if the weather is questionable, continue west on US 101 around Crescent Lake to the Sol Duc River valley. From the end of the Sol Duc Hot Springs Road, walk an easy mile through the rain forest to view the thundering spectacle of Sol Duc Falls before becoming the family hero and agreeing to spend the rest of the afternoon in the hot springs (a great rainy day activity).

Beach hiking near Cape Alava

If devoting several days to the park, the major points of interest are best seen by making a loop around the Olympic Peninsula. Drive to Olympia, go west to Hoquiam, then head north to start your tour at the Quinault Rain Forest. After exploring the trails around the Quinault Lodge, go west to Kalaloch and spend several hours playing on the sandy beaches and exploring tide pools. Continue your explorations by driving north to the Hoh Rain Forest. After checking out the visitor center and walking through the Hall of Mosses, drive out to Mora for an exhilarating walk on one of the rugged wilderness beaches. Continue northeast to Port Angeles, where you can culminate your tour with a trip to the crest of Hurricane Ridge. Of course, that was just the quick tour; if time allows add visits to the rain forests of the Sol Duc and Elwha Valleys to your explorations.

If you live within a couple hours' drive of the Olympic Peninsula, take advantage of its convenient proximity to view the park at a more leisurely pace. Each of the thirteen park accesses can be the object of a weekend excursion. As the kids become young adults, backpacking trips can be added to the agenda, allowing you to explore the other 95 percent of this mostly wilderness park.

Campgrounds and accommodations are easy to find around the periphery of the park. Park campgrounds are operated on a first-come basis and fill up every day during the summer. Reservations are recommended for all park-associated accommodations. For Kalaloch Lodge and Lake Quinault Lodge, call (360) 288-2900. For Lake Crescent Lodge, contact (360) 928-3211. For reservations at the Log Cabin Resort, call (360) 928-3245, and for Sol Duc Hot

Springs Resort, call (360) 327-3583. For lodging in the communities around the park, call the local Chambers of Commerce.

The Olympic Park Institute on Lake Crescent provides an ideal way for families with elementary school-age children to explore and study the park together. Accommodations, food, and materials all are part of the programs. Kids ages eleven to seventeen may learn some independence on an institute-sponsored backpack trip. For information, write to Olympic Park Institute, 111 Barnes Point Road, Port Angeles, WA 98363; or call (800) 775-3720.

Hurricane Ridge

Backpacking, camping, hiking, nature walks, scenic drives, views, visitor center

In recognition of its vast ecological and cultural diversity, in 1981 the United Nations designated Olympic National Park to be a World Heritage site. Like a giant ecological staircase, Olympic National Park encompasses a full range of environments, starting with the salt-laden ocean beaches, then climbing through the rich environment of the temperate rain forest to reach the delicate, yet incredibly hardy high alpine world, and ending in a desert of ice and rock at the crest of the Olympic Mountains.

The high alpine environment of the Olympics is most easily accessed at Hurricane Ridge. Although you won't get close enough to touch the glaciers, Hurricane Ridge offers an opportunity to explore the harsh and beautiful alpine world that was shaped by glaciers.

The name Hurricane Ridge is well founded. Even if hurricanes do not actually blow through this area, the ridge receives a great deal of wind and inclement weather. During the winter, winds can blow snow into massive mounds, covering roads and cars in a matter of an hour or so. During the summer, conditions are rarely that extreme; however, visitors must always be ready for rain, wind, and drenching mists.

Start your Hurricane Ridge visit with a stop at the Olympic National Park Visitor Center in Port Angeles. The movie there is a good way to introduce yourself to the alpine environment and learn how it relates to the rest of the park. Take time to wander around the displays; the elk is an impressive sight even if it is stuffed. The kids may prefer to head around the corner and check out a special place called the Discovery Room, where nature is explored through a series of hands-on displays: color, create a mask, be a salmon and work through a fish ladder, check out the computer, or just open all the room's hidden doors. To reach the visitor center, turn off US 101 at Race Street and follow the signs.

The trip to Hurricane Ridge is a memorable drive that begins at sea level in Port Angeles and arrives at the ridge tops 18 miles later and over 5,000 feet higher. This quick rush from sea level to the mountain tops may be the cause of some physical discomfort as the inner ear attempts to adjust to the decrease in air pressure. Babies adjust easily with a little crying. Everyone else can relieve inner-ear discomfort with a couple of big yawns.

Once you reach the ridge, plans should be as flexible as the weather is erratic. A walk with a park naturalist is fun and informative no matter what the meteorological conditions are. These walks are held at least twice a day from July through September. On your own, your family may want to go a little further for views from Klahhane Ridge or from Hurricane Hill.

For the exploration minded, the 7-mile Obstruction Point Road takes you away from the crowds at Hurricane Ridge to the highest point in the park that is accessible by car. From road's end you can take a top-of-the-world walk on Lillian Ridge or Elk Mountain. For longer trips or a family backpack, Grand Lake is an appealing destination. The drive to Obstruction Point should be considered only on sunny days when the narrow dirt road is dry. The trails from Obstruction Point are open and exposed, totally miserable in bad weather.

During the busy summer season, July through September, the Hurricane Ridge Visitor Center offers movies, food service, and a gift shop. The picnic area, located 1 mile beyond the visitor center, has running water, restrooms, and tables located to either fully enjoy the scenery or to hide in the trees and escape the brunt of the weather. The visitor center remains open the entire year, without food service and gift shop during the winter. The picnic area is closed after the summer season.

Hotels and motels are located at

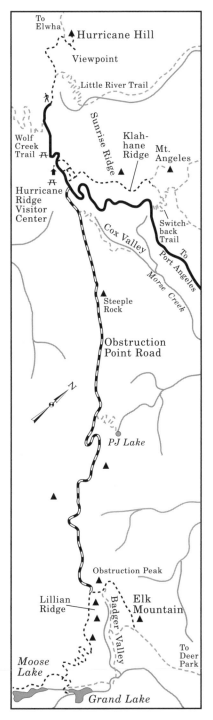

Port Angeles. Campers may choose between the 105-site Heart O' Hills Campground, located 5 miles up the Hurricane Ridge Road, or several private camp areas near Port Angeles. Heart O' Hills Campground is open year round and has campfire programs on the weekends during the summer. No camping is allowed above Heart O' Hills, except in the backcountry.

Hurricane Ridge Nature Trails

LOOP TRIP: up to 1.5 miles
TRAIL DIFFICULTY: easy
ELEVATION GAIN: up to 250 feet
ACTIVITIES: walking, views, wildlife, nature study
BEST: mid-June to September
MAP: Olympic National Park Handout
Map on page 205

First-time visitors to Hurricane Ridge should allot sufficient time to walk one or more of the short nature loops that tour the meadows across from the visitor center. Information signs along the trails point out various features, stressing the amazing adaptations plants have made to survive in this harsh environment.

Klahhane Ridge

For more information, take a walk in the company of a park interpreter. These walks last about an hour. Check at the visitor center for times.

Cirque Rim Trail: This short nature walk is paved and wheelchair accessible. The trail follows the edge of the ridge, overlooking a glacier-carved cirque (basin). Views from this trail extend over Port Angeles and the Strait of Juan de Fuca to Vancouver Island. Deer are often seen during the middle of the day, taking advantage of the shade offered by the thick branches of the subalpine firs.

Big Meadow Trail: Everyone will enjoy this 0.2-mile stroll on a paved trail through the meadows with views into the heartland of the Olympic Range. Deer are commonly seen along this trail also.

High Ridge Trail: Starting near the entrance of the Hurricane Ridge parking lot, this nature trail ascends 5,471-foot Alpine Hill to views of the Cascade, Coast, and Olympic Mountain Ranges as well as the meadows of Hurricane Ridge and the visitor center. This trail is moderately steep but the climb is mercifully short. Beyond Alpine Hill a dirt trail descends to a saddle and an intersection with the Klahhane Ridge Trail. Go straight for a short walk to Sunrise Point and a view over the Strait of Juan de Fuca. Back at the saddle, go right and complete the loop by switchbacking down through the trees to the ski lift and an intersection with the Cirque Rim Trail. Go right to complete the loop.

Klahhane Ridge

ROUND TRIP: 4.2 miles
TRAIL DIFFICULTY: moderate
ELEVATION GAIN: 1,000 feet
ACTIVITIES: hiking, scenic views
BEST: mid-July to September
MAP: Custom Correct: Hurricane Ridge
Map on page 205

Every hump, every dip, and every turn on this ridge-running trail has a view and every view is an outstanding one. If the children are not at the view-appreciation stage, you may have a hard time selling this hike to the younger family members. Some kids can be lured along by the possibility of spotting deer or marmots. Other kids succumb to food bribes. However you can do it, this trail is worth the effort.

Drive 18 miles up from US 101 in Port Angeles to Hurricane Ridge (5,230 feet). The trail starts at the east end of the parking area.

Walk the paved pathway through the meadow. When the trail divides stay right, and at the second intersection take a hard right and head up Alpine Hill. Pass a few subalpine firs and look for deer lingering in their shade.

The trail switchbacks, passing a couple of strategically placed benches before reaching the crest of Alpine Hill (5,471 feet). At 0.3 mile from the start a four-way junction is reached. Straight ahead is a 0.1-mile spur trail to Sunrise Point and views over the Strait of Juan de Fuca. Your trail is the one on the right, signed to Klahhane Ridge. Walk north, following the ridge crest through clumps of wind-sculptured alpine firs and across rocky meadows. Like all ridge crest trails, this one climbs then descends with the topography.

The final destination can be as far your feet or eyes want to take you. The trail will dance along the ridge offering views across the Olympic Range from the dark green rain forest in valley bottoms to the arctic environment of the glacier-clad summits. North across the Strait of Juan de Fuca is Vancouver Island and the San Juans. To the east, the icy summits of the Cascades pierce the sky.

A small TRAIL sign at 2.1 miles (5,250 feet) marks a perfect turnaround point. The spur trail heading around the sign is a scramblers' route up Mount Angeles. The Klahhane Ridge Trail leaves the ridge crest here and traverses around Mount Angeles to intercept the Switchback Trail before climbing back to the top of Klahhane Ridge (5,880 feet).

Hurricane Hill

ROUND TRIP: 3.2 miles
TRAIL DIFFICULTY: moderate
ELEVATION GAIN: 700 feet
ACTIVITIES: hiking, scenic vistas, wildlife viewing
BEST: July to September
MAP: Custom Correct: Hurricane Ridge
Map on page 205

An easily attainable summit with a 360-degree panorama of views is the lure that draws so many families to the old lookout site at the crest of 5,757-foot Hurricane Hill. In good weather this is an ideal picnic spot—if you keep an eye on your food. Chipmunks, ravens, camp robbers, and even a curious deer or two may wander by to check out your menu. Families with older children, and flashlights for everyone, may make this an evening walk and watch the sunset from the summit.

From US 101 in Port Angeles, drive uphill on Race Street. Pass the Olympic National Park Visitor Center then keep right when the road divides. After 5 miles reach the park entrance station and Heart O' Hills Campground. Continue the steady climb for 13 miles to the Hurricane Ridge Visitor Center. Go through the parking lot and continue along the ridge to road's end (5,057 feet).

The trail to Hurricane Hill follows the route of an old road and even has a strip of pavement for easy walking. It starts out along a rock- and grass-covered ridge crest then slips to the west side of the hill, maintaining a nearly

Hikers on the crest of Hurricane Hill

level traverse past upthrust and remarkably folded layers of sandstone. At 0.4 mile, the Little River Trail branches off on the right to begin its long descent to Little River Road.

Hurricane Hill Trail now begins a steady climb (steep for short legs), heading into a stand of subalpine firs then back to the open grasslands. When the trail starts a series of steep switchbacks, watch for crickets. They are numerous by late summer and it is not uncommon to see ravens boldly walking down the trail, among the hikers, looking for a tasty snack.

At 1.4 miles, the trail to the Elwha Ranger Station branches off on the left. Although few make the 6-mile trek to the Elwha River valley, many families follow the trail along the open ridge crest for a short distance to enjoy the view and find a quiet picnic site. The main trail continues to climb to the crest of the ridge where it divides. Head to the summit to check out the old lookout site and watch the ships cruising along the Strait of Juan de Fuca. Next, walk north to inspect the peak locator sign which pinpoints a vast array of summits, from the dry west side peaks to the glacier-covered massifs of Mount Olympus and Mount Carrie.

Lillian Ridge

RIDGE WALK
> ROUND TRIP: up to 3 miles
> TRAIL DIFFICULTY: easy
> ELEVATION GAIN: 600 feet
> ACTIVITIES: hiking, views
> BEST: July to September
> MAP: Custom Correct: Gray Wolf—Dosewallips
> Map on page 205

GRAND LAKE
> ROUND TRIP: 7.4 miles
> TRAIL DIFFICULTY: challenging
> ELEVATION GAIN: 1,700 feet
> ACTIVITIES: hiking, backpacking, fishing, views
> BEST: mid-July to September
> MAP: Custom Correct: Gray Wolf—Dosewallips

This is not only the most scenic ridge walk in the entire Olympic National Park, it is also one of the most child friendly. Lillian Ridge is broad, allowing little feet to rush ahead and explore or just stop to ponder a cricket or a beetle. Snowfields linger, often throughout the entire summer, ideal for impromptu sliding sessions.

Grand Lake is, as its name suggests, a grand destination. The lake lies in a forested basin with an easily accessible shore and sheltered campsites. Unfortunately, the trail to the lake is very difficult for young hikers. After leaving Lillian Ridge near the 1.3-mile point, the trail abruptly plummets into Grand Valley. It is not until heading back up that you find out just how really steep the trail is.

From US 101 in Port Angeles, drive 18 miles to Hurricane Ridge. At the entrance to the large Hurricane Ridge parking lot, find a dirt road on the left heading sharply back and downhill. This road is rough and narrow. Look for cars coming up before you start down; passing is difficult. The road ends, after 7 very slow miles, at Obstruction Point (6,125 feet).

You don't even have to get out of the car to appreciate the view. The mountains seem close enough to touch. Glaciers are all around, seemingly intermixed with dry, almost bony, rock-capped summits. Thousands of feet below are rich green valley bottoms, often shrouded with fog in the early hours.

Several trails originate from Obstruction Point. Yours is the most obvious, starting from the center of the parking lot and heading south along the ridge crest. Note: The ridge is very exposed. Always carry a jacket, even on a clear, calm day, in case of wind. If the clouds come in, turn around immediately and carefully follow the trail back. It is easy to get confused on this open ridge when a fog of white clouds obscures your vision.

As you walk, take time to stop and examine the vegetation. The flowers and plants are miniaturized, delicate, yet hardy. This could be the perfect moment to talk about the difficulties encountered by plants living at the edge of their adaptability, and how they do not need the extra stress of being walked on by people's feet.

After 0.7 mile of easy walking, a series of stone steps takes hikers down from the ridge crest. The trail then climbs around a rocky bump. When you reach the ridge crest again, the trail divides. Straight ahead is an unofficial trail which follows the ridge another 0.2 mile to a viewpoint and picnic spot. The main trail heads over the hill and descends.

The descent continues for 1.2 miles, dropping 1,200 feet before arriving at an intersection. Go left and continue down a grassy hillside for another 0.2 mile to another intersection. The trail to Grand Lake and the campsites is on the right. Alternative camping is found at Moose Lake, 0.5 mile upvalley.

Overnight campers may enjoy the strenuous, 2.6-mile climb to the 6,430-foot summit of Grand Pass. Views of the interior of the range are excellent. When you are ready to leave Grand Lake, do not allow yourself to be seduced by the easy-looking loop through Badger Valley. The climb is worse than the ascent back to Lillian Ridge. (Badger Valley is preferable only if the weather is terrible.)

MORE ACTIVITIES
Map on page 205

Heart of the Forest Trail: This ramble through an old-growth forest with huge ferns and giant skunk cabbages is delightful for the first mile. The second mile is spent descending, gradually at first, then steadily down Lake Creek drainage and is not recommended. The hike ends abruptly at the 2.3-mile point in a less-than-scenic clearcut. The trailhead is located at the upper end of Loop E in the Heart O' Hills Campground.

Switchback Trail: This shortcut into the high country of Klahhane Ridge starts on the north side of Hurricane Ridge Road, 10 miles above the entrance station. The trail charges up the hill, gaining 600 feet of elevation before intersecting the Klahhane Ridge Trail in 0.6 mile. From this point, just one more mile and innumerable more switchbacks rockets you up the next 800 feet to the ridge crest and views.

Cox Valley: If avoiding the crowds is your objective, then Cox Valley is your place. This little-used trail descends 1.8 miles, dropping 1,200 feet into Cox Valley. The trail disappears in the meadows. Campsites may be found from the 1-mile point on. The trailhead is located on the left side of Obstruction Point Road, 0.6 mile below the Hurricane Ridge parking lot.

PJ Lake: Somebody likes this lake; it even has a little campsite. The tiny lake is reached by a steep, nasty trail whose only redeeming feature is a pretty waterfall. The trail is 0.9 mile long. It drops 600 feet then climbs 200 feet. The

Badger Valley

trailhead is located on Obstruction Point Road, 4 miles from the Hurricane Ridge parking area, just opposite the unmarked Waterhole Camp.

Badger Valley: This grass- and wildflower-covered valley is the home of many well-fed marmots. Hikers on this trail will be treated to a beautiful meadow but must be ready to face the difficulties of a steep and narrow trail. The hike begins at the end of the Obstruction Point parking area in conjunction with the Elk Mountain Trail. At 0.2 mile is an intersection. Go right and head down the rocky slope. After descending 600 feet in 1 mile, reach a faint intersection with an alternate trail up Elk Mountain. At this point you have seen most of the open portions of the valley. Continue on for no more than 0.5 mile and stop before you begin descending steeply.

Elk Mountain: Sure-footed walkers will appreciate this scenic hike to the 6,764-foot summit of Elk Mountain. This is a challenging walk on a narrow, steep, and slippery trail. The trailhead is located at Obstruction Point. Start in conjunction with the Badger Valley Trail and follow an old road around the hillside 0.2 mile to an intersection. Continue straight, contouring the steep hillside for a short distance before heading almost straight up. Once past this very hairy section, the terrain and trail moderate. Near 0.8 mile, begin a long traverse over the open summit of Elk Mountain. The true summit is located at about the 1.6-mile point, a short distance off the trail.

Port Angeles: The City Pier and Park area is a great place to spend a couple of educational and relaxing hours. The park offers a boat-shaped play set for the younger children and a beach for everybody. The Arthur D. Fiero

Marine Science Laboratory has a hands-on tank for getting a feel of underwater life. At the observation tower at the end of the pier you can climb high enough to see over the breakwater at the harbor entrance and look across the Strait of Juan de Fuca. When in port, the Coast Guard cruiser may be toured. The waterfront park also has a bike path. To reach the City Pier and Park, drive US 101 to the center of town. Descend to the waterfront on Lincoln Street then turn right to find the parking area.

Elwha

Backpacking, camping, fishing, hiking, rafting

The Elwha Valley is green, intensely green from the fern-cloaked hillsides to the tops of the giant trees. Mosses grow everywhere, flowing off the trees in giant streamers, until even the sky seems green.

The valley has much more to offer than just beautiful forest scenes. Fishing is an ever-popular activity along the Elwha River and in Lake Mills. The shores of the lake (actually it is a reservoir) are brushy; however, fishing from a small watercraft can be rewarding. Note: The lake is subject to high winds

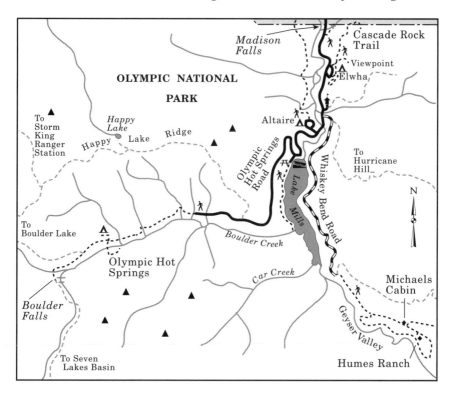

from 11:00 A.M. until late afternoon whenever the weather is fair. Those in canoes, kayaks, and even small dinghies need to exercise caution.

Want a few thrills? Try a half-day raft trip on the river with the Olympic Guide and Raft Service. This park-licensed concessionaire offers twice-daily trips down the Elwha River during the summer. Reservations are suggested.

Many people visiting the Elwha come to take advantage of one or more of the excellent trails. The most popular destination is Olympic Hot Springs. For a little more solitude, try the Geyser Valley Loop (sorry, it's just a name; no geysers in the Olympics). At Elwha Campground a nature loop can be followed through the rain forest, or you can have your senses equally overloaded with green if you walk the River Trail from Altaire Campground. For the truly energetic, trails head up the steep side of the valley to minor viewpoints.

Accommodations in the Elwha area include two campgrounds with a combined total of only seventy-one campsites; arrive early on weekends. Nearby Port Angeles has several large hotels and motels and plenty of restaurants. For backpackers, campsites are located within a couple miles of the trailheads.

Olympic Hot Springs and Lower Boulder Falls

OLYMPIC HOT SPRINGS
  ROUND TRIP: 5 miles
  TRAIL DIFFICULTY: easy
  ELEVATION GAIN: 300 feet
  ACTIVITIES: hiking, biking, bathing, backpacking
  BEST: June to September
  MAP: Custom Correct: Lake Crescent—Happy Lake
  Map on page 216

LOWER BOULDER FALLS
  ROUND TRIP: 7 miles
  TRAIL DIFFICULTY: moderate
  ELEVATION GAIN: 700 feet
  ACTIVITIES: hiking, biking, backpacking
  BEST: mid-June to September
  MAP: Custom Correct: Lake Crescent—Happy Lake

At one time, Olympic Hot Springs was the site of a ritzy resort, with golf course, hotel, and sanitorium. Eventually the resort was replaced by a campground and, over time, the road began to slump, then slide, down the steep hillside, forcing a closure on the final 2.2 miles.

One of several pools at Olympic Hot Springs

The happy result of the slides has been to make Olympic Hot Springs an ideal destination for a day of family fun and adventure. The hike to the springs is an easy one, and if the 2 miles spent walking on the paved road seem to be too much for the kids, parents can push strollers or pull wagons. Families with school-age children may make the trip on mountain bikes.

The hot springs has six main pools of various temperatures. The pools are shallow, less than twenty-four inches deep, with muddy bottoms. Bathing suits are required, but be prepared to encounter some nudity. Overnight stays are permitted in the old campground area.

Drive west from Port Angeles 10 miles on US 101 then turn left on Olympic Hot Springs Road. Go up the Elwha River valley for 10.6 miles and park at the gate that marks the end of the road (1,825 feet). (The final 4.7 miles of the drive are narrow and winding, unsuitable for vehicles pulling trailers.)

Head up the road on hard pavement for 2.2 miles. Some of the grades are steep, and younger bike riders may have to get off and push. Riders should use caution at all times to avoid entanglements with the numerous pedestrians.

At the end of the road is an outhouse. The campground is located up a steep hill to the right. The hot springs are straight ahead. The trail descends slightly to reach Boulder Creek in 0.2 mile. Cross the creek then head downvalley. The hot springs are located off the main trail. Follow the slight sulphur smell and

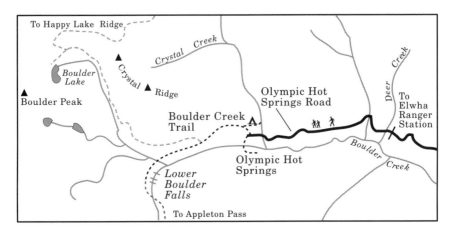

the well-beaten spur trails to the pools. The one pool below the trail seems to be the coolest and the best for younger children.

Boulder Creek Trail starts at the upper end of the camp area. Walk uphill from the road's-end outhouse then go left when the trail divides. Follow an old road to find the trail sign in 0.2 mile. Bikes must be left here. The trail heads through the forest, climbing gradually for 0.6 mile to an intersection. Go left on the Appleton Pass Trail for another nearly level 0.6 mile to the beautiful Lower Boulder Falls. Watch the younger children; some of the rocks around the falls are very slippery. Boulder Lake, found 2.6 miles up the right-hand trail, is a popular destination for fishermen.

Geyser Valley Loop

ROUND TRIP: 5.8 miles
TRAIL DIFFICULTY: moderate
ELEVATION GAIN: 650 feet
ACTIVITIES: hiking, backpacking, and fishing
BEST: June to September
MAP: Custom Correct: Elwha Valley
Map on page 217

History and scenery join together to make this an enjoyable hike for the entire family. The old pioneer cabins, numerous intersections, and abundant wildlife along the trail keep boredom at bay for even the most disinterested hiker. Add fishing poles to the pack and take advantage of the close proximity of the river to try for a fish or two. Backpackers can divide the hike into two very short days by making use of the riverside camp area at the halfway point.

From Port Angeles, drive west 10 miles then turn left and head up the Elwha River valley on Olympic Hot Springs Road. At 4.1 miles, pass the ranger

Old saw at Humes Ranch in Geyser Valley

station (backpackers stop and register). A short 0.1 mile beyond, go left on the gravel-surfaced Whiskey Bend Road for 4.8 miles to its end (1,198 feet).

Begin your hike by following the Elwha River Trail upvalley, climbing gradually along the side of the steep, forested hillside. The trail is wide enough for two people to walk side by side. At 0.9 mile, a spur trail descends to a rocky overlook of the valley below. In late fall and winter, elk graze in the meadow across the valley, otherwise the view is not remarkable.

At 1.2 miles go right and descend into Rica Canyon. The trail is steep for its entire 0.5-mile drop to the river. Young hikers with slippery soles may need a helping hand. Once down, the trail divides. Take the right fork and traverse

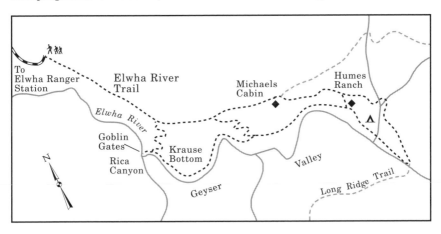

along the river for 0.1 mile to Goblin Gates. Here, with a lot of imagination, the globular rock formations can look like faces.

The loop route heads upvalley from the intersection, paralleling the Elwha River through an area once settled by the Krause family. This is a great place to look for deer and elk. At 2.7 miles the trail forks near an old orchard. Take the trail on the right and continue on 0.7 mile to Humes Ranch and a river campsite.

After checking out the old ranch house and artifacts, head left for a short 0.6-mile climb to Michael's Cabin, where you will go left and rejoin the Elwha Trail. After some contemplation about the life of a pioneer, head back. Spend the next 0.3 mile gradually climbing through the forest, then enter a brushy area burned by the Rica Canyon fire of 1977. At the 4.6-mile point, pass the Rica Canyon Trail, ending the loop portion of the hike. Continue straight and reach the trailhead at 5.8 miles.

MORE ACTIVITIES
Map on page 213

Madison Falls Trail: This 0.1-mile nature trail is wheelchair and stroller accessible. The trailhead is located 2.1 miles up the Elwha River valley, opposite the park entrance booth. Information signs along the route discuss the area's history. The trail ends at a scenic falls.

Viewpoint and Cascade Rock Trail: Parking is located in the Elwha Campground at the covered cooking shelter, 3.2 miles from US 101. You may also park across the road at the amphitheater. The trail immediately crosses a small creek then divides. Go left 100 feet then take the first right. After climbing 0.2 mile, the trail divides again. The trail on the right climbs another 0.2 mile then ends abruptly at a precipitous view over the very green Elwha River valley. To the left, from the intersection, the trail continues on for another 1.9 miles, gaining 1,200 feet, before ending at Cascade Rock. The view from the rock is nice, a sure bet for active teenagers who want to go for a hike just to get away from their parents.

Elwha Campground Nature Loop: This is a 0.8-mile walk through a forest of ferns. At this time, the walk is purely for enjoyment, uncluttered by informational signs or educational pamphlets. Families can discuss forest ecology, or the potential of this habitat for supporting a large population of elves, or whether young chipmunks with acne get any dates. Drive up the Elwha River valley for 3.2 miles from US 101. Park either in the Elwha Campground at the cooking gazebo or across the road at the amphitheater. Follow the trail across the creek then stay right at all intersections.

River Trail: Although used mainly by fishermen, this is a wonderful trail for a stroll over fern-covered hillsides to a riverside picnic site. The trailhead is located 4.6 miles up the Elwha River valley in Altaire Campground. No parking is available at the trailhead, so find a place to leave the vehicle outside the campground. The trail heads downvalley for 3 miles then ends at a road. Numerous river accesses are possible. Some sections are steep.

Lake Mills Trail: This easy-to-walk trail follows the west shore of the reservoir for 1.9 miles, ending at a point overlooking Boulder Creek and the lake. Although an obvious walk for fishermen, the lakeshore remains brushy for the entire distance. The trailhead is located on the Olympic Hot Springs Road, 5.8 miles from US 101 at the Lake Mills Boat Launch.

Lake Crescent

Boating, camping, fishing, hiking, swimming

The clarity of Lake Crescent is astounding. When the water is calm, walk out on any dock and peer down to the depths: It is like looking through a cobalt-tinted window. After a good look—jump in.

There are plenty of great family activities at Lake Crescent. Start your tour of the area with a visit to the Storm King Ranger Station located in a rebuilt 1909 forest service cabin. Inside is information about local trails as well as upcoming ranger walks and talks. The easy hike to the delicate curtain of mist called Marymere Falls is a must. Walk the trail on your own or join a ranger-led group for insight on local ecology. Storm King Trail, a strenuous hike, ascends to a glorious vista over the lake to Mount Baker.

If you enjoy mountain biking, Spruce Railroad Trail along the north shore of the lake is a challenging and fun way to spend an afternoon. Swimming, an activity reserved for the hardy or the young, is also popular, even though the waters are definitely chilly.

Canoes and small motorboats may be rented at the Fairholm Store at the

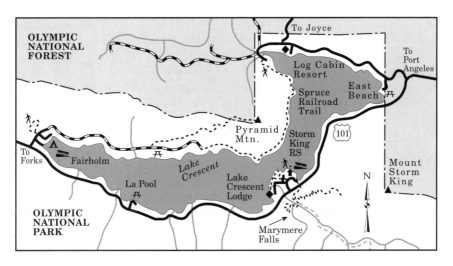

west end of the lake. Or bring your own boat and launch at Fairholm Campground, Storm King Ranger Station, or East Shore Picnic Area. The lake is often buffeted by high winds from midmorning to late afternoon, so small boats need to use caution.

Fishing will consume most of any spare time you might have left.

Fairholm Campground is the only public camp area on the lake. The campground has eighty-seven sites and frequently fills in the summer. It stays open all year with limited services from mid-September through May. Evening programs are held at the amphitheater on weekends during July and August. The boat launch has a roped-off area for swimming. Limited camping supplies and food service are available at the nearby Fairholm Store.

If you prefer daily showers, try the Log Cabin Resort or Lake Crescent Lodge. At the Log Cabin Resort you may choose between rustic log cabins and guest rooms in the lodge. There is also a full-service RV camping area here. Advance reservations are a must: (360) 928-3245. Lake Crescent Lodge has been an old favorite since 1926. Open year round. Call (800) 562-6672 for reservations.

Marymere Falls

ROUND TRIP: 2 miles
TRAIL DIFFICULTY: easy
ELEVATION GAIN: 400 feet
ACTIVITY: hiking
BEST: all year
MAP: Custom Correct: Lake Crescent—Happy Lake Ridge
Map on page 221

Even the most resistant walkers will have to work to keep from succumbing to the charm of this trail. Big trees, bridges, a couple of creeks, stairs, benches, and even a tunnel account for the high level of interest, and the lacy waterfall is a universally pleasing destination. If you are a camera buff, carry your tripod; on busy days people from around the world stand in line waiting for their chance to photograph the falls.

Drive 22 miles west of Port Angeles on US 101. About halfway around Lake Crescent, take the Storm King Ranger Station turnoff. When the road divides, go right. The parking lot (595 feet) often fills on weekends.

Walk past the ranger station then follow the wide path into the forest. If you have yet to check out the park's pamphlet on lowland forest communities, pick one up for perusal now or later. As soon as the trail enters the forest, it divides. Either fork works. The trail on the left descends stairs to the edge of the lake; the one on the right follows a gentler slope. The two trails rejoin in 75 feet to go under US 101.

Beyond the tunnel, the trail enters the forest where the ambient light drops dramatically and sunglasses are sure to come off in a hurry. Huge old stumps take on curious shapes in the halflight.

At the 0.4-mile point, the trail divides. Continue straight. (The trail on the right leads to Lake Crescent Lodge.) A giant tree on the left commands attention as you go by, and shortly beyond it the Storm King Trail branches off on the left. Next, pass a trail on the left which heads up Barnes Creek. Just beyond is a creek access where younger children appreciate a chance to throw rocks and maybe even fall in and get their feet wet. What could be more fun?

The trail crosses Barnes Creek on a narrow log bridge with two handrails, then immediately after crosses Falls Creek on a narrower log bridge with only one handrail.

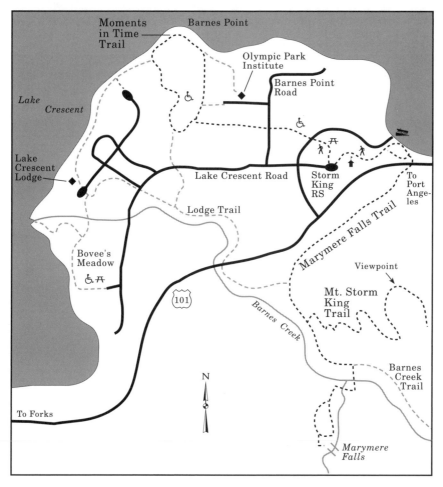

Upper viewing platform at Marymere Falls

Up to this point little elevation has been gained, but that changes as the trail begins its assault on the steep hillside. The big steps are part of the fun. After gaining 100 feet, the trail divides and starts a loop. The easiest ascent is to the right; however, the left is like an obstacle course and bound to appeal to the adventure-minded who like to squeeze around trees and clamber over cliffs. Benches along the way provide rest for the jaded.

The upper waterfall-viewing area has benches for resting and snacking before heading back down.

Spruce Railroad Trail

ROUND TRIP: 8 miles
TRAIL DIFFICULTY: moderate on foot; challenging on bike
ELEVATION GAIN: 150 feet
ACTIVITIES: hiking, mountain biking, swimming, fishing
BEST: mid-February to November
MAP: Custom Correct: Lake Crescent—Happy Lake Ridge
Map on page 219

Many railroad grades converted to trails are wide, level, easy to ride, and often lacking in scenery. The Spruce Railroad Trail is none of these. Although there are some easy sections, much of the trail is steep, rocky, and very narrow. The scenery is outstanding; one portion of the trail crosses an arm of the lake on an arched bridge, another narrow part skirts so close to the lake that one false turn of the handlebars would mean a cold swim.

Despite the difficulties, this is a popular hike and bike ride for adults and teenagers. Hikers must be prepared for a constant stream of bikes on weekends, suggesting that this is not the place for toddlers.

Note: Ticks have recently appeared in this area. They are a small variety and everyone should be doubly vigilant in looking for these tiny pests after any hike or ride. Poison oak is also found along the lakeshore: Watch for shiny leaves in clusters of threes.

The Spruce Railroad has two trailheads. Hikers who are not planning to walk the entire distance should start at the eastern end, reached by driving US 101 west from Port Angeles. Just before cresting the hill above Lake Crescent, turn right on East Beach Road, signed to the Log Cabin Resort. After 3.3 miles go left around the end of the lake to the well-signed trailhead (600 feet). To reach the west access, continue on US 101 another 15 miles. At the west end of the lake, go right on North Shore Road and follow it 4.9 miles to the trailhead.

The trail description is for hikers, or mountain bikers, starting from the east. If you and your family are good swimmers and do not have any great objections to somewhat chilly water, add swimsuits and towels to the pack.

The trail begins by heading up a grassy hillside. After 0.1 mile, intersect an old logging road which climbs gradually through dense tangles of brush. At the end of the first 0.5 mile the trail leaves the road and drops to the edge of the lake to join the old railroad grade. This is a fun section with several lake accesses around Harrigan Point. Mud holes are common.

At Devils Point, the old railroad avoided the steep cliffs by tunneling through them. Today the tunnel is considered unsafe and has been replaced by a narrow ribbon of a trail etched across the rock walls. A short, difficult descent at 1.3 miles leads to rock-bound Devils Bay and the arched bridge. On warm days this is a very popular place, where hikers and boaters and cyclists test their Silly Meters by jumping off the bridge into the frigid waters. The rocks along the shore are covered with sunbathers, warming up for another jump. (Watch where you sit; poison oak grows in this area.)

The trail heads back to the railroad grade and continues to follow the shoreline around the base of Pyramid Mountain. At 2.8 miles is another tunnel and once again you leave the railroad grade to follow a narrow trail to within a couple feet of the lake. Hikers will find this section of trail very scenic. Mountain bikers should ignore the scenery and carefully watch where they are going.

Beyond the tunnel, the trail rejoins the railroad grade for the final mile to the North Shore Road trailhead.

MORE ACTIVITIES

Maps on page 219 and 221

Swimming: Water access can be found all around the lake. The most popular swimming holes are at the Fairholm boat launch next to Fairholm Campground, Bovee's Meadow Picnic Area next to Lake Crescent Lodge, and East

Hikers near upper end of Storm King Trail

Beach Picnic Area on East Beach Road. The lake, which is over 600 feet deep at the center, never gets very warm so sunbathing (a short way to say "warming back up") is even more popular than swimming.

Boating: Free public boat ramps are located at Fairholm and Storm King Ranger Station. Boats may also be launched at Log Cabin Resort. Jet boats, ski boats, sailboats, kayaks, canoes, and even pedal boats can be seen on any busy weekend. Rental boats—canoes and small powerboats for fishing—are located at Fairholm, Lake Crescent Resort, and Log Cabin Resort.

Mount Storm King Trail: The hike up the shoulder of Mount Storm King gains 2,000 feet in 2.2 miles. The trail climbs relentlessly, and then ends way below the actual summit. Sounds like the kind of place that kids would hate, right? Not so; families are the most frequent trail users. The trail starts at Storm King Ranger Station and follows the Marymere Falls Trail for 0.5 mile before branching left. At the 2-mile point is a spectacular viewpoint. The official trail ends at 2.2 miles (3,100 feet). The view is disappointing here and many people are tempted to continue on in hopes of finding better views. Do not join them! Above are steep, slippery slopes that cannot be safely crossed without climbing gear.

Moments in Time Trail: This 0.5-mile loop passes through old-growth forest, goes by the site of an old homestead, checks out a hollow tree, then rambles along the lakeshore. It is an easy hike, perfect for strollers. Start by walking west from the Lake Crescent Lodge parking area. The trail may also be accessed from Storm King Ranger Station.

Fairholm Campground Nature Trail: This 1-mile loop starts at Fairholm Campground. Although the trail is easy, a good imagination is required to keep it interesting. The booklet is the ubiquitous "Lowland Forest Communities," fascinating for the mature audience, somewhat wordy for shorter attention spans. If you find interest flagging, make a game of finding slugs or counting moss-draped maples.

Pyramid Mountain Trail: The 7-mile round trip to the summit of Pyramid Mountain is a great place to exercise the teenagers or yourself. The trail is good but has few views on the 2,600-foot climb to the summit. The crest of the mountain is adorned with a World War II watch cabin. The watchman's duty was to look for enemy planes sneaking across the border. Today the cabin is ratty and has been badly abused. The trees have obscured much of the view. The trailhead is located off US 101 at the west end of Lake Crescent. Follow the North Shore Road 3.4 miles. Parking is found on the right, the trail is located on the left.

Sol Duc River Valley

Backpacking, fishing, hiking, relaxing, swimming

The Sol Duc area has the upbeat ambience more commonly associated with expensive resorts rather than a national park that is mostly wilderness. Certain amenities contribute to this atmosphere, the main one being a hot springs resort with a swimming area, hot pool for soaking, and children's play pool. If you are looking for something a little more upscale than the campground, the Sol Duc Hot Springs Resort has rental cabins (advance reservations are a must). The resort also has a restaurant, a fast-food outlet, and a small grocery store. There is even an RV campground.

If you get tired of swimming and soaking, you can explore the rain forest on one or more of the area's excellent

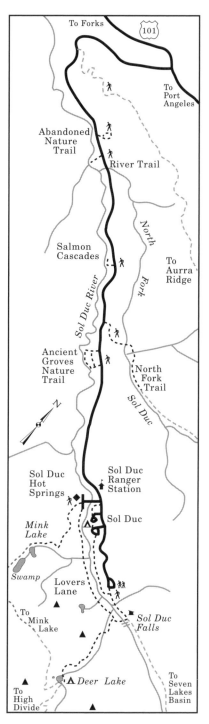

short walks. And, if you decide to spend more time walking than soaking, you can hike to one of the two mountain lakes near the area. For backpackers, Sol Duc is the starting point to Seven Lakes Basin and High Divide, one of the most popular extended trips in the park.

Ranger-led walks and evening campfire programs are daily affairs throughout the months of July and August. Check the posted schedule at the campground or stop in at the ranger station to inquire.

For reservations at Sol Duc Hot Springs Resort, call (360) 327-3583. The resort is open from mid-May to late September. It has thirty-two cabins, five with full kitchens. No reservations are accepted at the campground. Arrive early to secure one of the eighty sites.

Sol Duc Falls

SOL DUC FALLS
> ROUND TRIP: 2 miles
> TRAIL DIFFICULTY: easy
> ELEVATION GAIN: 50 feet
> ACTIVITIES: hiking, backpacking
> BEST: April to October
> MAP: Custom Correct: Seven Lakes Basin—Hoh
> Map on page 227

LOVERS LANE LOOP
> LOOP TRIP: 6 miles
> TRAIL DIFFICULTY: moderate
> ELEVATION GAIN: 340 feet
> ACTIVITIES: hiking, backpacking, fishing
> BEST: April to October
> MAP: Custom Correct: Seven Lakes Basin—Hoh

If you miss this short walk, you are missing the essence of the entire area. The trail passes through superb rain forest to reach a timelessly beautiful falls. You can even camp at the falls turning the simple hike into a simple backpack.

The 2-mile round trip to the falls is an easy walk on a wide, well-graded trail with enough bridges, slugs, ferns, and odd fungi to keep even toddlers interested. The old shelter near the falls provides an excellent rest or play area for those in need. Don't be surprised if the preschoolers are more interested in the shelter than the falls.

From US 101, drive northeast on the Sol Duc Hot Springs Road 14.4 miles to the road end parking area (1,900 feet). From this point it is an easy walk upvalley to the falls.

If looking for a longer trip, try Lovers Lane Loop. This hike may be started from your campsite or the amphitheater parking lot. Pack a towel and swimsuit and watch how fast the hike goes when you promise a swim in the hot spring near the end.

For the Lovers Lane Loop, start at the amphitheater parking area located 13.1 miles upvalley from US 101 (1,650 feet). Walk past the amphitheater to the campground. Stay right on the paved road through Loop A to find a trail at the far end which leads to Loop B. When you reach pavement a second time, stay right and walk to the far end of the campground where a well-marked trail heads up the forested valley. At 1.7 miles from the parking area, the loop route joins the main trail to Sol Duc Hot Springs. The forest becomes even thicker and moss is the predominate life form. Green, green, green, with a few crystal-clear creeks keeping the scene from becoming monotonous. For anyone who enjoys flower identification, look for the forest beauties like trillium in the spring and dogwood in the summer.

The shelter and an intersection are reached 2.4 miles from the amphitheater. Go right and descend toward the roaring falls. The rocks below the viewing area look tempting for play along the river; however, a slip would be fatal. Walk upriver if looking for water access.

Beyond the falls, the loop trail heads to the right for 0.1 mile to an intersection. Once again, take the right fork, heading downvalley on Lovers Lane. This trail is rough with big steps, rocks, and roots. A bridge and beautiful falls

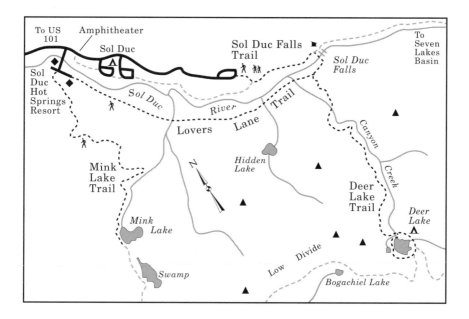

Small creek along trail to Sol Duc Falls

at Canyon Creek are the next attraction, located at the 2.9-mile point. The way continues through the forest, passing large trees and head-high ferns.

You will walk right along the edge of the hot spring resort area at 5.3 miles. It's fun to watch the swimmers and even more fun to walk on the final 0.1 mile to the end of the trail then go jump in yourself. To complete the loop, follow the road past the resort cabins then across the Sol Duc River. Go right at the end of the bridge and head back upvalley. Several small hot springs can be found on the gravel bar at the edge of the river, opposite the RV campground. Peek down the old metal pipe and watch the bubbles roll to the surface before returning to the amphitheater parking lot at 6 miles.

North Fork Trail

ROUND TRIP: 2.4 miles
TRAIL DIFFICULTY: moderate
ELEVATION GAIN: 800 feet
ACTIVITIES: hiking, fishing
BEST: May to October
MAP: Custom Correct: Lake Crescent—Happy Lake Ridge
Map on page 225

A quiet picnic spot away from the general throng of tourists, a glimpse of the rain forest, and a chance to relax along the edge of a frothy river: The North Fork Trail has all these virtues plus the added incentive of being short. In just 1.2 miles you may set out your sandwiches in a grassy meadow overlooking the emerald ponds of the North Fork Sol Duc River.

From US 101, drive 8.6 miles up Sol Duc Hot Springs Road. Park on the right side of the road opposite the trailhead (1,475 feet).

The trail begins climbing immediately, heading through heavy timber and up fern-cloaked hillsides. After 0.6 mile and a gain of 400 feet, reach the crest of the ridge and, like the bear that went over the mountain, head down the other side.

The descent is steady through a narrow drainage filled with towering devil's club. If any of the group are bored you can tell them the story of the hiker who tried using leaves for toilet paper. This hiker looked around and picked the biggest leaf he could find—devil's club. It's a true story; I heard it from the ranger who was on duty that day and had to pick out the thorns. (On second thought, maybe don't tell the story.)

The trail reaches the North Fork Sol Duc River at 1 mile and crosses it on a log bridge. Head upvalley another 0.1 mile to the meadows where, if you do not see deer or elk, you may at least see signs of their passing. After lunch, continue upvalley for another 0.1 mile to a point where the river brushes the edge of the trail. This is a great place to look for spawning salmon in spring or fall.

MORE ACTIVITIES
Map on page 225

Abandoned Nature Trail: Located 5.1 miles from US 101 up Sol Duc Hot Springs Road, this 0.1-mile loop is not only short, but also fun. Without guides or signs, walkers are free to use their own imagination to supply information, factual or fanciful, about the trees and moss-covered soil. The trailhead is a little hard to find. Park on the right side of the road before the sign marked TRAIL. The trail is on the left.

River Trail: This short walk goes 15 yards through the forest to the confluence of the Sol Duc and the South Fork Rivers. The cascades here are worth the walk any time; however, when the salmon are coming upriver, this is a magical location. The trail is located 5.6 miles from US 101 up Sol Duc Hot Springs Road, on the right side of the road. A parking area has been provided.

Salmon Cascades: This is a definite must stop in the spring and fall when the salmon are running. It is a thrill to spot one of these beautiful fish on their mandated journey up the river. The Salmon Cascades are located 7.5 miles up the Sol Duc Hot Springs Road from US 101. This is a popular stop and the parking area is well signed.

Ancient Groves Nature Trail: This is a 0.5-mile stroll through a lowland forest community. The skunk cabbage are beautiful in April or May. The trail begins 9.2 miles from US 101 on Sol Duc Hot Springs Road. A second parking area and trail access is located 0.2 mile beyond.

Mink Lake: This surprisingly delightful lake is set in an open basin between forested hills. The hike is 5 miles round trip on a challenging trail that climbs steadily, gaining 1,500 feet of elevation. The lake is a great day hike; however, there are several official campsites if you desire a longer stay. The trailhead is located 13.6 miles up the Sol Duc Hot Springs Road in the resort area. Parking may be difficult by the afternoon. Alternate parking is found at the amphitheater.

Deer Lake: This 8-mile round trip is a great day or overnight hike. See backpack trips section for more information.

The Northwest Corner:
Ozette and Neah Bay

Backpacking, boat camping, boating, car camping, fishing, hiking, swimming

Miles of narrow and twisting roads must be driven to reach either the Ozette access or the Neah Bay access to Olympic National Park. The long drive is discouraging and certainly does not fit into the schedule of anyone trying to see the park in just a couple of days.

Despite the exhausting road trip, these are extraordinarily popular areas. At Ozette, the small, fourteen-site campground fills up every night in July and August. A nearby resort offers additional campsites as well as a small store and deli.

The 3.1-mile hike from Ozette to Cape Alava is exceeded in popularity only by the 2.8-mile hike to Sand Point. Both beach trails are certified easy to walk by the thousands of children who annually find the prospect of a sandy beach at the ocean seductive enough to complete these hikes at a young age (5-year-olds are as common as sandfleas). The beach is also a popular destination for backpackers—so popular that the park has set a quota of eighty persons per day from June through mid-September, and backpacking permits are hard to get without advance reservations. A 9-mile loop can be made by tying Cape Alava to Sand Point with a 3-mile beach walk, which passes a famous group of pictographs called Wedding Rock. There is also a "hole-in-the-rock" to be explored, and deer to be spotted lounging among the driftwood to ensure the interest of the entire family.

Ozette Lake is ideal for canoe and kayak trips. Boaters have access to several excellent campsites and two trails to the ocean. The lake is shallow so even non-swimmers have a chance for a good splash. Fishermen are generally well-rewarded for their efforts.

Neah Bay is the jump-off point to the very popular Shi-Shi Beach and beautiful Point of Arches area. No park facilities exist at Neah Bay. The trailhead is on Makah lands and they control parking and access. The town of Neah Bay is the home of the Makah Cultural and Research Center, a wonderful museum that houses artifacts from the 500-year-old ruins of Ozette Village. The museum provides an amazing glimpse of the incredibly rich and varied culture of the native coastal people and is worth the drive. At the tip of Cape Flattery a 0.5-mile trail tunnels through a tangle of rich coastal forest to the most northwestern point of the continental United States. Viewing platforms overlook massive

Beach time near Sand Point

sea caves along the coastal cliffs and vigilant viewers will often spot puffins fishing in the offshore waters.

Lodging is available at Neah Bay, but reservations are recommended as the motels are often full during fishing season. Camping is available at several private camp areas.

Ozette Lake—Boat Trip

ROUND TRIP TO TIVOLI ISLAND: 14 miles
PADDLING DIFFICULTY: easy
ACTIVITIES: boating, camping, fishing, hiking
BEST: March to October
MAPS: Custom Correct: North Olympic Coast
Map on page 233

Canoes, kayaks, sailboats, and powerboats take advantage of the exploration opportunities on this grand lake. Although the scenery is less than remarkable and clearcuts are visible on all but the west side of the lake, camping is excellent, swimming delightful, and fishing good. However, it is the hiking opportunities that really make this trip unique and exciting. Not only do you have the chance to paddle and explore, you also have the opportunity to walk to one of the most beautiful wilderness coasts in America.

Drive US 101 west from Port Angeles 5 miles, then turn right on Highway 112, signed to Joyce and Neah Bay. Pass by Sekiu at 36 miles and continue another 3 miles. Turn left at a well-signed junction for the final 21 miles to the road's end at Ozette.

If planning to be out for one or more nights, pick up a backcountry permit at the ranger station (no reservations required, just a fee). Water bottles and containers can be filled near the beach trailhead. Unload at the launch area then take your car back to the hikers' parking area where you have to pay a fee to park.

If you are on a normal schedule, you will be ready to go about noon, right in time to be blasted by the afternoon winds. If there are whitecaps on the water, wait until they die down in late afternoon or early evening. If the water is just a little bit rough, hug the west shore.

Eagle Point is the first jut of land on the west side of the lake. The water is very shallow here and the waves can really roll. When whitecaps are present, pull in to shore. Campsites are scenically placed on the point if you end up spending the night.

Beyond Eagle Point, the water remains rough for a mile until you round

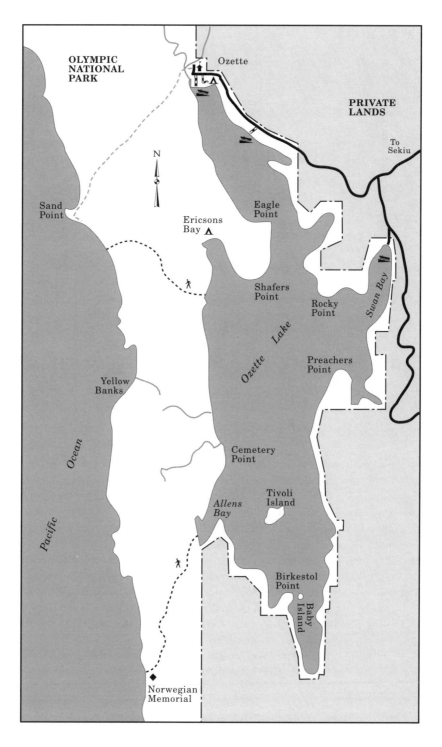

Family canoeing near Tivoli Island in Ozette Lake

Shafers Point and can duck into Ericsons Bay. At the north end of the bay is a beach and campground with privy, fire grates, picnic tables, and wire for hanging food. HANG YOUR FOOD! The varmints (mice, chipmunks, raccoons, deer, and bear) are real pests. Urinate only in the privy; deer are attracted to the salt and will hang around the camp area looking for guys using trees.

Just 0.7 mile south of Ericsons Bay campground is a 2.2-mile trail to the Pacific Ocean. The trailhead is marked by a white sign and is easily visible from the water. The trail is well maintained; however, the boardwalks are narrow. The trail ends at a sandy beach just 0.6 mile south of Sand Point.

Continuing down the lake, campsites are located south of Cemetery Point and at the head of Allens Bay, and there is a primo location on the sandy spit at the northeast corner of Tivoli Island.

The second trail to the ocean starts at the southern end of Allens Bay, just north of the slough area. This 2.4-mile trail was abandoned in 1994 and is deteriorating fast. Long legs and a tolerance for brush are needed. Watch for rotting wood on the old boardwalks and bridges. The trail ends at the Norwegian Memorial on a section of coast that is prickly with sea stacks.

Cape Alava, Sand Point, and Loop Hike

CAPE ALAVA AND SAND POINT
   ROUND TRIP: up to 6.2 miles
   ACTIVITIES: beach fun, wildlife
   TRAIL DIFFICULTY: moderate
   ELEVATION GAIN: 500 feet
   BEST: March to October
   MAP: Custom Correct: North Olympic Coast
   Map on page 236

LOOP HIKE
   LOOP HIKE: 9.2 miles
   ACTIVITIES: beach fun, wildlife, petrogylphs
   TRAIL DIFFICULTY: moderate
   ELEVATION GAIN: 500 feet
   BEST: March to October

This is the best hike in the state for families. Families with very young children (three to five years old) should plan to do the hike as a backpack and keep the distance traveled per day to a minimum. The six-to-ten age group can do the Cape Alava or Sand Point trip in a day, provided there is plenty of play time at the beach. Older kids, age eleven and above, can generally do the entire loop in a single day.

The trails to Cape Alava and Sand Point are fascinating. Both trails are boardwalks for almost the entire distance. The boardwalks turn into bridges at swamps and streams, with occasional glimpses of muck, gluck, and giant skunk cabbages. Both trails end at excellent campsites that are overrun with raccoons. (If you do not see one, try laying your pack down for a couple of minutes and waiting behind a tree.) You will also see deer, especially at Cape Alava, where they like to nap among the drift logs along shore.

Drive to Ozette Lake (see directions in boat trip earlier) and park. Pay the parking fee and, if backpacking, the permit fee and per-night fee, then put all the fees behind you and head out for some fun.

The trail begins by crossing Ozette River on an arched bridge then heading into the forest. After a couple hundred feet the trail divides. To the right is Cape Alava. Before long the boardwalk begins. The boardwalk is tiring to the feet, but well appreciated by those who remember wading through the muck before it was all boarded over. Use caution; the boards can be slippery when wet and a skating rink when frosty.

The trail heads northwest, climbing over low ridges and diving down steep stairs to boggy little ravines. At the 2-mile point, cross Alhstroms Prairie, part natural bog, part pasture for Alhstroms's abandoned farm. The buildings have disappeared, but it is fun to linger a moment or two and wonder how a farmer thought he could survive in this jungle.

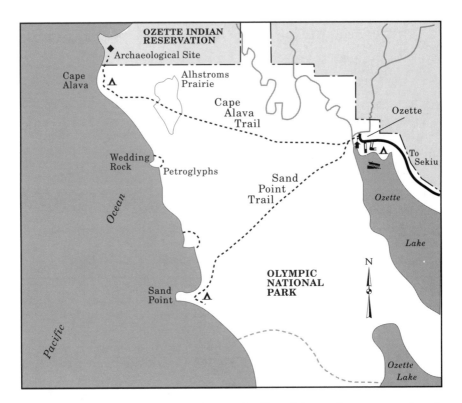

At 2.9 miles the trail leaves the boardwalk and descends to a grassy bench at the edge of the beach. This area was inhabited by the Makahs for several thousand years before hikers and campers started to visit. If you follow the beach or trail north 0.3 mile, you will find the ranger station and Ozette Village site where archaeologists have dug up houses buried in a mudslide 500 years ago. Their findings are housed in a museum at Neah Bay; however, you may visit a memorial just north of the ranger's residence here.

Sand Point is reached by a 2.9-mile tramp on the boardwalk. The trail stays in the trees until it reaches the south side of the point. Numerous campsites are found throughout the area. Hang up all valuables as soon as you set your pack down. Raccoons have been known to undo pack zippers. On warm days, kids will probably make a beeline straight for the water, complain about the temperature, and refuse to come out until bribed with a favorite food. Note: No fires are allowed at Sand Point.

If hiking the entire loop, the 3.3-mile section between Sand Point and Cape Alava is the most challenging. The rocky beach makes for slow walking; additionally, the tide pools are alluring, the forty or more petrogylphs at Wedding Rock require time to thoroughly explore, and the rock with a hole in it is entrancing. Avoid hiking at high tide, when it can be difficult, if not impossible, to get around the rocky points. Several nice campsites are passed en route.

Shi-Shi Beach and Point of Arches

ROUND TRIP: 8 miles
TRAIL DIFFICULTY: moderate
ELEVATION GAIN: 200 feet
ACTIVITIES: beach play, tide-pool exploration, photography
BEST: May to October
MAP: Custom Correct: North Olympic Coast
Map on page 238

This is an extremely family friendly beach hike. For kids, there are miles of sandy beaches, tide pools full of anemones, starfish, and crabs, rock arches, and caves to crawl through. For adults, there are all of the above as well as birds nesting on offshore rocks and an exotic mixture of sea stacks and wave-sculptured rocks.

This is a wonderful place for a day hike and an even better location for a backpack trip. Backpackers need to note that the largest sites are located just behind a protective wall of spruce trees at the 1.5-mile point, where the trail first descends to the beach. The campsites at Petroleum and Willoughby Creeks are limited in size. Most have room for one small tent, the rare site being large enough for a larger, four- or five-person tent.

The easiest and safest trail to Shi-Shi Beach and the Point of Arches is from Makah Nation lands at Neah Bay. The only access through Olympic National Park is from Ozette and requires a difficult river crossing. Families with experienced, high school-aged kids may enjoy the challenge. Families with younger kids should not consider this access.

When starting the trip from Neah Bay, please remember that you must cross private lands before you reach the park. The Makah Nation has been

Keeping feet dry on a beach hike near Sand Point

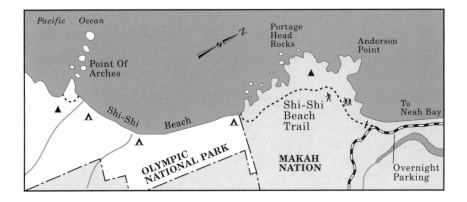

exceedingly generous in allowing access over their lands. Please follow all posted rules and park in official areas only.

The trail can be extremely muddy, drying out occasionally in August. Young children should have rubber boots. Sturdy shoes or waterproof hiking boots are a must for everyone else.

Drive US 101 west from Port Angeles 5 miles then turn right on Highway 112, signed to Joyce and Neah Bay. Pass by Sekiu at 36 miles. Continue another 18.1 miles to the west end of Neah Bay. At the base of a hill the road divides; go left following signs to Fish Hatchery and Hobuck Beach. After 2.5 miles go left on a dirt road, which crosses the Waatch River to meet the Truck Route. Go right, following signs to the Fish Hatchery. After 4.3 miles the road makes a 90-degree bend to the left. Straight ahead is a gate, a warning about car vandalism, and a No Parking sign. Unload people and gear here, then drive back 0.2 mile to the first house and park in the backyard. Pay the per-day fee—a reasonable $4 in 1997—then head out.

The trail begins on an old logging road that climbs over Portage Head. When faced with giant mud holes, look for bypass trails on the right. At 1.5 miles the trail enters Olympic National Park. Backpackers are required to fill out a self-registration permit and mail in their fee. The trail then plummets to the first camping area and Shi-Shi Beach. This is an extremely steep descent; be prepared to help the younger children and show them how to grab onto roots for support.

Once down, head for the beach. If your family is up to a bit of rock scrambling, go north over rocky ribs to impressive sea stacks, tide pools, and a shipwreck at the south end of Portage Head. Watch for birds nesting and swimming offshore, as well as an occasional harbor seal in the water.

To the south is 2.5 miles of sandy beach. When the tide is out, the damp sand offers easy walking all the way to the double-headed Point of Arches. You cannot mistake this place; there are arches and caves everywhere. After passing cliffs for a mile the terrain levels enough to permit camping. Reliable sources of water are located at Petroleum and Willoughby Creeks.

Observation platform on the Cape Flattery Viewpoint Trail

MORE ACTIVITIES

Makah Cultural and Research Center Museum: This nationally recognized museum houses the artifacts found at the Ozette village site. The discovery of the mud-covered village is considered to be one of the most significant archaeological finds in North America. The museum shows a representation of traditional Makah life throughout the year and is a fascinating place to spend an hour. Young children may be quickly bored; "touch" areas are limited and rooms are dark.

Cape Flattery Viewpoint Trail: This wonderful, 1-mile round-trip walk to the northwest tip of the continental United States has something for every age group. There is a boardwalk trail for young hikers, and vistas, exotic birds, and pounding surf for everyone else. The four principle viewpoints are located on top of rocky cliffs and are surrounded by fencing for safety. A picnic area is located in the trees.

In 1997, trail signage was missing. To reach the trailhead, drive to the west end of Neah Bay and follow the paved road left for 3.5 miles. When the pavement ends continue on a wide but rough dirt road for another 4.7 miles. The parking area is on the left. The trail begins by descending. Stay on the widest trail at each intersection.

Mora

Backpacking, hiking, nature walks, sandy beaches, tide pools

Perched on the edge of one of the last remaining stretches of wilderness coast in the continental United States, beaches near Mora are both wild and scenic. Sea stacks dot the coast, tide pools abound along the rocky shore, and beaches are covered with colorful pebbles and sculptured drift logs. Erosion is unusually rapid in this area and the shoreline is in a constant battle with the ocean. Sitka spruce cling to what soil they have and turn their backs to the water, creating a dense wall of vegetation at the high-tide line.

Ranger-led walk from Rialto Beach to Hole-in-the-Wall

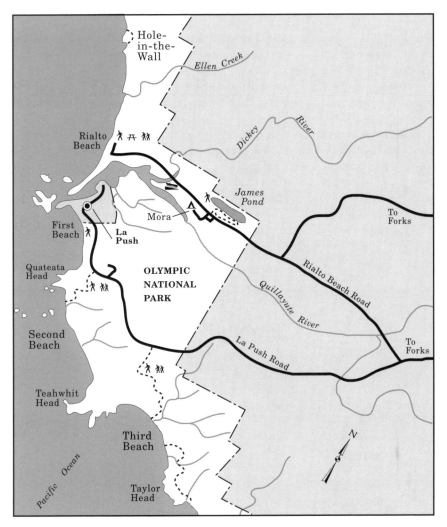

The rocks and sea stacks along the shore are part of a large marine sanctuary designed to protect nesting birds as well as the sea lions, otters, and whales that use these waters. Overhead, bald eagles are seen circling and hunting for prey.

Although immensely popular, the Mora area lacks the easy coast access found at Kalaloch. The terrain makes trails to Second and Third Beaches challenging, with steep descents and long climbs. First Beach and Rialto Beach are easy to access, but, except at low tide, the walking is difficult. It is suggested that you save this area until the children are all old enough to be sturdy walkers.

Activities at Mora revolve around the ocean. Hiking the beaches fills the days of most visitors. Ranger walks to the tide pools at Hole-in-the-Wall are extremely interesting and insightful. When the weather is inclement, walking the trails to Second and Third Beaches, through incredible tangles of coastal forest, may be more enjoyable than exploring the windblown coast. In addition to the beach trails, there is a short nature loop to a lily pad–covered pond and the Slough Trail along the Quillayute River.

Accommodations can be found at the nearby Indian Reservation in the town of La Push, scenically located on First Beach, or inland 18 miles at the town of Forks. Restaurants, grocery stores, and Laundromats are all located in Forks.

Mora Campground is situated on the Quillayute River, 2 miles from the coast, and is open year-round. This forested area has ninety-four sites and frequently fills on weekends. Campfire programs are offered during the summer months on Friday, Saturday, and Sunday nights. A small ranger station at the campground is open during the summer with rangers available to answer any questions you may have. Private campgrounds with showers may be found at Forks and La Push.

Second Beach

ROUND TRIP: 1.5 miles
TRAIL DIFFICULTY: moderate
ELEVATION GAIN: 240 feet
ACTIVITIES: hiking, backpacking, beach exploration
BEST: all year
MAP: Custom Correct: South Olympic Coast
Map on page 241

On stormy winter days, Second Beach is a wild place, washed by pounding surf, blown by howling winds, and sculpted by bits of flying sand. In the calm of summer, the more ferocious forces of nature are easy to overlook as you laze in the sun and build a sand castle or two. The high cliffs and mudstone bluffs surrounding the beach isolate the visitor from the surrounding world, focusing attention on the peacefulness and beauty of the here and now. At the north end of the beach is a nearly perfect rock arch. Off shore, birds can be seen squabbling over territorial rights on Crying Lady Rock. Beyond, the Quillayute Needles are scattered across the horizon like a fence to keep boats from falling off the end of the world.

Amidst this beautiful scenery, look for children having a great time on the sand. Building dams on the small stream to the south of the trail is a favorite pastime. Don't expect them to look toward the water; dams are best built facing inland. Seashells do not survive long in the rough waters off Second Beach; however, rocks and sculptured wood are fun to look at. Use caution if entering the water: Currents, submerged logs, and undertow make swimming hazardous.

Several campsites can be found in small nooks and crannies along the beach. Bring as much of your own potable water as possible as water availability is limited.

Drive 2 miles north of Forks on US 101, then west toward La Push for 14 miles. The trailhead is located on the left as the road makes its final drop to First Beach and La Push town center.

The trail starts by skirting a hatchery then heads up a forested hillside. After 0.1 mile enter the national park where the trail soon levels off. This section can be very muddy. If you have not already done so, check the tide chart at the backpackers registration station.

A few feet beyond the registration board, the trail turns into a boardwalk

No time to look at scenery, there are dams to be built.

and heads down 130-plus steps. These steps are slippery when wet; use caution. Once down, pass a pit toilet then prepare for the final hurdle: a balancing act across the 100 feet or so of beach logs tossed up by winter storms.

Once on the sand, the beach extends more than 1.5 miles to the south. Watch the tides or you may get stranded. Do not try to go around the headlands at the north or south end of the bay—both are very dangerous.

Hole-in-the-Wall

ROUND TRIP: 3 miles
TRAIL DIFFICULTY: moderate
ELEVATION GAIN: 4 feet
ACTIVITIES: hiking, backpacking, ranger walks, tide pools
BEST: all year
MAP: Custom Correct: North Olympic Coast
Map on page 241

Pounding surf, tide pools teeming with life, a natural tunnel, sea stacks, rocks to clamber over, otters, sea lions, whales, and eagles soaring overhead: Everything a beach-exploring family could want, except solitude.

This easy day hike can be turned into an easy backpack. Camping is allowed

Hole-in-the-Wall

north of Ellen Creek, so you only have to walk a short mile to have a great overnighting experience. Be warned—these scenic campsites are popular and fill early.

Plan your hike for low tide. During high tide you may have to scramble over logs to make your way along the beach. Rangers lead daily walks to Hole-in-the-Wall. Times vary. Check at Mora Campground for scheduled walks and current tide tables.

Drive 2 miles north from Forks then turn west on La Push Road. After 9 miles go right on Mora Campground–Rialto Beach Road for a final 5 miles to road's end at the Rialto Beach parking area.

Follow the paved trail from the bathroom to the beach, passing through the old campground-turned-picnic-area that is soon to become shore. Where the trail ends, drop down to the beach and head north. Each large rock deserves exploration, and your walk will be interrupted by numerous checks for octopi and sea stars. At 0.9 mile, Ellen Creek cuts across the beach sands. By mid-summer, feet will splash across the creek without noticing it. However, for much of the year the creek is a major obstacle. The safest way to cross is to remove shoes, roll pants up to the knees, and wade across. The alternate method is to walk upstream to find a log on which to cross, then return to the beach on a well-trodden trail. Remember, logs are often slippery.

Beyond Ellen Creek, a pair of fang-like sea stacks create shadows over the beach. Take time to clamber on the rocks before heading on around the corner for the final sandy stretch to Hole-in-the-Wall. During the winter months, when the tides rarely are low enough to allow passage through the Hole, hikers often use the steep bypass trail on the right. During the summer, the Hole is dry for several hours of the day and can easily be walked through. Beyond Hole-in-the-Wall, low tide exposes hundreds of tide pools. Being careful to walk only on bare rock or gently over the barnacles and mussels, head out to an exposed sea stack. Count the thousands of small anemones and a hundred or more colorful sea stars as you go. Look for hermit crabs in every pool as well as crabs of all other sizes.

Good hikers and rock scramblers can go beyond the Hole-in-the-Wall. Check the tide tables carefully before you round the next head. It can be a long wait for low tide.

MORE ACTIVITIES
Map on page 241

First Beach: Easy access makes this mile-long beach very popular for walking, surfing, and kayaking. This beach is mainly rocks and driftwood in the winter but does show some sand in the summer. Massive James Island and the Quillayute Needles provide a wild and scenic backdrop for beach explorers. To reach the beach, drive west from US 101 for 14.2 miles on La Push Road. Take the first turnoff on the left when the road descends to the ocean.

The road ends at a rough parking area with beach access. First Beach is also reached from the community buildings in downtown La Push.

Third Beach: Although mentioned as part of the Toleak Beach Hike (see the backpack section), Third Beach is a destination in its own right. Sea stacks, a lacy waterfall, sandy shore, and sculptured driftlogs create a true wilderness beach experience just 1.4 miles from the road. Several campsites are available. The trailhead is located 12 miles west of US 101 on the road to La Push.

James Pond: This 0.4-mile loop starts next to the ranger station at Mora Campground and ambles out to lily pad–covered James Pond. The pond is accessible from an old log that extends out onto the water. This loop is especially good for youngsters working on their Junior Ranger Activity Books.

Slough Trail: This forest trail parallels the Quillayute River, heading upstream for over a mile. At the 0.9-mile point, a side trail descends to the grassy riverbank. The trail is of most interest to fishermen. Access it from the entrance of the maintenance and residential area at Mora Campground.

Hoh Rain Forest

Backpacking, camping, hiking, nature walks, visitor center, wildlife viewing

Between the snow- and ice-coated Olympic Mountains and the frothing, churning waters of the Pacific Ocean lies a darkly shadowed jungle called the temperate rain forest. Only a small portion of this once-imposing forest has escaped the loggers' ax; these remnants are preserved in the national park.

The Hoh is one of the two wettest areas in the continental United States. (The Verlot area, also in Western Washington, is the other.) Rainfall averages 148 inches a year. Fortunately, the months of June, July, and August are relatively dry, receiving only three inches apiece, allowing for a (possibly) dry summer visit.

A large herd of Roosevelt elk lives in Olympic National Park and, during the winter, many of these big animals move into the sheltered Hoh River valley. Fall, winter, and spring are good seasons to look for elk near the Hoh Visitor Center or around the campground. Most of the herd move up to the high meadows during the summer and chances of seeing elk are reduced. Check at the visitor center for current information on the herd's location.

Favorite activities at the Hoh include checking out the displays in the visitor center and walking one or more of the three nature trails. Despite the grandeur of the forest, the activity most preferred by children is playing along the gravel bars that line the silty waters of the Hoh River. (Luckily, forest vs. river arguments can be resolved with a walk on the Spruce Nature Trail, which offers both.) The Hoh River Trail begins its 17.5-mile upvalley trek at the visitor center. The trail ends at the snout of the Blue Glacier on Mount Olympus and is considered to be one of the most beautiful hikes in the world. This trail

Elk in the rain forest

offers excellent year-round day hiking and backpacking opportunities for families with children nearing the middle school age, and for scout troops.

Other activities at the Hoh include daily ranger walks through the rain forest, campfire programs, and the Junior Ranger program.

The Hoh Campground has only eighty-nine sites, which fill up every night during the summer. The two DNR campgrounds and one private campground located just outside the park catch the overflow. Both Bogachiel State Park Campground and Rain Forest Hostel are within easy driving distance. The closest lodging is 12 miles north of the Hoh River turnoff at the town of Forks.

Hall of Mosses Nature Trail

ROUND TRIP: 0.8 mile
TRAIL DIFFICULTY: easy
ELEVATION GAIN: 150 feet
ACTIVITIES: walking, nature study
BEST: all year
MAP: park handout
Map on page 249

Massive old maples with long, flowing moss streamers reminiscent of Grandfather Time's scraggly old beard form a beautiful hall that would not be out of place in an old-world cathedral. The moss is at its rain-soaked best in the spring; however, the hall is a "must-see" at any time.

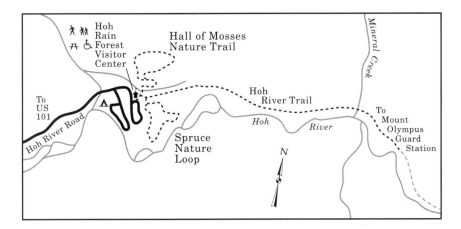

The Hall of Mosses Nature Trail travels through a temperate rain forest that has reached a venerable old age. In addition to long banners of moss trailing off massive trees, there is a beautiful understory growth of ferns, lichens, moss, and oxallis. Excellent examples of nurse logs, an important component of the rain forest, are seen, supporting trees that vary in age from seedlings to stately colonnades of mature trees.

Drive to the end of the Hoh River Road and park. Walk past the visitor center and follow the paved trail into the forest, staying left at all intersections. Stop to look for fingerlings in the small creek before heading up a steep hill to the start of the loop portion of the walk. The loop is a one-way walk to aid with traffic flow—please respect the arrows during the summer season.

Spruce Nature Loop

LOOP HIKE: 1.2 miles
TRAIL DIFFICULTY: easy
ELEVATION GAIN: 30 feet
ACTIVITIES: hiking, wildlife viewing, river play
BEST: all year
MAP: park handout
Map on page 249

The Spruce Nature Loop offers more variety but less grandeur than the Hall of Mosses. If time allows, walk both. This trail starts in the ancient forest then descends a few feet to enter a younger forest. Another short drop takes you to grassy parklands along the edge of the Hoh River, where early succession

Rain forest along the Hall of Mosses Nature Trail

vegetation such as alders, maples, and birches grow. The trail then climbs, almost imperceptibly, back to the ancient forest, completing a giant circle of life.

Elk are occasionally seen along the river and their presence is felt everywhere. Look for prints and droppings along the trail. You may also sense their presence when you look at the cropped ferns and grasses that serve as testimonial to their passing.

Drive to the end of Hoh River Road and park (580 feet). The most direct route to the Spruce Nature Trail is to follow the paved path that heads into the forest on the southeast side of the parking area. However, you can't go wrong if you start at the visitor center; all intersections are well marked.

Leave the paved trail and cross a small stream. The trail bends right then divides; to the left is the Hoh River Trail. Stay right and after a few feet go left at the start of the loop. The trail climbs over a low hill then begins its gradual descent to the river. Watch for tracks of elk as well as deer, bear, and raccoon in the soft soil. Counting nurse logs and trees that were raised by nurse logs can keep the entire family busy.

At 0.8 mile, the trail reaches the edge of the Hoh River channel. Except during the spring floods, it is easy to walk out on the gravel river bar to the main channel. Throwing rocks, skipping stones, building small dikes, and floating drift logs are popular activities. Stay out of the water; the river current is swift and unsafe for swimming or wading. Early morning or late afternoon visitors may spot elk.

The trail heads back into the forest passing an impressive colonnade of trees. After a final study of the infinite shades of the color green, follow the trail as it loops back to the start.

MORE ACTIVITIES

Hoh River Trail: A 4-mile round-trip hike up the Hoh Valley is a great introduction to this impressive trail that begins in the rain forest and ends 19 miles later at the edge of the Blue Glacier. The meadow opposite the confluence of Tom Creek is an excellent picnic spot and turnaround point. Enjoy the park-like atmosphere created by grazing elk. Does the park pay them for their immaculate gardening efforts? If desired, you may continue for miles up this peaceful valley. At 8 miles, the Hoh River Guard Station makes an excellent campsite.

Big Spruce: This large tree is easily visible from a turnout on the Hoh River Road, located 16.4 miles east of US 101. Big Spruce merits at least a quick look.

Hoh Spring Interpretive Trail: Designed by a private timber company, this 0.2-mile trail showcases their efforts to rehabilitate streams in clearcuts and aid endangered salmon runs. Although it is an easy walk, there is very little of interest here except, perhaps, for kids who have recently studied salmon streams at school. This trail is located on the Hoh River Road, 9.4 miles east of US 101.

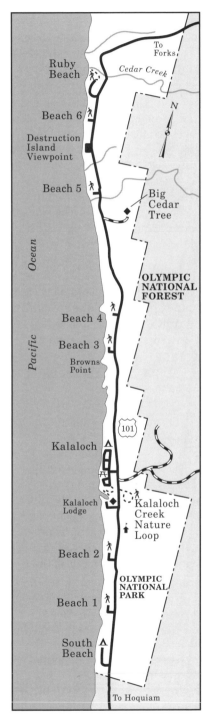

Kalaloch

Beach walking, camping, nature trails, picnicking, surf fishing, tide pools

If you are the chief vacation planner for the family, you probably already know that a trip to the beach, any beach, is a hit. For the children, there is the seemingly endless fascination of sand and surf. For the parents, there is the ultimate relaxation of a happy family entertaining themselves. The constant sound of the surf releases tensions you never even knew you had. Relaxed and rested, the entire family will find tide pool exploration fascinating and wave chasing totally invigorating.

Kalaloch has one of the most entrancing beaches on the entire Washington coast, with lots of sand for building castles and burying toes as well as plenty of rocks for sheltering tide pool gardens. The perfection of the area is marred only by the number of people who know about it. Do not expect solitude.

Despite Kalaloch's location on a remote section of the coast, there are complete resort facilities including forty cabins with kitchenettes, some overlooking the ocean. A dining room provides meals and a coffee room offers snacks. The small grocery store has all the basics and gas is available at the service station. Reservations are a must: (360) 928-3211.

For everyone else, the Kalaloch Campground has 177 campsites and usually fills every night during the summer. The overflow campground at South Beach has eighty additional, unstructured sites along the edge of the beach. The overflow area is free (in 1997), and a fantastic deal. Water containers may be filled at Kalaloch and bags of garbage may be put in the dumpsters there. The wind rolls straight off the water, so bring a sturdy tent and strong tent pegs that can be hammered into the hard ground. The only thing South Beach lacks is a paved road for roller blading and bike riding.

Campfire programs are held nightly at Kalaloch Campground in July and August and rangers lead daily tide pool walks. In addition to exploring the seven beaches, try a 1.2-mile-long nature walk and a short stroll to a big cedar. The local ranger station is small; however, the staff can answer any questions you may have about the park in general or the Kalaloch area in particular.

Kalaloch Creek Nature Loop

LOOP TRIP: 1.2 miles
TRAIL DIFFICULTY: easy
ELEVATION GAIN: 30 feet
ACTIVITY: walking
BEST: all year
MAP: Custom Correct: South Olympic Coast
Map on page 251

Just a few feet from the vast openness of the Pacific Ocean lies a nearly impenetrable tangle of vegetation. This wall-like mat of salt-hardy spruce protects the plants behind it from the ocean spray, creating an environment where cedars, hemlocks, and firs can grow to giant proportions. Although the largest trees were harvested years ago, the young, second-growth forest has already reached an impressive size.

The nature loop is accessed from Kalaloch Campground. If not camping, leave your vehicle at the picnic area and walk south through Loop A. At the restroom, the road divides. Stay left and continue to the trailhead.

Just a few feet from the start, the trail crosses US 101. Use caution; most cars are not prepared to stop. Once across, follow the well-signed trail into the forest. Giving imaginary names to the trees you pass is a fun way to keep the disenchanted from staging a sit-down strike. Be sure to have a lot of synonyms for the word "tall" at the tip of your tongue: lofty, giant, towering.

At the 0.3-mile point, the trail divides and the loop portion begins; go left. The trail heads into a marshy area where a boardwalk was built to keep hikers' feet dry. The trail dips then climbs, and soon after begins a broad loop around a meadow near the edge of the Kalaloch Creek. To visit the creek, you must leave the trail and follow a well-trodden path through the brush. By midsummer

Exploring the rocks at Beach 4

the creek level is low enough to expose a rocky beach. Back on the loop, the trail continues through the forest, passing a viewpoint of a tree with giant burrows. The loop closes at 0.9 mile. Go straight ahead to return to the campsite.

Beach Walks

ROUND TRIP: up to 17 miles
TRAIL DIFFICULTY: easy
ELEVATION GAIN: up to 200 feet
ACTIVITY: beach exploration
BEST: all year
MAP: Custom Correct: South Olympic Coast
Map on page 251

Long or short, beach walks at Kalaloch can be tailored to fit your desires. At low tide you may walk the entire 6-mile stretch from Ruby Beach to Kalaloch Campground. South of the campground are 2.5 more miles of broad sandy beaches before reaching private property at the Quinault Indian Reservation boundary. The beach access trails range from 30 feet to 100 yards long, acceptable distances for even the most adamant anti-walker.

Parking spaces are located along the edge of US 101. Most of the parking spots have spaces for a couple of cars only. Larger parking areas are found at Kalaloch Campground, Beach 4, and Ruby Beach.

Beaches 1 and 2 are located south of the Kalaloch resort area. The access trails go from US 101 through a wall of salt-tolerant Sitka spruce to sandy beaches. Beach wood abounds and fires are permitted as long as they are started away from the logs.

Beaches 3 through 6 are located north of the Kalaloch resort. The Beach 4 trail ends on a sandstone rock outcropping riddled with hundreds of small holes created by the boring of piddock clams. The rock outcrop to the north has excellent tide pools. The beach is also a popular smelt netting area, an interesting activity to watch if you have never seen it before.

Ruby Beach, at the north end of the beach strip, is the most exotic. Cedar Creek empties into the ocean here, creating a small cove with a couple of sea stacks for drama. Winter visitors should use caution: At high tide the beach access trail may flood, leaving beach visitors stranded on the beach logs or forcing them to wade the frigid waters to return to their cars.

MORE ACTIVITIES

Big Cedar Tree: Although this tree does not hold any records for size, it was remarkable enough for the park to build a road 0.3 mile from US 101 so visitors can gawk at it. The access road is located 4.7 miles north of Kalaloch Campground on US 101.

Queets

Fishing, hiking, primitive camping

Queets is one of the least-visited areas in Olympic National Park. This quiet and intensely green valley lies at the heart of the temperate rain forest and is an ideal place for thoughtful contemplation of the glories of the world and the incredible vitality of nature. Obviously, it is not the best location for the average, active pre-teenager.

The list of amenities at Queets is a short one: a primitive, fifteen-site campground with tables, a pit toilet, a rock-covered river bar, and no drinking water.

Two trails start at the roadend. Sams River Trail (also called the 3-Mile Trail) is a must for every visitor. Queets Valley Trail, which heads upvalley to some of the most dramatic forest in the Olympics, begins with a dangerous ford of the Queets River. Even at optimal conditions, the river bed is slippery and the cold water very fast moving—not recommended for families with young children. The valley trail is one of the places that should wait until the kids are sturdy teenagers and can hold their own in the swift current.

Sams River Trail

Drive US 101 south from Kalaloch 13 miles or north from Amanda Park 18.5 miles, then head east on Queets River Road. (This dirt road is well graded but often very muddy.) The campground is reached at 14.4 miles, the end of the road is another 0.2 mile beyond.

Sams River Trail

LOOP TRIP: 2.7 miles
TRAIL DIFFICULTY: easy
ELEVATION GAIN: none
ACTIVITY: hiking
BEST: all year
MAPS: Custom Correct: Queets Valley
Map on page 256

From overgrown arbors hung with long streamers of moss that look like entrances to decrepit troll houses, to hidden glades of thick grass where settlers once tried to farm—Sams River Trail is a great introduction to the history and ecology of the Queets Valley. The settlers soon became discouraged by the immense work required to clear enough land for crops to grow among the massive trees. The abandoned fields are now favorite haunts of elk and deer. Hikers have a chance of spotting these animals, even during the summer.

Sams River Trail is little more than a path hacked through the dense brush. Expect a considerable amount of mud after any storm. Waterproof footwear is recommended at all times.

In this description, the hike begins at the end of the road; however, the trail may be picked up at the campground or the ranger station. From the end of the road, walk past the pit toilet then follow the narrow trail through the dense underbrush along Sams River. After 0.2 mile the trail bends right and heads into a forest of evergreens, alders, and maples. Watch for signs of elk—prints and droppings—as you go.

At 1.5 miles the trail meets the main road at the edge of a large clearing.

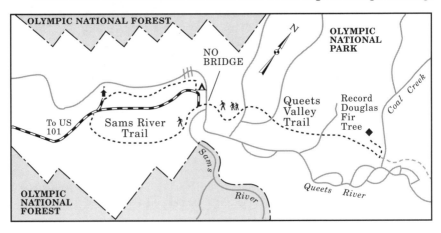

Look carefully for elk and deer, then cross the road and walk to the ranger station. Just before the cabin, take the first trail on the right and begin the 1.1-mile trek back upvalley. This trail passes several huge cedar stumps which serve as reminders of what the forest was like when the first settlers arrived. At 2.6 miles the trail meets the road and ends. Go left and walk the road for the final 0.2 mile back to the trailhead to close the loop.

Quinault

Backpacking, camping, canoeing, fishing, hiking, kayaking

For family adventuring, the Quinault is mighty close to perfect. Located at the southwest corner of the park, this is the heart of the rain forest and, at the same time, it's only 30 miles from the ocean beaches. Just outside the park boundary lies Quinault Lake, the location of several resorts, the most renowned being the Quinault Lake Lodge. If resorts are not your style, take your pick from three forest service campgrounds, three national park campgrounds, and one private campground, all located near the lake.

Hiking is the most popular activity in the Quinault area. Most of the trails meander through the moss-hung forests, providing wondrous looks at the temperate rain forest. These trails range from 0.5 mile to 8 miles in length; however, if you are looking for something more strenuous, you can continue on an extended backpack to the Enchanted Valley, or climb to the 4,492-foot summit of Colonel Bob. The 28-mile drive, or mountain bike ride, around Quinault Lake is

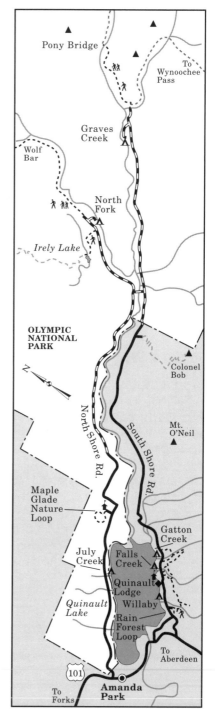

an interesting jaunt, as long as you add a few stops to check out waterfalls, size yourself up against the world's largest spruce tree, look for elk in the meadows, visit the national park visitor center, and walk the Maple Glade Rain Forest Nature Loop.

The Quinault area is located 44 miles north of Hoquiam and 30 miles southeast of Kalaloch. If camping during the summer months, it is best to arrive early to secure a site. The three forest service campgrounds have a combined total of only fifty-five sites. The three national park campgrounds have a total of sixty-seven sites; the thirty sites at July Creek are walk-ins, and the small, no-fee, seven-site North Fork Campground is without water. The private Rain Forest Resort on the south shore has thirty-one additional sites and accepts motor homes.

During the summer months, rangers lead hikes in the Quinault Lake area every weekend. Choose between a walk through the rain forest or a walk and discussion to learn about geology along the lakeshore. Also on weekends, evening programs are given at Quinault Lake Lodge and are open to everyone.

Quinault Rain Forest Loop Trails

RAIN FOREST NATURE TRAIL
    LOOP TRIP: 0.5 mile
    TRAIL DIFFICULTY: easy
    ELEVATION GAIN: 50 feet
    ACTIVITIES: walking, nature study
    BEST: all year
    MAP: Custom Correct: Quinault—Colonel Bob
    Map on page 259

QUINAULT RAIN FOREST LOOP TRAIL
    LOOP TRIP: 4 miles or more
    TRAIL DIFFICULTY: moderate
    ELEVATION GAIN: 300 feet
    ACTIVITY: hiking
    BEST: all year
    MAP: Custom Correct: Quinault—Colonel Bob

Loops within loops help you customize your exploration of the Quinault Rain Forest. This popular forest service trail system is located off South Shore Road, 1.6 miles east of US 101. The parking lot/picnic area is usually a busy place. When full, continue on another mile and park at the forest service office.

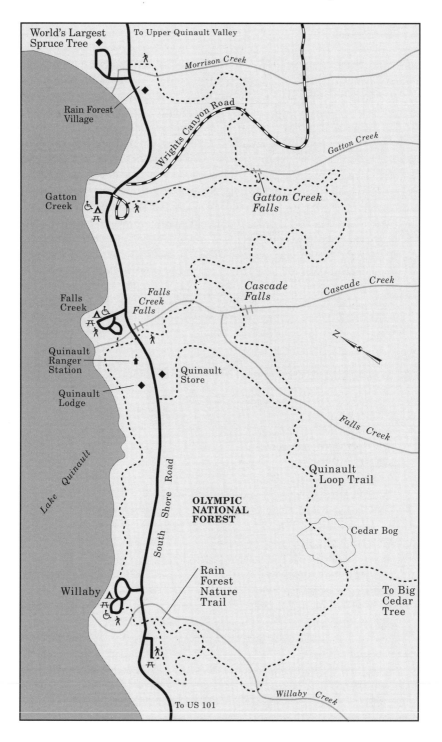

World's Largest Spruce Tree ◆

To Upper Quinault Valley

Morrison Creek

Rain Forest Village

Wrights Canyon Road

Gatton Creek

Gatton Creek

Gatton Creek Falls

Gatton Creek

Falls Creek Falls

Cascade Falls

Cascade Creek

Falls Creek

Quinault Ranger Station

Quinault Store

Quinault Lodge

Falls Creek

Falls Creek

Quinault Loop Trail

Lake Quinault

South Shore Road

OLYMPIC NATIONAL FOREST

Cedar Bog

Rain Forest Nature Trail

To Big Cedar Tree

Willaby

To US 101

Willaby Creek

The Rain Forest Nature Trail and the Quinault Rain Forest Loop Trail begin together, paralleling Willaby Creek. It is fun to peer down into the fern- and moss-draped gorge to spy the creek below. Plants grow to giant proportions; look for massive devil's club along the trail. After 0.2 mile the trail divides. The Rain Forest Nature Trail Loop heads to the right and meanders its way around some big trees before ending at the parking lot in 0.3 mile. The Quinault Loop Trail continues ahead to the first of many creek crossings.

At 1.1 miles is an intersection with the trail to Big Cedar Tree. The tree is located 1.7 miles off the main loop and can be a fun side trip for good walkers. Along the way, the trail crosses a huge old tree which spans a swamp and there is an arch tree (a tree that grew on an old stump that later rotted away, leaving a natural path right through the base of the tree) to walk through. At 1 mile, the trail makes an unbridged crossing of Willaby Creek, best done on slippery rocks, then climbs steeply to an anticlimactic end at the big old cedar tree.

Beyond the Big Cedar intersection, the Quinault Loop Trail crosses a cedar bog, a great place to check out skunk cabbage—the skunky smell is said to be in the leaves. At 2.8 miles the trail divides again. Energy allowing, the right fork is the most fun, with four bridged creek crossings before reaching the South Shore Road at 3.8 miles. Cross the road, go right a few feet, then head down to the lakeshore. Walk west pass the Quinault Lodge and some private cabins. At Willaby Campground follow the paved road through the camp area. Return to the trail to recross Willaby Creek and head back to the trailhead.

Wolf Bar

ROUND TRIP: 4.8 miles
TRAIL DIFFICULTY: moderate
ELEVATION GAIN: 60 feet
ACTIVITIES: hiking, backpacking, fishing
BEST: March to October
MAP: Custom Correct: Quinault—Colonel Bob
Map on page 257

If you can imagine a prairie with ferns and a few large trees, you will come fairly close to visualizing the North Fork Quinault River valley. Once your imagination gets going, the stately trees can turn into old mountain men clothed in fancy green buckskins with trailing fringes of moss.

Imagination aside, the goal of this hike is Wolf Bar, a backcountry camp area located on a wide gravel and rock bar along the edge of the North Fork Quinault River. The campsites, which work equally well as picnic spots, are scenically located along the river bank. On good days, several hours can be spent among the rocks on the river bar or playing hide and seek in the fern prairie.

From US 101, follow South Shore Road around Quinault Lake for 8 miles on pavement and 4.7 miles on dirt to an intersection. Go left and cross the Quinault River then take the first right and drive up the North Fork Valley 3.7 miles to road's end.

The trail heads upvalley from the end of the road, cutting across a nearly level river terrace. Ferns cover the ground, leaving scant space for grass, an occasional dogwood flower, or cow parsnip. At the end of a short 0.5 mile, the river swings across the valley, forcing the trail up the steep hillside. Before long, the river meanders back to the south side of the valley and the trail descends to the first of several groves of stately old trees.

At 1.5 miles a flood channel is crossed. Except when it is running out of control during the spring run-off, the riverbed is dry. Shortly after, climb over a low rib then descend to the very green Wolf Bar area. A small sign marks the spur trail to the camp area: however, the presence of the friendly looking gravel bar will offer an excellent clue to your location at least 0.1 mile before you get there.

Maple Glade Nature Loop

LOOP TRIP: 0.5 mile
TRAIL DIFFICULTY: easy
ELEVATION GAIN: none
ACTIVITIES: walking, nature study
BEST: all year
MAP: none
Map on page 257

Every visitor to the Quinault area should take time to feast their senses on the Maple Glade Nature Loop. The stately bearing of the moss-hung alders and maples gives the impression of walking through a venerable old-world cathedral. Light filters through the leaves as if they were the most intricate of stained glass windows. The floor of nature's cathedral is carpeted with velvety green grass and delicate ferns, kept trimmed by the caretakers (deer and elk).

The Maple Glade Nature Loop starts at the national park's Quinault River Ranger Station, located 5.9 miles off US 101 on North Shore Road. The ranger station is open 9:00 A.M. to 5:00 P.M. during the summer only. The nature trail is open the entire year.

The trail begins across the parking lot from the ranger station. Cross the marsh on a wooden bridge then enter the forest where you may pick up a trail brochure from the trailside box. Even children can sense the quiet vitality and strength that fills this glade. Some may want to shout and attempt to impose a human presence on the pervasive peacefulness. Perhaps a prize for the first person to spot a deer or elk will help to ensure attention. After you have completed the loop and gleaned all the information from the trail brochure, consider walking around again, just looking.

MORE ACTIVITIES
Map on page 257

Swimming: Quinault Lake is a popular place for kids to splash and swim. Campgrounds have small beaches and some resorts have rafts. The water temperature may take a little getting used to.

Boating: Boat launch facilities are located at Willaby and Falls Creek Forest Service Campgrounds on the South Shore Road of Quinault Lake. Afternoons are often windy.

Bicycling: The 28-mile loop around the lake is an excellent ride for wide-tire bikes. The ride is mostly level, with 14.3 miles on pavement and 13.7 miles on compacted dirt and gravel. Expect some traffic throughout. There is an organized ride around the lake once every summer, usually in late July. Check with the Quinault Ranger Station for details.

Gatton Creek Falls: The falls is a scenic destination, and at 0.6 mile, well within reach of most families. The hike may be started from a trailhead opposite Gatton Creek Campground or 0.4 mile on up South Shore Road at a small parking lot located just past the Rain Forest Resort.

World's Largest Spruce: This immense tree is located in the Rain Forest Resort Campground on South Shore Road, 3.5 miles east of US 101. Park on the south side of the road, just beyond the resort. Cross the road, then walk through the resort to reach the tree.

Graves Creek Campground Nature Loop: This 1-mile trail circles the nearly level flood plain below the campground. Along the way, pass through groves of moss-hung trees, skirt the Quinault River, and cross a wide meadow covered with snarly grass. Deer, elk, and slugs are the most common forms of wildlife; however, an occasional bear may wander through. Mornings and evenings are best times for wildlife viewing. Numbered posts along the trail are keyed to a pamphlet that may be picked up at the trailhead in the campground.

Pony Bridge: The destination of this hike is a bridge over a narrow gorge of the Quinault River. It is a beautiful canyon, with lacy curtains of water cascading off hillsides blanketed with ferns then tumbling to the torrent below. The canyon is steep, the hillsides slippery, and the rocks along the edge of the river are perpetually damp. Children should be cautioned, several times over, to keep their explorations to a minimum. Several campsites are located at Pony Bridge. The hike begins at the Graves Creek trailhead, located 18.5 miles up South Shore Road from US 101. The round-trip distance is 5 miles and the trail difficulty is moderate.

Irely Lake: This is a popular 2.2-mile round trip to a marshy lake. The reason for the popularity of this hike is not obvious. The lake has virtually no shore but does have a discouragingly large population of mosquitoes. If interested, follow South Shore Road east to its intersection with North Shore Road.

Pony Bridge

Go left, then go right on the narrow North Fork Road for 2.8 miles. The trailhead to Irely Lake is located on the left-hand side of the road, parking is on the right. The trail is moderately difficult with several steep and rough sections.

Staircase

Camping, fishing, hiking, nearby boating

With two easy walks, numerous river access points for fishing, and sand bars for picnicking and play, Staircase is a mecca for families with young children. For those with boats, the nearby Lake Cushman is a great place for a morning paddle before the wind kicks up.

The road-end campground has fifty-nine sites and there are additional spaces available at the nearby Big Creek Forest Service Campground and Lake Cushman State Park (reservations are accepted). Lake Cushman Resort has cabins for rent.

Drive US 101 to Hoodsport then head west on the well-signed road to Lake Cushman and Staircase. If this is your first visit, stop at the combined Forest Service and National Park Information Center for maps and updates on fishing regulations and trail conditions.

Staircase Rapids Loop Trail

LOOP TRIP: 2 miles
TRAIL DIFFICULTY: easy
ELEVATION GAIN: 200 feet
ACTIVITIES: hiking, fishing
BEST: April to October
MAP: Custom Correct: Enchanted Valley—Skokomish
Map on page 266

Do not let all the strollers, baby packs, and toddlers at the trailhead discourage families with older children or no children at all from walking this easy loop along the banks of the North Fork Skokomish River. Babies to grandparents will enjoy this forested trail.

Staircase is on the dry side of the Olympic Mountains and receives a whopping forty inches less rain annually than the west side valleys do. That means the ferns and moss and solid mass of understory vegetation must survive on only one hundred inches of rain a year, and they do so beautifully.

Big Cedar on Staircase Rapids Loops

The trail begins at the day-use parking area and follows the paved road across the gated North Fork Skokomish bridge. Well-read toddlers will find the bridge perfect for a game of Pooh Sticks—so stock up on twigs and pinecones before heading across. On the far side, angle to the right and walk across a grassy meadow, the former site of the Staircase Resort, currently the park service residential area. Just before heading into the woods, pick up a trail guide from the trailside box.

In a few feet, pass a side trail to a small hydroelectric plant, a must for all mechanical-minded hikers. The display of old water pipes is also interesting. Back on the main trail, it is only a short distance to the Big Cedar spur trail which leads to a marvelous old tree.

Continuing on, the trail passes river overlooks, cascades, the Staircase Rapids, and an interesting geology display. Just before the toddlers get terminally bored with toddling, reach an intersection. The trail on the left continues upvalley another 1.2 miles and has little to offer unless you are looking for a picnic location on the wide gravel bar 0.2 mile upvalley.

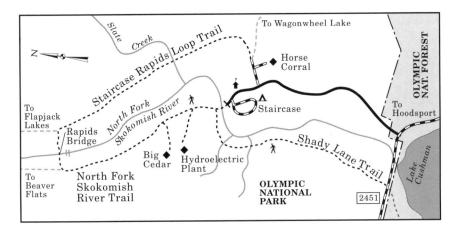

The loop hike follows the right fork and tunnels under a huge overhanging boulder before heading out over an unusual-looking bridge. On the far side, continue straight through the jungle-like forest to intersect the main valley trail then go right to head back to the ranger station. The trail downvalley follows the route of an old road and is wide enough to walk two abreast.

The only major challenge of the hike is met at Slate Creek, which is crossed on a single log bridge. Toddlers should have their hands held and hand holders should hold on to the handrail. The trail ends at the overnight parking area. Go right and descend to the day-use area.

Shady Lane Trail

ROUND TRIP: 2.4 miles
TRAIL DIFFICULTY: easy
ELEVATION LOSS: 30 feet
ACTIVITIES: hiking, fishing
BEST: April to October
MAP: Custom Correct: Enchanted Valley—Skokomish
Map on page 266

This trail crosses the real Staircase, which was located on a large rock wall at the edge of the river. Early trail users clambered over the top of this rock on rough cedar steps, pulling their reluctant pack animals along behind. Thanks to a bit of dynamite, the stairs were replaced by a level trail, and hikers now walk along the rock face rather than climb over.

From the day-use parking area at Staircase, walk the gated road across the wide bridge. Immediately after crossing the North Fork Skokomish River, go left and follow the wide trail downvalley. Before long an old mining shaft is passed, a reminder of why the original trail was built. Next, skirt the open rock face that was the location of the original staircase. Can you imagine how hard it must have been to coax heavily laden mules, donkeys, and horses up and down shaky wooden steps?

Beyond the rock cliff, the trail heads away from the river and into a peaceful forest. Several big trees (a maple and a couple of cedars) are passed. At 0.9 mile the trail joins a gated road which provides accesses to some vacation cottages. You may continue on another 0.3 mile to Road 2451.

At Road 2451 you have a choice: Go back the way you came, or loop back on the road. To loop, go left and walk the dike across the upper end of Lake Cushman to an intersection. Head left again. Use caution on the road; it may be busy.

MORE ACTIVITIES
Map on page 266

North Fork Skokomish River Trail: The trail begins at the overnight parking area at the end of Staircase Road. The initial 3.7 miles are on an abandoned road and are very tedious. However, if you persevere, this trail will take you into the heart of the wilderness portion of Olympic National Park, where you will find Flapjack Lakes, Sundown Pass, Lake La Crosse, and Anderson Pass.

Wagonwheel Lake: Despite its listing in this section, this is not a recommended trail. With an elevation gain of 3,200 feet in 2.9 miles, it is more of a scramble than a hike. The most enthusiastic description I have ever heard of the lake itself is "Ho Hum"; personally, I could only manage a "Hum"!

Ugh, a slug

Hamma Hamma

Backpacking, camping, fishing, hiking

The Hamma Hamma River valley lies outside the national park and would not receive mention here if it were not for Lena Lake. Hidden between nearly vertical hills, this forested lake is the destination of an endless stream of families throughout the summer. At times it seems that the number of children at the lake exceeds the number of adults.

There are two major Forest Service campgrounds in the Hamma Hamma Valley: Hamma Hamma and Lena Creek. Both fill by Friday night on summer weekends. Other than fishing, the main family activity in the valley is hiking. Of the three trails heading out of the valley, only one, Lower Lena Lake, is recommended for families.

Children playing in Lower Lena Lake

Lower Lena Lake

ROUND TRIP: 6.4 miles
TRAIL DIFFICULTY: moderate
ELEVATION GAIN: 1,100 feet
ACTIVITIES: hiking, fishing, backpacking
BEST: mid-June to October
MAP: Custom Correct: The Brothers
Map on page 269

Even though the forest service has scattered a remarkable twenty-seven campsites along the west and north sides of Lower Lena Lake, it still may be hard to find a place for your tent on a sunny summer weekend. This obscure little lake is a rarity in the backcountry: It is accessed by an outstanding trail that is easy for youngsters to walk. The trail is so well graded that it is not uncommon to see sturdy three-year-olds chugging the entire distance on their own two feet, and rambunctious five- to eight-year-olds seem to be everywhere.

For the preschoolers, a backpack trip with an overnight stay at the lake seems to work the best. School-age kids will be able to do the entire distance in a day, if you start early and plan for a three- to four-hour break at the lake for water play or fishing.

Drive US 101 along the west side of Hood Canal, 2.6 miles north of Eldon. Head up the Hamma Hamma River on Road 25 for 7.7 miles to find the trailhead on the right (685 feet). A forest service parking pass, purchased at any forest service office and most sporting goods stores, must be displayed on your windshield.

The trail begins in the trees and remains cool and shady all the way to the lake. The climb starts immediately, gaining elevation in a leisurely fashion as

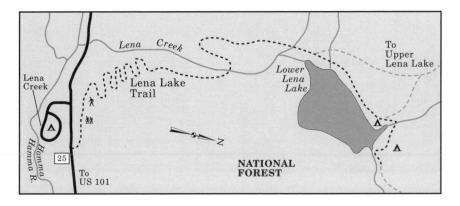

the trail makes sixteen long switchbacks up the steep hillside. At 2 miles the mysteriously dry Lena Creek is crossed. (The creek flows vigorously above and below this point.)

After three more switchbacks, the trail settles in for a nearly level traverse. At 2.7 miles, sharp-eyed hikers will see the lake waters sparkling below through the trees. Continue around the lake, passing the first fourteen campsites before recrossing Lena Creek. The remainder of the campsites are located at the north end of the lake. The best lake access is a sandy cove at the end of the trail.

Experienced hikers may be interested in the steep and difficult trek to Upper Lena Lake. This trip should be reserved for strong hikers who are willing to work hard for the cerebral pleasure of excellent scenery.

Dosewallips

Camping, fishing, hiking

The Dosewallips entrance to Olympic National Park is used mainly by backpackers. Only from late May through June, when the display of native rhododendrons turns the trail into a flowering garden, is this a popular area for day hikers. All who brave the rough access road will find a campground located in

Native rhododendron in bloom

an impressive grove of trees where hide and seek, tree climbing, and obstacle Frisbee are popular activities. When other games pall, fishing is an accepted pastime, even though the tree-hung banks of the river do tend to collect a lot of bobbins and lures. Note: The road washed out in 1997; check with the park before heading out.

From the town of Brinnon on the east side of Hood Canal, turn off US 101 and drive up the Dosewallips River valley for 7 miles on pavement, followed by 7.9 miles on gravel. The final 4 miles are narrow and steep, and are not recommended for vehicles pulling trailers. For overnighting, thirty campsites can be found at the national park campground, open May through October. The Forest Service Elkhorn Camp, located 4 miles from road's end, and Dosewallips State Park in Brinnon offer additional sites.

Dosewallips River Trail

TERRACE LOOP TRAIL
　　LOOP TRIP: 1.5 miles
　　TRAIL DIFFICULTY: moderate
　　ELEVATION GAIN: 300 feet
　　ACTIVITIES: hiking, fishing
　　BEST: June to September
　　MAP: Custom Correct: Gray Wolf—Dosewallips
　　Map on page 271

DOSE RIVER TRAIL
　　ROUND TRIP: 3 miles or more
　　TRAIL DIFFICULTY: moderate
　　ELEVATION GAIN: 300 feet
　　ACTIVITIES: hiking, backpacking, fishing
　　BEST: June to September
　　MAP: Custom Correct: Gray Wolf—Dosewallips

　　Dosewallips (commonly referred to as The Dose) offers a great place to bring the extended family together for a hike. The numerous intersections, fishing opportunities, rhododendrons in June, and minor elevation gain provide interest for everyone from preschoolers to their grandparents.
　　At road's end, you have two hikes to choose from: the Terrace Loop Trail and the Dose River Trail. The Terrace Loop is a rough, narrow trail that parallels the river. Although offering few views, is does have two river access points. The Loop joins the wider Dose River Trail for the final 0.5-mile descent to the

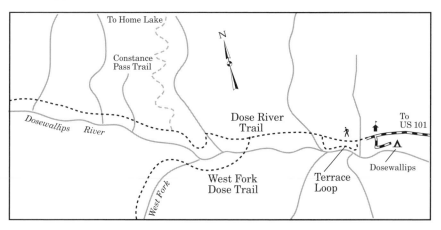

campground. The Dose River Trail is the wider of the two options and the easier to walk, but has no river contact for almost two miles. Younger hikers will require some supervision on the narrow log bridges. In its favor, the numerous intersections along the trail make excellent rest stops or turnaround points.

Both hikes begin by following the Dose River Trail up from the ranger's residence. After the initial steep ascent, the trail divides. The Terrace Loop goes left, traversing around a rhododendron-covered hillside overlooking the river. Deer are often spotted here.

The Dose River Trail continues straight ahead, gradually climbing along the forested hillside. At 0.5 mile, pass the intersection with the Terrace Loop. At 1.4 miles reach Dose Forks. Here the West Fork Dose Trail descends to a river crossing and camp area then continues on to cross the West Fork at a spectacular gorge in 1 mile. In June, when the rhododendrons are in bloom, stay with the main Dose Trail. At the 2.5-mile point, pass the Constance Pass intersection. Continue straight for another 0.2 mile to reach a tremendous display of flowers.

Deer Park

Camping, hiking, views, wildlife viewing

Deer Park is the most obscure of the thirteen Olympic National Park accesses, and for good reason. The access road is dangerously narrow and facilities at Deer Park are extremely limited. But even with all its difficulties and disadvantages, the view makes the tortuous drive worthwhile.

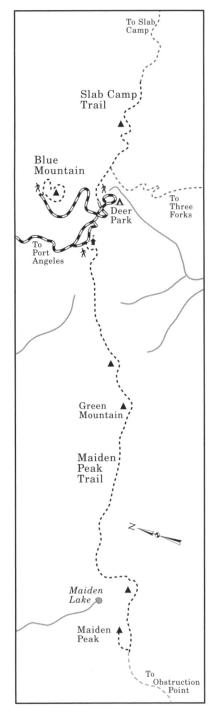

The view. The view is incredible, unequalled anywhere in the Olympics. From the crest of Blue Mountain the salt air of the Strait of Juan de Fuca mixes with the rarified alpine breezes of the glacier-covered Olympic Mountains. The lowlands spread out below your feet like a maritime map of islands and waterways. Beyond is a giant relief map of the snow- and ice-covered Cascades and the even icier Coast Range in British Columbia. Swing around south to trace the rugged topography of the Olympic Range, looking down thousands of feet to forested valleys then straight out to massive glaciers at elevations even lower than your 6,007-foot vantage point.

Deer Park is a very small area, with limited activities. You can camp, picnic, explore a couple of trails, or just look at the view. Most families will be able to see the entire area in a single day or a leisurely weekend. On a clear day you may want to bring dinner and stay for the sunset.

The campground is primitive. Its best feature is the great view. It also has two well-used shelters, pit toilets, and eighteen sloping campsites with tables and fire pits. Bring your own firewood. Running water is usually available during the summer season. No fee is charged. The access road is not suitable for motor homes or trailers. The closest lodging is in Port Angeles.

A small ranger station is located near road's end; however, the ranger's duties are varied and do not allow for full-time staffing of the facility.

Directions to Deer Park and a few words about the road: The Deer Park turnoff is located just east of Port Angeles at US 101 milepost 253, and is marked with a small sign. The very large Deer Park Cinema complex, just west of the turnoff, is a better landmark. Once on Deer Park Road, head south to the mountains. The paved two-lane road lasts for 7.5 miles then turns into a wide dirt road. At the 9-mile point, the road enters Olympic National Park and begins climbing steeply, switchbacking and narrowing as it goes. Before long the road is barely wide enough for one car and there are no guardrails to give the

The deer at Deer Park

agoraphobic even a small sense of security. Extreme caution should be taken on blind corners. Concentrate on staying to your side of the road, even when traversing the steepest of hillsides. Keep your speed down.

At 16.8 miles the road divides. The ranger station and Observation Point Trail are located to the left. The road continues up, passing a second access to the ranger station. The road splits again when it reaches a small bench at 17.2 miles. Deer Park Campground and Three Forks and Slab Camp Trails are to the right; the viewpoint is to the left. The left fork climbs through the meadows to a high point on the side of Blue Mountain and ends 18.1 miles from US 101.

WALKS AND HIKES
Map on page 272

Blue Mountain: Every visitor to Deer Park should plan to walk some or all of this short loop over the 6,007-foot summit of Blue Mountain. The hike begins at the parking area and the views begin at the same time. The trail follows an old road through meadows. A large herd of deer live here and it is rare not to see at least one. At the top of Blue Mountain a steep, narrow trail loops back to the parking lot. Families with young walkers may find it easier to turn around and go back the way they came.

Slab Camp Trail: This is an easy walk through rocky meadows. Along with wildflowers, hikers are treated to views of rich, velvet-green trees in the Cameron Creek and Gray Wolf River valleys, and of the wind-blasted summits along Gray Wolf Ridge. Views start right away; in fact, the best part of this trail is near the start. After 1 mile of ridge wandering, the trail begins to descend. If you have some over-energetic teenagers in tow, you may want to continue on for another 0.5 mile. Definitely turn around when the trail heads into the forest. The trailhead is located on Loop B of the Deer Park Campground. The Slab Camp Trail starts in conjunction with the Three Forks Trail. At 0.2 mile the trail divides. Stay left and continue along the ridge. (The Three Forks Trail descends through the forest, dropping over 3,000 feet in 4.1 miles to end at the Cameron Creek Trail. The return trip is great exercise.)

Maiden Peak: At one time the park planned to build a road along the ridge from Deer Park to Obstruction Point. Luckily, good sense intervened and the project was abandoned. Today a very scenic trail connects the two locations. The trail begins near the Deer Park Ranger Station and follows the rolling ridge crest with quick descents and steep climbs. At 1.3 miles, traverse around Green Mountain, descend, then climb again. Views increase as the forest gives way to meadows. After crossing a saddle at 2.5 miles, the trail climbs to a grassy bench then traverses around the south side of Maiden Peak. Follow the trail around the peak then go right and head cross-country for the final short stroll to the summit. This hike is rated as challenging.

Backpack Trips

Toleak Point

ROUND TRIP: 12 miles
TRAIL DIFFICULTY: challenging
ELEVATION GAIN: 500 feet
ACTIVITY: backpacking
BEST: all year
MAP: Custom Correct: South Olympic Coast
Map on page 275

Here is an opportunity to see the Pacific Ocean at its best with sea stacks, waterfalls, and thundering surf. Although this hike is both fascinating and fun, this is a true wilderness coast, so expect challenges galore, like planning your days around the tides, steep climbs over headlands, and muddy trails. The rewards are beach-side campsites with enthralling views, tide pools rich in life and color, sea birds, bald eagles, wave-carved logs, brilliant sunsets, sand, and fun.

Although most children love the ocean and many will walk astonishing distances to prove it, this hike is definitely reserved for the older ones. Several sections of the trail are difficult, including a couple of places where you must use a rope to ascend the steep hillsides. Scrambling over slippery rocks and even slipperier logs is common, and depending on the tide, you may have to scale a couple of ten-foot high cliffs.

Drive US 101 to the La Push turnoff, located 2 miles north of Forks. Head

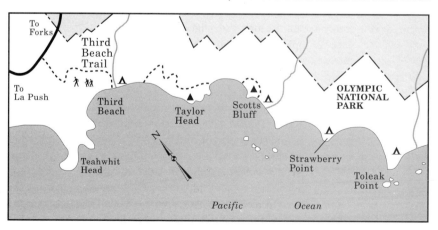

Exploring a tide pool

west 12 miles to the Third Beach trailhead and park on the left-hand side of the road (240 feet). Note: trailhead vandalism is common. Take all valuables with you.

Follow the trail through the forest until, at 1.2 miles, it drops abruptly to Third Beach. Cross the creek and pass several small campsites before letting your feet sink into the sand. Hike south on the beach 0.7 mile until you spot a marker on the hillside indicating the location of the trail over Taylor Head. (It is not possible to walk around Taylor Head). Scramble up the tide-eroded base of the bluff to find the well-maintained trail above. Head uphill to the ladder, then grab the rope and walk to the top.

Once on the crest of Taylor Head, the trail descends to cross a creek then climbs again through forest. At 3 miles from the road, return to the beach at a small bay guarded by a rocky point. The rocky point can be rounded at low tide. If your timing is off, you can follow a narrow trail over the top. However, if the tide is high, you may have to wait for it to go out before walking on.

At 3.5 miles are the massive cliffs of Scotts Bluff, a point which can be walked around at very low tides or crossed by trail. On the south side are campsites and a creek which must crossed. If your balance is good, use the logs; if not, you will need to wade. Just beyond is another rocky point which can be rounded at a medium tide or climbed over. At 4.7 miles reach Strawberry Point, which marks the start of the scenic beaches, tide pools, and best campsites.

Beyond the point, the beach bends into a moderately deep cove before reaching Toleak Point at 5.7 miles. Campsites are located in the trees or on the beach. The best source of water is Jackson Creek, 0.2 mile south. An old shelter is located next to the creek.

Deer Lake and High Divide Loop

DEER LAKE
    ROUND TRIP: 8 miles
    TRAIL DIFFICULTY: moderate
    ELEVATION GAIN: 1,600 feet
    ACTIVITIES: hiking, backpacking, fishing
    BEST: July to September
    MAP: Custom Correct: Seven Lakes Basin—Hoh
    Map on page 277

HIGH DIVIDE LOOP
    LOOP TRIP: 18.5 miles
    TRAIL DIFFICULTY: challenging
    ELEVATION GAIN: 4,000 feet
    ACTIVITIES: backpacking, fishing
    BEST: late July to September
    MAP: Custom Correct: Seven Lakes Basin—Hoh

The well-graded trail, good scenery, and delightful lakeside campsites combine to make Deer Lake an ideal first backpack. Once camp is set, you can then spend several days exploring the alpine world in the hillsides above.

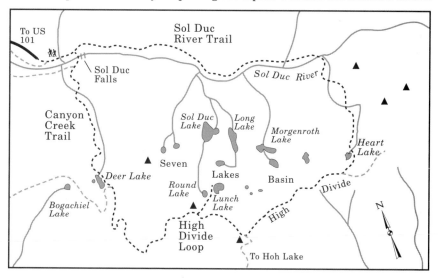

Enthusiastic hikers on their way to Deer Lake

For experienced hikers, the High Divide Loop is one of the most popular trips in the park. The loop incorporates many of the most spectacular features of the Olympics: old-growth forest, rivers, lakes, waterfalls, high alpine meadows, exhilarating vistas, and abundant wildlife. Advance reservations are recommended.

From US 101 drive up the Sol Duc River valley 14.4 miles to the road's end parking area (1,900 feet). (Backcountry permits may be picked up at Eagle Ranger Station, 2.3 miles before the end of the road.)

The first 0.9 mile of the Deer Lake Trail and High Divide Loop are spent heading upvalley on the popular trail to Sol Duc Falls . When the trail divides near an old shelter, go right and walk the bridge over the falls, then continue on 0.1 mile to an intersection with the Lovers Lane Trail. Stay left and begin climbing the forested hillside. At 1.7 miles cross Canyon Creek on a sturdy bridge and pass a forested campsite. The ascent remains steady all the way to the Deer Lake intersection, reached at 3.8 miles. Campsites are located all around the lake; the eastside sites are forested and tend to be drier. Deer Lake is a great base camp for an 8.8-mile round-trip hike to the summit of 5,474-foot Bogachiel Peak, or a 7.8-mile round trip to Lunch Lake in Seven Lakes Basin.

For those doing the loop, pass the junction with the spur trail to Deer Lake and Bogachiel River Trail, then continue climbing out of the forest to the high alpine world of straggly trees and flower-covered meadows. At 6.8 miles (4,900 feet) the trail to Seven Lakes Basin branches off to the left. The basin is a very popular destination and an entire day can be spent wandering from lake to lake.

The loop trail continues its increasingly scenic climb along Bogachiel Ridge then swings around the west side of Bogachiel Peak. At 7.7 miles (5,200 feet) is a major intersection. The High Divide Loop continues straight, maintaining its traverse. To the right, a trail descends 1.5 miles to Hoh Lake. At 7.9 miles, pass a trail on the left, which climbs to the 5,474-foot summit of Bogachiel Peak, the site of an old fire lookout and 360-degree views that include Mount Olympus and, on clear days, the Pacific Ocean.

The loop now enters one of the most beautiful areas in the park. Following the crest of the High Divide, hikers are treated to abundant wildflower fields to the north, and views of the Olympus massif and Bailey Ranges to the south and east. After a couple of magical miles, an intersection with the Sol Duc River Trail signals the start of the descent. At 10.4 miles reach Heart Lake (4,800 feet), scenically situated at the upper end of Sol Duc Park. The trail then descends 2.6 miles to the Sol Duc River valley and follows the river through stands of large trees to return to the trailhead at 18.5 miles.

Enchanted Valley

ROUND TRIP: 26 miles
TRAIL DIFFICULTY: challenging
ELEVATION GAIN: 900 feet
ACTIVITIES: backpacking, fishing
BEST: March to November
MAP: Custom Correct: Enchanted Valley
Map on page 280

Miles and miles of forest, groves of giant firs, park-like stretches of alder and maple, frothing creeks, and a crystalline river combine to create an almost spiritual ambience in the deep East Fork Quinault River valley. The destination is an alpine cirque where, in early season, waterfalls stream off the nearly

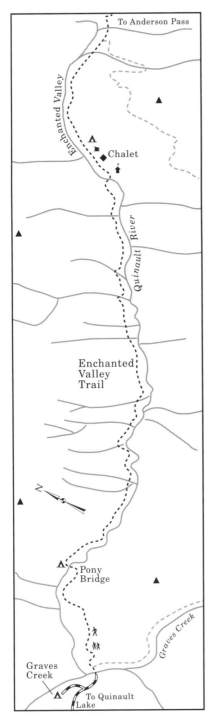

vertical hillsides and, later in the summer, the meadows are covered with mats of colorful wildflowers. Enchanted is a perfect name for this valley.

Although this is a long hike, numerous campsites along the trail allow you to custom tailor your itinerary. Four days or an entire week can be spent hiking, exploring, and just enjoying this area. Because this is a low-elevation trip, it is open most of the year and hikeable to all who are shod to handle a trail covered with an amazingly gooey form of mud.

Drive US 101 to Quinault Lake, then follow South Shore Road 18.5 miles to its end at Graves Creek trailhead (646 feet). The hike begins with a crossing of Graves Creek on a spectacular bridge that is supported by a single log. Head uphill on an old road for a couple hundred feet to an intersection. Continue straight, hiking though a forest of giants. Old stumps attest to even larger trees in the past.

At 2 miles you will arrive at a 1,200-foot high point on a forested saddle. A picnic table here marks the end of the old road and the beginning of trail. Descend for the next 0.5 mile to reach Pony Bridge (906 feet) at 2.5 miles. After checking out the gorge from the bridge, cross to find campsites and two steep but well established boot trails to small beaches on the river's edge. Any families opting to spend the night here should be prepared to keep strict watch on the children. Numerous less-exposed campsites can be found in the next 2 miles.

The trail climbs and descends, avoiding any chance of monotony as it heads over river terraces, old moraines, and heaps of gravel. Campsites are generally found whenever the trail approaches

Enchanted Valley chalet

water. The exception is O'Neil Creek Camp at 6.8 miles, which is reached by a 0.2-mile side trail.

At 10.5 miles the trail abruptly leaves the deep forests and enters subalpine meadows surrounded by peaks towering over 6,000 feet above. Initially the meadows are full of scrub alder and other assorted tangles of brush. The brush gives way to flowers further up. At 13 miles cross the East Fork and shortly beyond reach the old three-story Enchanted Valley Chalet (2,000 feet), built in the 1930s as a luxury hotel. Today the building is a shelter for hikers. But don't plan your trip around a stay in the chalet; it is often full.

Exploring the valley can easily take an entire day. Just 2 miles above the chalet is the world's largest western hemlock. Three miles beyond it is the summit of 4,464-foot Anderson Pass.

Winter

Winter brings snow to the higher reaches of the Olympic National Park and a nearly steady downpour of rain to the lower valleys and rain forests. Access to the high country is limited to Hurricane Ridge, where the blast of the winter storms can be tremendous and the trees along the crest of the ridge are often encased in a beautiful armor of snow. On weekends, a small ski area provides some challenging runs for downhillers, telemarkers, and snow boarders. Cross-country skiers tour the closed road beyond the visitor center, and backcountry skiers find challenge on the steep slopes of Hurricane Hill. Snowshoers can explore the area on their own or take a walk with a ranger. These walks are held on weekends from late December through March. Snowshoes are provided free of charge. Call ahead to the visitor center in Port Angeles for times and road closure information.

Many of the park's winter visitors come to escape the snow. The low-elevation valleys and the coast are suitable for hikes throughout the winter. The Hoh River and Quinault Lake areas are ideal winter destinations. Although neither is immune to snow, it generally does not linger for more than a week or so. By March, these two areas are ideal destinations for spring breaks. The coast is another place that remains inviting throughout the year. Take careful note of the winter tides, which are much higher than in the summer, and bring more clothes than you or your family could possibly wear; hypothermia is common in this damp environment.

Be sure to call ahead at (360) 452-4510 to check out road conditions and closures before you start your trip.

Index

About the Authors

Tom Kirkendall and Vicky Spring started their outdoor adventuring at very young ages. Vicky started backpacking when she was three months old. Tom was a late bloomer, who didn't hit the trail for an overnighter until reaching a venerable age of three. Throughout the years they added climbing, bicycle touring, mountain biking, canoeing, and skiing to their list of favorite things to do. When their own children arrived on the scene they took them in stride and kept going. Their son took his first hike at five days old and was on his first backpack at three weeks. Their daughter carried on the tradition by refusing to be carried on family hikes after she turned three and proceeding to prove she was ready by hiking eight miles.

Tom Kirkendall and Vicky Spring live in western Washington with their two children where they work as photographers focusing on landscape and adventure sports.

About the Mountaineers

Founded in 1906, The Mountaineers is a Seattle-based non-profit outdoor activity and conservation club with 15,000 members, whose mission is "to explore, study, preserve, and enjoy the natural beauty of the outdoors . . . ."The club sponsors many classes and year-round outdoor activities in the Pacific Northwest, and supports environmental causes by sponsoring legislation and presenting educational programs. The Mountaineers Books supports the club's mission by publishing travel and natural history guides, instructional texts, and works on conservation and history. For information, call or write The Mountaineers, Club Headquarters, 300 Third Avenue West, Seattle, Washington, 98119; (206) 284-6310.

Send or call for our catalog of more than 300 outdoor titles:

The Mountaineers Books
1001 SW Klickitat Way, Suite 201
Seattle, WA 98134
1-800-553-4453
e-mail: mbooks@mountaineers.org
website: www.mountaineers.org

Other titles you may enjoy from The Mountaineers:

WASHINGTON'S BACKCOUNTRY ACCESS GUIDE: National Parks, National Forests, Wilderness Areas, *Ken Lans*
An extensive compilation of Washington backcountry information, fully updated for access, trail conditions, permit and new user fee information. Includes general descriptions, a listing of maps to reference, driving directions, and information on climate, campgrounds, nearby services, ranger district addresses and telephone numbers, emergency contacts, and regulations.

BEST HIKES WITH CHILDREN, IN WESTERN WASHINGTON AND THE CASCADES, VOL. 1, Second Edition, *Joan Burton*
A completely revised edition of the best-selling book in the *Best Hikes with Children*, series, with approximately 20 new hikes, including day hikes plus some overnight backpack trips.

BEST HIKES WITH CHILDREN, IN WESTERN WASHINGTON AND THE CASCADES, VOL. 2, *Joan Burton*
A guide to day hikes and overnighters for families, with tips on hiking with kids, safety, and fostering a wilderness ethic. Includes points of interest, trail descriptions, information on flora and fauna, campsite locations, and maps.

KIDS IN THE WILD: A Family Guide to Outdoor Recreation,
Cindy Ross & Todd Gladfelter
A family-tested handbook of advice on sharing outdoor adventures with children of all ages and skill levels, with recommendations on equipment, food, safety, and family activities.

EXPLORING WASHINGTON'S WILD OLYMPIC COAST, *David Hooper*
Most detailed guide available to hiking the beaches of Olympic National Park, with advice on camping, safety, wildlife, human history, and shipwrecks.

MAC'S FIELD GUIDES, *Craig MacGowan & Sauskojus*
   Northwest Park/Backyard Birds
   Northwest Trees
   Pacific Northwest Wildflowers
Two-sided plastic laminated cards developed by a teacher of marine science, with color drawings, common and scientific names, and information on size and habitat. Part of a series with more than thirty titles.

ANIMAL TRACKS: PACIFIC NORTHWEST, Book & Poster,
Chris Stall
Both book and poster offer information on 40-50 animals common to the Pacific Northwest region.

WASHINGTON STATE PARKS: A Complete Recreation Guide,
Marge & Ted Mueller
One of the series of multi-season, multi-activity regional guides, with maps, directions and information on park facilities.